The problem of pornog

Can a commitment to free speech be reconciled with the regulation of pornography? In *The Problem of Pornography* Susan M. Easton argues that it can. Pornography poses a particularly difficult challenge to legal and feminist theory: at what exact point does the freedom of the individual come into conflict with the legal regulation of free speech?

Susan Easton explores and evaluates the arguments used within feminism and liberalism for the regulation of pornography by taking John Stuart Mill's harm principle as a starting point. Given the difficulties of proving harm in the case of pornography, the author turns to the concept of autonomy as an alternative foundation for regulation and argues that incitement to racial hatred legislation might offer the best model for the regulation of pornography. Objections to having any regulation at all, including the appeal to moral independence and the right to free speech, are considered, and the text includes a review of the English and American laws governing obscene materials.

Susan Easton is a barrister and Lecturer in Law at Brunel University, London. She has written on Hegel and feminism and is the author of *The Right to Silence, Disorder and Discipline* and *Humanist Marxism and Wittgensteinian Social Philosophy*. She is Editor of the *International Journal of Discrimination and the Law*.

The problem of pornography

Regulation and the right to free speech

Susan M. Easton

London and New York

First published 1994
by Routledge
11 New Fetter Lane, London EC4P 4EE

Simultaneously published in the USA and Canada
by Routledge
29 West 35th Street, New York, NY 10001

© Susan M. Easton

Phototypeset in Garamond by Intype, London

Printed and bound in Great Britain by T.J. Press (Padstow) Ltd,
Padstow, Cornwall

British Library Cataloguing in Publication Data
A catalogue record for this book is available from the British Library.

Library of Congress Cataloging in Publication Data
Easton, Susan M.
  The problem of pornography: regulation and the right to free speech/Susan
  M. Easton.
  p. cm.
  Includes bibliographical references and index.
  1. Obscenity (Law)–United States.   2. Pornography–United States.
  3. Freedom of speech–United States.   4. Obscenity (Law)–Great Britain.
  5. Pornography–Great Britain.   6. Freedom of speech–
  Great Britain.   I. Title
  K5293.E27 1994
  344′.0547–dc20
  [342.4547]   93–37378
                                                          CIP

ISBN 0–415–09182–9 (hbk)
ISBN 0–415–09183–7 (pbk)

Contents

Acknowledgements viii
Introduction ix

1 The liberal defence of pornography 1

2 The types of harm 10

3 Proving harm 32

4 Diversity and autonomy 42

5 Feminism, truth and infallibility 52

6 Free speech and majoritarianism 59

7 The slippery slope 65

8 Feminism and puritanism 79

9 The protection of free speech 85

10 Interpreting the First Amendment 94

11 The civil rights Ordinances 109

12 Freedom of speech and the regulation of pornography in
English law 122

13 The 'right' to consume pornography 145

14 Incitement to sexual hatred 158

15 Conclusion 175

Notes 179
Bibliography 184
Table of statutes 189
Table of cases 190
Index 193

For Storm, Baskie and Daisy

Acknowledgements

I am grateful to David Lamb and Andrea Hyde for editorial assistance and Michael Hames for information on policing. I would also like to thank Esmond for voluntarily exercising constraints on his right to free speech, allowing me to complete the manuscript.

Introduction

The dispute over pornography and censorship has split both liberals and feminists. The problem of pornography has been of great concern within feminism, especially in relation to violence against women, and has been a major dimension of critiques of patriarchy. It has raised questions regarding the role of perfectionism within feminist thinking and within liberal thought. As well as stimulating theoretical debates, the problem of pornography has also generated political activism, culminating in pickets of sex shops and clubs, 'off the shelf' campaigns directed at high-street retailers, and vigorous demands for legal constraints on the free market in pornography. In the process the broader issue of the use of the law as a feminist strategy has been raised. Feminism has split on the desirability of constraints and on the use of the law as a feminist strategy.

It has been argued by Smart (1989), for example, that the use of the law to regulate pornography in the United States has adversely accentuated the differences between feminists in public. But one might argue that this demonstrates the strength and dynamism of feminism: the fact that it contains a rich diversity of perspectives rather than one dominant paradigm shows that it constantly reflects on its ideas and strategies. Once the issue is in the public arena, it may strengthen the political effectiveness of women by mobilising support and cooperation on that issue.

The significance of pornography compared to the wider representations of women in popular culture, including advertising, as the key site of women's oppression, has also been debated using theories drawn from a number of disciplines and schools, including semiotics and literary criticism.[1] The emancipatory potential of pornography in liberating sexual inhibitions and providing affirmation to sexual minorities has also been considered. The demands for the regulation of pornography have also raised the spectre of censorship, which has been seen as a weapon of the state which may be used against minority groups or against feminist writers. The problem of pornography has been a central issue within liberalism, and arguments both for and against the regulation of pornography may utilise classical liberal ideas. Mill's *On Liberty* offers a useful source of concepts and methods, including the harm principle, which have been used by both sides in the pornography and censorship debate (Mill, 1970). It is principally the defenders of pornography who have deployed Mill's notion of moral independence, his plea for toleration and analysis of the link between freedom of thought and freedom of publication, and his focus on the importance of a range of opinions for social and individual improvement, to allow for the possibility of learning through errors and experience. The Millian commitment to freedom of opinion and freedom to publish is a bulwark of the defence of pornography offered by representatives of the industry and may also be found in modern jurisprudential defences, for example, the work of Ronald Dworkin (1986a).

Mill's distinction between self-regarding and other-regarding action as a basis for social intervention has been used by both defenders and critics of pornography; we find fundamental differences in the characterisation of pornography as to whether it should be located in the self-regarding or other-regarding realm. This in turn rests on the question of whether or not pornography is harmful to others. We also find differences in the emphasis placed on autonomy and the effects of pornography on the promotion and stunting of autonomy. Although the harm principle is used extensively by advocates and critics of regulation, Mill's analysis of diversity and individuality, which has received less attention in discussions on pornography and censorship, is relevant to the debate.

The liberal defence of pornography relies principally on the argument that the consumption of pornography falls squarely within the self-regarding sphere, in which the individual is sovereign. Even if pornography is harmful to the consumer, this will not be a sufficient ground for regulation. A commitment to liberalism means embracing the principle of moral independence so that even if others think one's ideas are foolish, mistaken or offensive, then one should not be prevented from freely expressing those ideas, provided that no tangible harms to others result directly from that expression. Freedom of thought is meaningless without the freedom to publish. Toleration demands acceptance of a range of views of sexuality and sexual preferences. A slippery slope argument is also invoked in support of the pornographer's right to publish. If sexual material is restricted, then sex education in schools may be exposed to the risk of control and political ideas, and literary and artistic works will also be under threat. Moreover, it is argued that a free market in ideas and opinions is essential to the public good in affording the possibility of acquiring knowledge of satisfying ways of living.

The proponent of regulation has to address each of these arguments. A case for regulation may be advanced from within a liberal perspective, derived from Mill's arguments in *On Liberty*. However, defenders of pornography have also made use of the harm principle, but the assessment of harm in the two approaches diverges considerably. The harm principle may also present problems: the Supreme Court in *American Booksellers* v. *Hudnut* 475 US 1001 (1986), when considering the constitutionality of the Indianapolis Ordinance, affirmed the opinion of the Court of Appeals in *American Booksellers* v. *Hudnut* 771 F 2d 323 7th Circuit (1985), which had accepted evidence of harms to women and objective causation, but concluded that the harms to women were outweighed by the need to protect First Amendment speech rights. This contrasts with the approach of the Canadian Supreme Court in *R.* v. *Butler*, 89 Dominion Law Reports 449 (1992), where it was held that section 163 of the Criminal Code, dealing with obscenity, did violate the Charter of Rights and Freedoms, but was justified as a reasonable limit prescribed by law. Although it was difficult to establish the precise causal link, it was reasonable to presume that exposure to pornography affected attitudes and beliefs; legislation aimed at preventing harm to women and children and to society as a whole was of fundamental importance and could justify infringement of the right to freedom of expression.

But the harm principle is not the sole foundation of the argument for regulation. Given the problems of proving harm and causation and of balancing competing rights and interests, it may be worthwhile appealing to other grounds, namely, the arguments for autonomy, rationality and diversity.

Millian principles have often been invoked in defence of free speech. Free speech has been seen as essential to the functioning of democracy and representative government, to the promotion of autonomy and the pursuit of the truth. Applying these justifications of free speech to pornographic materials has proved difficult. Yet pornography has attracted considerable and vigorous support from defenders of free speech. The question of regulation has been construed in terms of a Manichean opposition between free speech and censorship, with the defenders of free speech and pornography construed as the forces of good and feminist demands for restraint representing a sinister shift towards censorship.

Yet the major justifications of free speech found in English and American law and jurisprudence are difficult to apply to pornography. However, while these justifications are severely strained when applied to pornography, the exceptions to the protection and coverage of the free-speech principle in Anglo-American law and theory may justifiably and rationally be seen as relevant to the exclusion of pornography.

DEFINING PORNOGRAPHY

Pornography is often described as hard to define but easy to recognise. Justice Stewart said in *Jacobellis* v. *Ohio* 378 US 184 (1964) that he was unable to define pornography, but he knew it when he saw it. The word 'pornography' originates from the Greek and means writing about prostitutes. Pornography should be distinguished from obscenity, which means the filthy or disgusting. Obscenity rather than pornography is the term normally found in legal instruments. The original meaning of obscene was 'filthy'. *The Oxford English Dictionary* defines 'obscene' as filthy, indecent, offensive to modesty or decency, expressing or suggesting lewd thoughts. It defines pornography as the description of the life and manners of prostitutes and their patrons and the pornographer as one who writes of prostitutes or obscene matters. Legal usage does not conform to everyday language or to dictionary definitions. The United States Supreme Court has construed obscenity narrowly as pornography. Frederick Schauer (1982) favours a definition of pornography in terms of sexual depiction rather than obscenity, as obscenity could, but need not, be pornographic and pornography may, but need not, be obscene. In England the Obscene Publications Act 1959 has been used to prosecute publishers of leaflets extolling drug use but has been primarily directed at pornography and increasingly at child pornography. The law has also distinguished between possession and publication or dissemination. Obscenity is defined in the Act in terms of its tendency to deprave and corrupt, that is, in terms of its impact rather than content, but in practice the law is usually used in relation to materials containing bestiality, children and homosexuality.

The definition of pornography found in feminist literature for the most part follows that of Catherine MacKinnon and Andrea Dworkin used when drafting the Minneapolis and Indianapolis Ordinances. Pornography is defined by them as sexually explicit material which subordinates women through pictures or words. It would include scenes of women enjoying pain, humiliation and rape and penetration by objects or animals, or shown as bruised or hurt in a context which makes these conditions sexual. Examples cited by MacKinnon as commonly available include materials which are not overtly sexual, for example, women hanging from trees without exposing their genitalia and not engaging in sexual acts, women's bodies scarred by radiation treatments, pictures of quadriplegics, women's limbs being slowly severed, or women being hunted down and shot. She stresses that pornography encompasses much more than conventional definitions of sexual behaviour. But all the above should be seen, she says, as sexually explicit because:

> This term 'sexually explicit' acknowledges the sexually dynamic quality of the material without using subjective sexual arousal as a standard for it, and makes it feasible to develop a case-by-case jurisprudence based in existing law but appropriate to a new concept and real cases.
>
> (MacKinnon, 1984: 32)

She emphasises that she is not defining it as the representation or depiction of subordination but 'as an active practice of the subordination of women', that is, an act in the form of words. The fact that some acts may take a verbal form is already recognised by the courts in other contexts such as blackmail and libel. Pornography is active in the sense of serving as a sexual stimulus. The notion of sexual explicitness is already used to clarify meanings of obscenity. In *People* v. *Mature Enterprises* 73 Misc 2d 749 (1974) the court referring to *Deep Throat* observed that 'the explicit sexual activity represents the "hard-core" feature of the material'; the activity here included group sex and anal sex.

Recurring themes found in pornography include multiple rape, men planning and executing a rape which the victim enjoys despite initial resistance, sadism, and the profaning of the sacred. The latter dimension has received less attention in the current debate, but in the past has been used as a strong motif in pornographic works, featuring in the writings of de Sade. The view of pornography as liberating, radical and challenging has developed partly because of the shock and outrage caused by profaning of the sacred.

Although much of the pornography and censorship debate has focused on the degradation of women in the material, this perception of pornography has been subjected to criticism from academic commentators. While acknowledging that pornography, including magazines aimed at a mass market, has become more violent since the 1960s, Joel Feinberg (1987a) argues that one may find materials without depictions of subordination where the material is just sexually arousing without the added dimension of domination and subordination. But for most writers this would then fall within the definition of erotica. He also points out that there may be materials containing scenes of domination of men by women:

> there are pornographic materials intended for men, that appeal to their masochistic side exclusively, in which they are 'ravished' and humiliated by some grim-faced amazon of fearsome dimensions.
>
> (Feinberg, 1987a: 145)

But while there may be a specialist market for this material, the majority of materials depict female subordination, and it is the reinforcement of the routine subordination of women that is of importance in the debate. Furthermore, the humiliation and assault of men in the production of pornography would have grounded an action under the MacKinnon-Dworkin Ordinance and fallen within their definition of 'actionable' pornography.

Feinberg distinguishes three definitions of obscenity. 'Obscenity' may be used in a pejorative, judgmental way, to suggest the offended state of mind of the maker of the statement; it is also used by the courts to mean material aimed at producing an erotic response in the consumer. Third, it may be used in a neutral way to classify material, for example, describing the fact that it contains certain words.

Obscenity is construed by Feinberg as a particular form of offensiveness, suggesting both disgust, producing what he calls a 'yuk' reaction, and allurement. It may refer to objects, natural or created, persons and actions, and is usually very blatant. Feinberg distinguishes his account of obscenity from that of David Richards, who defines obscenity in terms of abuse of bodily function: 'The obscene identifies a special class of the possible objects of shame which are explained by reference to certain defined notions of competence in bodily or personal function' (Richards, 1977: 61). The obscene traditionally refers to a way of thinking about human conduct, for example, masturbation has been seen as a misuse of sexual parts. Feinberg sees this as both too narrow and too broad, too narrow because the common use of the word 'obscene' includes, for example, the public torture of victims, which has nothing to do with bodily function. Other abuses of bodily function such as smoking are not seen as obscene, so Richards' definition is too broad.

Feinberg is critical of the identification of pornography with obscenity. Although the two may overlap, they are not identical. Because 'pornography' is used descriptively to refer to sexually explicit writing and pictures, he says, it is narrower than 'the obscene'. Pornography is confined to sex, while obscenity is more than sex. But it may be difficult to maintain such a sharp distinction, as disgusting materials might still be intended to produce a sexual response and have that effect, however bizarre the taste or the audience. For example, films of autopsies, human dismemberment and surgery containing no overt sexual references or pictures of the genitalia are circulating in Britain. Presumably the audience finds them simultaneously alluring and disgusting, and exploring the forbidden world of the mortuary might be part of the attraction.

Feinberg emphasises that obscene materials will cause shock and repugnance, whereas pornography is confined to sexually arousing material, and many things seen as obscene are not sexual at all. Some pornographic materials may not be obscene. He is therefore critical of the use of 'obscene' to refer to the pornographic, in the Supreme Court's jurisprudence, initially in *Cohen* v. *California* 403 US 15 (1971), where it was stated that obscene meant pornographic. But the Court, says Feinberg, has not given us a means of identifying obscenity. This may not be necessary, as it may be be easily recognisable by juries, but it may be harder to find and identify the redeeming features, which will give the work First Amendment protection.

Feinberg also examines the relationship between pornography and literature, identifying three main approaches: (i) pornography and literature are quite distinct, although pornography may be useful provided that we are clear that it is not literature, a view associated with Burgess (1970: 5); (ii) pornography may be seen as a corruption or perversion of genuine literature as judged by literary standards, a view he associates with George Steiner (1970: 47); (iii) pornography can be seen as a form of literature and sometimes has literary merit, a view associated with Kenneth Tynan (1970: 111). On this third view pornography may be art if it is well executed. Feinberg favours a distinction between literature and pornography in terms of primary use. Pornography is as predictable as a dictionary or telephone book, even if at a high level. As he says:

> That 'high porn' is still pure porn, no matter how you slice it, is a point well worth making in reply to all the pretentious critical hogwash that would find some mysterious literary merit in the same old stuff when served up by fashionable names.
>
> (Feinberg, 1987a: 131–2)

Even if it is done well, he argues, it is still pornography rather than literature. He cites the films of Just Jaeckin, *Emmanuelle* and *The Story of O*, as cases of 'artful pornography', which are beautifully filmed, but do not reach the level of dramatic art; they may rather be likened to a beautifully illustrated cookbook. However, *Emmanuelle* is not clearly obscene in the sense that there are no close-ups of sex organs, and male sex organs are not shown. But he accepts that pictorial art could be pornographic, aiming at sexual arousal, yet still constituting art; but this could not be applied to literature, because literature and pornography are mutually exclusive. The most they may have in common, he says, is that they are books. Literature reflects critically on the human condition, while pornography aims to stimulate masturbation.

A distinction is also often drawn between erotica and pornography: the former represents the world of the sensual and depicts sexual activity, but does not present sexual relations in a degrading or dehumanising way. Linton (1988) defines erotica in terms of the depiction of the pleasure of sexuality within a positive emotional relationship, while pornography dehumanises and degrades sex, by separating sex from love and treating people as things (Linton, 1988: 123). However, while the distinction is well established in Western culture, in other cultures such as that of China, erotic or even romantic material may be seen as pornographic. The serious-ness with which pornography is viewed is also reflected in the use of the death penalty in China for traffickers in pornography.

Linton considers why people find pornography offensive when the treat-ment of people as things in other areas of life, for example, commercial contexts, is accepted. He argues that ultimately it is because people see sex as something which should be solely a matter of personal relations. Pornography is 'a symbolic threat to the social order ... the *consumption* of pornography represents an indulgence of licentious sexual tastes which itself symbolises freedom from or rebellion against social constraints.' (Linton, 1988: 124). Pornography is also threatening because it brings sex into the public sphere of the market place. It is anomalous in the sense of blurring these categories, but also because it may be seen as active rebellion against the social structure. But this is problematic because pornography might be seen as reflecting patriarchal, hierarchical and unequal social orders.

Linton argues that it is not the sexual explicitness of pornography which renders it offensive but the fact of sexual explicitness out of place. He identifies various devices by means of which sexual explicitness *per se* is defused, including defining it as possessing artistic merit, and through routinisation, the gradual acceptance of images. Artistic works which transcend these boundaries may be received with hostility. He cites the example of Manet's *Dejeuner sur l'herbe*. What made it outrageous was not its sexual explicitness – for representations of naked women in rustic scenes had long been acceptable – but rather the fact that the men were fully dressed; the suggestions of sexual availability and impersonality were also seen as shocking. However, through time what is seen initially as obscene may come to be redefined as a work of art.

A distinction is often drawn between soft-core and hard-core material. The former would include depictions of heterosexual relations but exclude violence and sado-masochism, buggery and the use of children and animals. It would not encompass Linton's definition of erotic material, as it could still present normal acts in a dehumanised way. A distinction could also be drawn in terms of markets and outlets, soft-core being available in corner shops and high-street retailers and hard-core obtained through box numbers and dealers. But the distinction has been challenged not least because of the continuity in practice between the two sources. Barry (1984) argues that so-called 'soft' material still consists of sexual objectification, reducing women to their sexual attributes.

Pornography is defined by the Campaign against Pornography and Censorship (1988) to include both soft-core and hard-core material. The group rejects the sharp distinction between the two in favour of a continuum of representations of women, including the depiction of the enjoyment of rape and torture. The definition follows closely the one used in the Ordinances, namely the graphic sexually explicit subordination of women through pictures and/or words that also includes one or more of the following: women portrayed as sexual objects, things or commodities, enjoying pain, being reduced to body parts and penetrated by objects or animals.

Given the proliferation of definitions and distinctions it may be useful to use the concise classification referred to in *R. v. Butler* 89 Dominion Law Reports 449 (1992), which distinguishes between materials depicting the following: (i) explicit sex with violence, (ii) explicit sex without violence but which subjects people to treatment that is degrading and dehumanising and (iii) explicit sex without violence which is neither degrading nor dehumanising. The concerns of feminist campaigners and the demands for prohibition are directed at the first two categories.

RESEARCHING PORNOGRAPHY

In researching the impact of pornography, various methodological problems arise. As well as the problems of establishing a causal relation between the consumption of pornography and harms to women, there is also the wider problem of access to information. Pornography may be obtained through private networks and clubs and distributed through mailing lists not easily accessible to the researcher. Interviewing consumers may be difficult where material is illictly obtained. Victims of pornography may also be difficult to contact or apprehensive about discussing their experience, although research on victims' experience is now being undertaken.[2] This may reflect the general invisibility of women workers in the sex industry and of those involved in the practice of sexual slavery, which has been defined by Kathleen Barry (1984) as the objective social condition of sexual exploitation and violence, and the reluctance of official organisations to release information or to investigate the problem. It is difficult to find a sample population to survey and draw generalisations from or to engage in participant observation, she says, and established methods of sociological research are difficult to apply in studies of the sex industry.

A further reason for the invisibility of women's exploitation in the sex industry is the development of myths and ideas which serve to marginalise their experience, for example, that they freely chose that way of life, which precludes an examination of the structural objective conditions of their lives. Attention has been focused primarily on the exploitation of children, whose position is usually contrasted with that of adult women, who, it is presumed, must have freely chosen to participate in the production of pornography or in other sectors of the industry such as prostitution. In this respect the approach of some commentators on pornography has reflected social and judicial attitudes towards rape, in which a presumption of consent has led to a denial of a problem rather than a focus on the causes of such behaviour and the responsibility of the perpetrators.

Demands for the regulation of pornography raise philosophical, empirical and legal questions. The philosophical issues include the question of whether pornography constitutes speech, the boundaries between speech and conduct, the nature and scope of the free speech principle, and the relationship between the state and the individual. The empirical problems centre on the measurement of the effects of pornography. Legal problems have arisen over the drafting of appropriate legislation to allow free speech in other areas, evidentiary problems regarding the burden and standard of proof, the appropriate remedies for those harmed by pornography, and procedural issues concerning the responsibility for determining the impact of pornography in a particular case, whether this should lie with expert witnesses, the jury or the judiciary.

Chapter 1 will consider the liberal defence of pornography. This will be followed in Chapter 2 by a discussion of the types of harm which arguably may result from the free market in pornography. The difficulties of applying conventional legal models to harms allegedly arising from the production and consumption of pornography will be examined. The merits and problems of using harm-based arguments as the foundation of the case for regulation will also be considered. Chapter 3 focuses on the problems of proving harm. Chapter 4 considers the issues of diversity and autonomy, drawing from the work of Mill (1970) and Raz (1986). This is followed in Chapters 5, 6 and 7 by discussions of questions of infallibility, majoritarianism and the slippery slope argument. The relationship between feminist and puritan critiques of pornography is considered in Chapter 8. It will be argued that while the moral right's critique relies on the sanctity of the family and the harms to marriage and the family, the feminist argument is concerned with the effects on women rather than the family *per se*. Chapter 9 examines some of the problems which arise in determining the scope of free speech protection, and Chapters 10, 11 and 12 review the relevant legal materials in England and the United States and consider proposals for reform, including the Indianapolis Ordinance and the Williams Report. Dworkin's critique of the Williams Report and his defence of the right to consume pornography is critically examined in Chapter 13, where the possibility of using Dworkinian ideas in favour of regulation is explored. Chapter 14 examines incitement to racial hatred legislation as a possible model for the regulation of pornography. In the Conclusion the merits and pitfalls of using the law to solve the problem of pornography are reviewed.

Chapter 1

The liberal defence of pornography

CLASSICAL LIBERALISM: SELF-REGARDING AND OTHER-REGARDING ACTION

Millian arguments have dominated debates on free speech and censorship. The major justifications of free speech found in English and American jurisprudence, including the democracy and truth justifications, are eloquently advanced in Mill's writing and have been used by defenders of pornography. The harm principle has been at the forefront of the debate.

Mill's objective in *On Liberty* was to chart 'the nature and limits of the power which can be legitimately exercised ... over the individual' (Mill, 1970: 126). Stimulated by his fears over the new majoritarianism, Mill saw it as crucial to identify a clear limit to interference from the state and from custom, otherwise life for the individual would become intolerable. What is needed, said Mill, is one very simple principle to govern the relationship between society and the individual. The principle he offers is that 'the sole end for which mankind are warranted, individually or collectively, in interfering with the liberty of action of any of their number, is self-protection' (Mill, 1970: 135). The only ground on which intervention is justified is to prevent harm to others and 'His own good, either physical or moral, is not a sufficient warrant' (Mill, 1970: 135).

Mill's argument is expressed in the two maxims:
(1) The individual is not accountable to society for those actions affecting only his or her own interests. The most which others can legitimately do is engage in persuasion, instruction, advice or avoidance.
(2) the individual is accountable to others for actions which prejudice their interests and may justifiably be punished whether through legal or social means.

The feminist demand for regulation of pornography, a matter which properly concerns only the passive consumer, would be seen by defenders of pornography as a clear example of the unwarranted intrusion of public opinion and constraints into the self-regarding sphere. Pornography is seen as 'harmless' in so far as no compelling evidence has been offered of any tangible harm to others. Ronald Dworkin (1986a) posits the hypothetical situation where excessive consumption of pornography might lead to absenteeism, which would justify the state imposing restrictions. If one can find no evidence of harm to others, there will be no grounds for punishing a private indulgence.

Of course, a critic of pornography might well argue that it may be better for consumers to refrain from this activity, and therefore to restrict access to pornographic materials because they are demeaning to users and of such poor intellectual quality that they divert them from more worthy self-enhancing occupations. It is precisely this type of argument for restriction which is ruled out on Mill's principle, for here the focus would be on the consumer and 'in the part which merely concerns himself . . . over his own body and mind, the individual is sovereign' (Mill 1970: 135). For Mill, no matter how degrading and depraved an activity is, if no one else is affected by it, the fact that others may think that forgoing this activity would make an individual a happier or better person is not sufficient to justify the imposition of sanctions. Mill exempts from his doctrine immature and mentally impaired individuals, so children and those who are incapacitated are excluded, but adults' preferences clearly fall within the principle of liberty. Within this domain of personal liberty lie the realms of consciousness, thought and feeling. Where opinions are concerned, whatever the subject-matter, absolute freedom is essential.

On Mill's argument moral entrepreneurs such as the Temperance Movement or the modern anti-pornography movement would seem to be engaged in unwarranted interference. The appropriate guardian of the individual's mental, spiritual and physical health is the individual. If the effect on others infringes their rights or substantially affects their interests, then regulation of the harmful activity might be appropriate, but otherwise the appropriate sanction would be mere criticism and 'there should be perfect freedom, legal and social, to do the action and stand the consequences' (Mill, 1970: 206).

Confronted with this type of argument, the feminist critic of pornography would appear to be on shaky ground. Legal regulation of the kind embodied in the Indianapolis Ordinance would seem to be an unjustified intervention, as sexuality is the most private area of self-expression and self-realisation. Consequently attempts to control pornography have been firmly resisted by liberal theorists. Persuasion in the form of demonstrations and vigils outside sex shops would be acceptable unless the customers were actually prevented from entering. Any increase in state power is seen as evil in itself, and the spectre of state officials investigating private activities and thoughts accounts for much of the liberal fear of feminist protest. This fear of state power has also diffused certain radical and feminist approaches, influenced by Foucault (1979), and partly accounts for scepticism over the use of the law as a feminist strategy.

In defending the realm of personal sovereignty, Mill stresses that he is not undervaluing the exercise or development of higher faculties, or seeing all pleasures as equal. A crude form of utilitarianism cannot be attributed to Mill. Certainly, it would be difficult for anyone to deny the poor quality of pornography. Most liberal commentators who emphasise the right to consume pornography, in the absence of proven harm, including Ronald Dworkin (1986a) and Bernard Williams (1979), have acknowledged the low quality of the material, while Feinberg (1987a) describes it as simply boring. But the 'lowest' preferences deserve protection: no one is warranted in preventing other adults from adopting a particular activity, from doing what they like with their own lives, when they are the best judges of their own feelings. The outsider may offer observations on more edifying pursuits and seek to persuade, but ultimately individuals must decide for themselves and be the arbiters of their own tastes. Mill recognises that these tastes may be unpleasant:

> There is a degree of folly, and a degree of what may be called . . . lowness and depravation of taste, which, though it cannot justify doing harm to the person who manifests it, renders him necessarily and properly a subject of distaste, or in extreme cases, even of contempt.
>
> (Mill, 1970: 207)

In such cases we may consider the person a knave or a fool, shun him or her and warn others to do so, but we should not limit the individual's freedom of action to behave as a knave or fool. Similarly the liberal pornographer would accept the right of other parties to express their views, to organise anti-pornography meetings and panels to exchange views. But the fear for the liberal defender of pornography is the prospect of such disapproval being hardened into legal and physical restraints on actions, into civil or criminal sanctions. Mill recognises that 'A person . . . who pursues animal pleasures at the expense of those of feeling and intellect – must expect to be lowered in the opinion of others', but the worst he or she should expect is the inconvenience of disapproval, not the forcible prevention of his or her actions (Mill, 1970: 208).

Mill illustrates his argument by examples such as drinking and gambling, where the addiction may affect the gambler's family or creditors. Here intervention is justified not on the grounds of extravagance, but because of the breach of duty of those to whom the addict owes obligations. 'No person ought to be punished simply for being drunk', says Mill, 'but a soldier or a policeman should be punished for being drunk on duty' (Mill, 1970: 213). Whenever there is a direct harm or risk of harm to either society or another individual or the public in general, 'the case is taken out of the province of liberty, and placed in that of morality or law' (Mill, 1970: 213).

If society does interfere unjustifiably, the chances are that it will 'get it wrong'. He gives the example of the sale of poisons, arguing that if the only use for poisons were murder then prohibition might be legitimate, but poisons may also be used for innocent purposes.[1] Prohibition is an indiscriminate weapon: one cannot restrict the potential murderer without also denying the innocent the freedom to choose. Similarly, the pornographer might argue that even if *some* pornography is used for improper means, as an aid to rape, by an unbalanced individual with a prior disposition to harm others, this does not justify denial of access to pornography to the vast majority of law-abiding consumers, who use pornography for private non-criminal activities, for example, as harmless fantasy or sexual aids. We might just as well stop the sale of kitchen knives because on occasion they are used to commit murder. If there is a danger of misuse of the item in question, then all one may properly do is warn.

Claims of a causal link between the circulation of pornography and violent crime have met with considerable scepticism from pornographers and commentators and investigators, including the Williams Committee (1979) and the President's Commission (1970). But some defenders of pornography go further than this. Rather than simply denying harm, they argue that pornography has positive benefits in contributing to individual and social well-being, including liberating individuals from taboos and constraints at the harmless level of fantasy, promoting personal growth and awareness and providing a catharsis for individual sexual tensions.[2] Pornography may also be used in therapeutic programmes to re-educate sex offenders away from negative perceptions of sexual relations into more positive attitudes and behaviours.

But even if one acknowledges the potential to harm in rare cases, the reliance on a warning to control the misuse of potentially dangerous substances and materials is problematic when applied to pornography. For it is difficult to see what form it could take when attached to a video-recording or magazine. A warning regarding the degradation and depravity of the acts witnessed, the effects on the user or the implications for the humiliation of women is unlikely to succeed if this is what is being sought by the consumer. Already warnings of the strong 'adult' nature of the contents may be used to tempt buyers of magazines, combined with wrapping them in cellophane to make them appear more enticing. This contrasts with the case of smoking, for example, where smokers do not smoke in order to develop cancer even if this is a highly probable effect. If the threat of death and cancer are insufficient to deter people from smoking, a warning regarding the effect on one's 'moral well-being' is unlikely to have any impact on the avid consumer of pornography. A warning will be meaningless if it refers to the specific effect desired by the consumer.

The use of warnings may be appropriate to Mill's example of poison, where one can label clearly the content and its dangers and reasonably assume that they will be effective, but is weaker when applied to pornography.

An alternative option within the scope of Mill's argument is registration. But registration of pornography-users would be a Herculean task for those responsible for registration given the facilities for copying videotapes and passing round magazines through informal networks. The registration of imports would be possible, assuming they could be identified, but for materials manufactured within the jurisdiction it would be harder to impose a system of registration. The plentiful supply is a product of technological changes and the profitability of the commodity. Consumers of pornography might be registered, just as owners of fire-arms and users of certain drugs may be registered, although this is likely to be unpopular. Most people would see the registration of their purchases of magazines and videos as Orwellian.

But restrictions have found more favour with liberal commentators. The Williams Committee advocated restricting the public display of material which others find environmentally unattractive and denying access to sex clubs to minors, while leaving adults a free choice whether or not to buy the goods or to enter those clubs. Restrictions were also imposed by the Indecent Displays (Control) Act 1981.

Mill recognises that there may be hard cases which lie on the boundary between self-regarding and other-regarding action, such as gambling dens and brothels. But it is precisely because of such difficulties that a wide range of opinions is necessary, in order to find the best policy to adopt consistent with respect for individuals' rights and interests. 'Fornication, for example, must be tolerated, and so must gambling', says Mill, 'but should a person be free to be a pimp, or to keep a gambling-house?', he asks (Mill, 1970: 231–2). If activities such as drinking and gambling are acceptable in private, why should we condemn them because they operate as a business, governed by commercial considerations? Similarly one might argue that if sexual relations conducted by consenting and loving adults constitute a social good, then individuals working in the sex industry should not be attacked simply because the cash nexus is involved. Janet Radcliffe Richards (1982), for example, argues that if sex meets with public approval, there would seem to be no strong ground for seeing it as wrong to earn money through sexual activity. But the fact that activities occur as part of a commercial enterprise is significant, as in the examples of both gambling and pornography, their profitability has meant that they have attracted the interest and involvement of organised crime in the United States. The need to maintain profitability arguably builds in a 'hardening' effect, ensuring that the material contains a more violent content through desensitisation as familiarity results in falling sales, which are remedied by new and more extreme materials. Mill recognised that commercial motives and financial interests could lead proprietors to encourage excessive drinking and gambling. The commercial exchange of goods and services also normally means a public exchange which, in the case of drinking or pornography, may have adverse environmental effects.

Controlling activities such as drinking, gambling or pornography through the price mechanism, by increasing the price through taxation, might be an option. But this is a *de facto* prohibition for poorer members of society, and arguably discriminatory and elitist, in assuming that the middle-class consumer can handle pornography without problems but that the working-class consumer cannot. If the state needs revenue, says Mill, it makes sense to tax luxuries rather than necessities and to tax those pursuits the state sees as harmful. This needs to be distinguished from making the commodities available only to certain groups. Moreover, one of the 'virtues' of pornography today, a pornographer might argue, is that mass production enables access at relatively low cost to all, while in the nineteenth century it was available only to the elite. The minimal cost also means that individuals' responsibility to fulfil their obligations to their families will not be threatened.

But there might be scope for restraint on Mill's argument where there are immediate implications for public order. The example he gives of incitement to violence is addressing an unruly mob outside the corndealer's house where the likelihood of violence is immediate rather than speculative (Mill, 1970: 184).[3]

Frederick Schauer (1982) questions whether a meaningful distinction can be drawn between self-regarding and other-regarding action but says that if it can, then speech is normally other-regarding with the potential to cause harm or good to others. One speaks primarily to affect others. The effects may be positive, for example, reassurance, or negative, in the case of deception; acknowledgement of the other-regarding nature of speech is reflected in the civil law of defamation, and the criminal law of incitement. The harms of words, argues Schauer, may in certain cases far exceed harms from physical injuries, if one's whole livelihood, for example, is affected by a libellous statement.

The effects of speech may be extensive, affecting community relations or gender relations, for example in the cases of 'hate speech' directed at ethnic minorities and women, as well as inciting immediate violence or hatred. Mill recognises the effect of speech on others and formulates the problem of free speech in terms of calculating the negative consequences of speech against the ill-effects of speech suppression. As Schauer observes, the protection of free speech in American law and jurisprudence may be given not because it is self-regarding but despite the fact that it is other-regarding and in some cases harmful or offensive to others. Offensiveness will not always justify restraints on speech, and toleration of offensive speech may be the price to pay of living in a democratic pluralist society.

Once one sees speech as other-regarding, the fact that a harm is identified as resulting from speech does not resolve the issue of regulation. The type of harm and extent of harm would have to be sufficiently serious to warrant intervention, and one would need to take account of the nature and strength of the opposing rights and interests. Consequently, the pornography and censorship debate has focused on the identification of harms, measuring the extent of harms, their proximity and remoteness, and balancing these harms against the harms arising from suppression of pornography.

MODERN LIBERTARIAN DEFENCES OF PORNOGRAPHY: CONSENT, CONTRACT AND CHOICE

Modern defences of the sex industry have relied upon contractual arguments and on the *volenti* argument that, if individuals consent to an activity which others find offensive, the state should not intervene provided that consent is freely given. The 'consent' doctrine is also reflected in some feminist defences of pornography and prostitution which stress the importance of women choosing their own forms of work and sexual relations.

The doctrine of consent has provided a useful way of accounting for the existence of the market in sexual services, including pornography and prostitution. In prostitution the exchange of services for money is simultaneous, but in pornography, the consumer pays for the depiction of sexual activities, so that the other parties to the contract are more remote. Provided the contract for payment of services is made by free consenting adults, and occurs within the framework of the law, then the contract has validity and should not be criticised or overturned simply because the commodity in question is sex. One should be free to enter into a contract even if others disapprove. Furthermore, it is argued, the commercial exchange of sexual services may benefit individuals and society. For example, the argument is often advanced that pornography may prevent crime by providing a way of channelling sexual desires and relieving sexual tensions privately; it may also provide sexual satisfaction to those otherwise unable to form relationships, because they are housebound, for example, or because they are separated from their normal sexual partners. Provided that participation is voluntary, there can be no valid objection. From a contractarian perspective voluntariness is the only issue to consider. One should not distinguish sex from other commodities exchanged on the market. But this atomistic model of exchange overlooks the structural determinants underpinning the market, the fact that women's choices may be conditioned by fundamental structural inequalities which affect their life chances and earning capacity. The sex industry in all its various forms, including prostitution, third world sex trips and pornography, is controlled by and for men. Furthermore, given the involvement of organised crime in the sex industry in the United States, the notion of a private contractual arrangement is difficult to sustain. By focusing on the voluntary nature of participation in the sex industry, choice theorists overlook coercion and the various techniques to ensure participation. Kathleen Barry (1984), for example, identifies five major patterns of procuring, including befriending, actions of gangs, syndicates and organised crime, recruiting agencies for work and marriage, direct purchase and kidnapping.

If we focus specifically on the pornography industry we find that it depends on the exploitation of the weakest groups, including children, women in third world countries, victims of sexual abuse and prostitutes, who may be forced by poverty and racism into the industry. There are also problems with the presumption of choice if seen in the context of a lifetime of cultural pressures and expectations. Real choice may be possible only in a social structure without sexual discrimination.

Contractarianism also ignores the subordinate position of women in the labour market, which may influence their 'free decision' to participate in order to raise their standard of living. For this reason, a consent defence was excluded when drafting the Indianapolis Ordinance. Barry (1984) is sceptical of economic theories which see prostitution as a viable economic alternative for women given the loss of their earnings. She treats pornography as a form of prostitution in which producers and distributors function as pimps living off the earnings of participants. Both would fall within her definition of female sexual slavery, which embraces:

ALL situations where women or girls cannot change the immediate conditions of their existence; where regardless of how they got into those conditions, they cannot get out and where they are subject to sexual violence and exploitation.

(Barry, 1984: 40)

What requires examination is the social acceptance of such practices, which she explains in terms of the ideology of cultural sadism.

Even if there is a contract between private individuals, it may be hard to enforce because some of the activities may be illegal. The sex industry, far from being an aggregate of consenting buyers and sellers, can be viewed as both reflecting and perpetuating gender inequalities, institutionalising access to women's bodies.

Also important to the contractual model is the assumption that a market will develop wherever there is demand, and as sexual desire is a constant feature of human behaviour, inevitably the provision of sexual services will flourish. In this way the universality and ubiquity of prostitution and pornography in all types of societies are explained, although consumption will be greater in market economies.

The assumption of inelastic demand is problematic when applied to sexuality. The view that sexual desire is a constant, essential, biological feature fails to take account of the way in which sexuality is mediated by cultural expectations. The essentialist argument has also been criticised. As Pateman (1988) points out, no one ever died of sexual frustration, and most people are able to cater for their own sexual demands if they lack a sexual partner. Sexual impulses do not necessarily require entering into a sexual relationship, commercial or otherwise. The sale of women's bodies through the mechanism of prostitution, she argues, is a typical feature of patriarchal capitalism. Although Pateman focuses on prostitution rather than pornography, a similar point could be made in relation to the pornography industry. Women's provision of sexual services, whether in the form of prostitution or participation in pornographic films and magazines, could be seen as the most extreme form of alienation and dehumanisation as the body becomes a commodity and subordination is confirmed in every act. The buying and selling of images of women's bodies as commodities open to all on the market with sufficient disposable income to purchase those services reinforces the right of access to women. As the former socialist societies embrace free-market principles, the sex industries are flourishing, including the expansion of the pornography market. In 1993 a Russian edition of *Penthouse* was introduced, containing a section featuring Russian women.

A feminist critic of pornography might accept the pornographer's argument that interference cannot be justified on the ground of harm to men. But harm to men is not a bulwark of the feminist argument, although one might point to the ways in which pornography affects the consumer, inhibiting the development of fulfilling sexual relationships by generating distorted expectations of female behaviour and precluding an understanding and appreciation of other dimensions of women's characters.

Feminists and liberal anti-feminists may agree on these effects but diverge on whether intervention is warranted. The harms which concern feminists are rather the alleged harms to *women*. But a Millian argument in favour of regulation may be grounded in the fact that pornography may be seen as a practice rather than speech or ideas, as other-regarding action which is harmful to others. Mill's concept of harm embraces more than direct physical damage. He includes duplicity and the unfair use of advantage as well as the infliction of direct physical harms. We also find in Mill's writing a concept of individuality which cuts across the self-regarding and other-regarding distinction and extends beyond physical harm which may be relevant to the assessment of the impact of pornography. This will be considered following a discussion of the types of harm which may be linked to pornography.

Chapter 2

The types of harm

Various types of harm arising from the production and consumption of pornography have been identified. These include direct and indirect physical and emotional assaults, raising issues of proximity and remoteness, effects on community morality and offence caused by the display of obscene materials.

To elucidate the harms arising from pornography, one needs to be clear whose interests are being harmed: those of the consumer, whose capacity for self-development could be undermined by consumption, and those of women and society as a whole. Here we might distinguish between women's interests as participants in pornographic productions, as real and potential victims of sexual assaults and as citizens of a society in which pornography flourishes, as part of a general pattern of gender inequality. We might also distinguish between physical and non-physical harms. One could point to effects on women's self-esteem and the truncation of personal development engendered by the widespread sale and consumption of pornography. When considering the interests of society as a whole, we might consider the impact of pornography on community morality or the quality of the environment.

The types of harm may include physical harm, psychological effects, minor or serious harm, direct or indirect, proven or speculative harms. Psychological effects were recognised by Mill as harms to take into account in considering issues of regulation. They have also become increasingly important in legal contexts as the law of tort has come to recognise the importance of 'nervous shock' as mounting a claim in tort in some cases when the incident causing the shock is not directly viewed by the plaintiff.[1]

These distinctions are important both at the level of philosophical debates and also in terms of the specific problems in construing legislation in Britain and the United States. For example, considering *who* is liable to be depraved and corrupted is important in interpreting and applying the Obscene Publications Act 1959 and in determining community standards using the test formulated in *Miller* v. *California* 413 US 15 (1973). There may also be difficulties in applying legal concepts of harm, based on tort models, when considering the impact of pornography on women as a group – as tort models are essentially atomistic and linear models. If we are dealing with harms to women as a class, the harms may be indirect rather than direct and the concept of a group injury is undeveloped in English law. On the pure liberal view, if the consumer's interest is the only issue, then there is no ground for social intervention, no matter how degrading the effects of the activity. The key question in considering whether the regulation of pornography is justified is whether a free market affects the interests of others in ways which are sufficiently harmful to necessitate constraint. The case for regulation has principally relied on the claim that obscene or pornographic materials may cause anti-social or illegal acts including sexual offences. A number of claims and counter-claims have been advanced, and attempts to establish a causal link raise methodological and evidential problems.

The major sources of evidence in the debate have been the results of experimental studies undertaken by social psychologists to test the impact of pornography on subjects' attitudes and behaviour, two major governmental inquiries into the impact of pornography in the United States, the President's Commission (1970) and the Meese Commission (1986) and the testimony of victims at the Minneapolis Hearings (1983). Research on sex offenders and the differentials in crime rates for sexual offences compared both cross-culturally and through time, in societies which have relaxed controls on pornography, have been cited in the debate. A review of the research on the impact of pornography was commissioned by the Home Office in Britain and undertaken by Howitt and Cumberbatch (1990), who could find no compelling evidence in the materials surveyed of a causal link between pornography and sexual violence. They concluded that the evidence was more ambiguous than commentators suggest: 'Inconsistencies emerge between very similar studies and many interpretations of these have reached almost opposite conclusions' (1990: 94). They point to major methodological difficulties in the experimental studies, raising doubts regarding their internal and external validity. There are also gaps in our knowledge of the relevant variables: for example, not enough is known about the attitudes which may encourage sexual attacks or the role of pornography in psychosexual development. We do not have sufficiently detailed records of sexual offences to plot changes through time in relation to changing patterns of pornography consumption. Most of the available research is based on Canadian and American experience rather than European studies. Although reluctant to infer a causal link, the authors were nonetheless sceptical regarding claims of the advantages of pornography:

it would be overgenerous to the research evidence to argue a case for the benefits of pornography. The idea that pornography might serve as a substitute for the direct expression of sexual violence has not really been subject to the necessary empirical tests ... However, it is probably unrealistic to believe that there is a major contribution made by pornography in this respect since there is no substantial evidence of any reduction in sexual crime where pornography circulation rates have increased.

(1990: 95)

The President's Commission on Obscenity and Pornography was set up in 1967 and reported in 1970. It made a number of recommendations which reflected the liberalisation of sexual morality at that time. It reviewed the effectiveness of the existing laws on pornography and obscenity and examined methods of distribution, the effect on the public and its relation to crime and made recommendations accordingly. The Commission could find no empirical research to establish firmly a causal relationship between the consumption of pornography and criminal behaviour. It therefore recommended the repeal of existing legislation prohibiting the sale, exhibition and distribution of sexual materials to the consenting public. It could find no grounds for state interference with the reading or viewing materials of adults. The Commission's Report was criticised for its selective use of statistics, and a further study undertaken by the Meese Commission came to quite different conclusions.

The question of harm was also central to the Meese Commission's inquiry. This Federal Commission was briefed by Edwin Meese, the Attorney-General, in 1985, to find new ways of controlling pornography. It reported in 1986 and recommended stronger enforcement of existing obscenity legislation as well as enactment of new measures. The Report concluded that pornography does cause individual, social, moral and ethical harm and proposed further restrictive measures. Sexually violent pornography, it concluded, is causally related to anti-social and possibly unlawful acts of sexual violence. The chair of the Commission was an anti-vice prosecutor and the majority of the Commission were already opposed to pornography, which led some critics to argue that its conclusions were predetermined. It was also criticised for presenting women as helpless passive victims and for its conservatism. Vance (1986), for example, argues it was used by the Reagan Administration as a sop to the moral right, to compensate for the Administration's failures on the issues of abortion and school prayers. The moral right had been very critical of the earlier President's Commission on Obscenity and Pornography (1970), which had found no evidence of a connection between pornography and anti-social behaviour and which had argued for a weakening of restrictions.

The Meese Commission rejected the use of Ordinances and the repeal of existing obscenity laws, arguing that those laws could deal with the violent and degrading material which the Ordinance wished to combat, especially if they were supplemented by civil remedies using existing obscenity standards. The Commission also supported the work of citizen action groups seeking to use non-legislative measures to reduce the availability of pornography. While the Meese Commission did not undertake its own research, it did examine research undertaken by others, including that of Malamuth and Donnerstein,[2] who testified to the Commission.

Although controls on the basis of the likelihood of physical harm have been difficult to achieve, limits on the free market on the grounds of offensiveness have succeeded. Regulation in the form of restrictions might be sought on grounds of offensiveness to others caused by the public display of obscene materials. The offence principle is described by Feinberg in *Offense to Others* as follows:

> It is always a good reason in support of a proposed criminal prohibition that it would probably be an effective way of preventing serious offense [as opposed to injury or harm] to persons other than the actor, and that it is probably a necessary means to that end.
>
> (Feinberg, 1987a: 1)

The prevention of offensive conduct on this principle '*is* properly the state's business' (1987a: 1).

In determining whether an offence is sufficiently serious to warrant intervention, we need to take account of its magnitude, which is determined with reference to its intensity, duration and extent. We also need to consider its reasonable avoidability, because the harder it is to avoid without great inconvenience, the more serious it is. We also need to consider how reasonable the offender's conduct is by reference to its social utility, the availability of alternative opportunity, whether it is motivated by spite or malice, the nature of the locality in which the conduct occurs, and the importance of free expression. Generally the free speech principle would take precedence over offensiveness. A legislature or judge will balance the reasonableness of the offender's conduct against the seriousness of the offence. Bare knowledge of offensive conduct, where that conduct is unwitnessed, would not normally be sufficient to intervene. For intervention to be justified it would need to be a profound offence rather than a mere nuisance or inconvenience. Included in profoundly offensive acts would be Nazi demonstrations in Jewish communities, where one would be outraged by the act even if it did not personally affect oneself. The circulation of pornographic materials might be seen on the feminist argument as comparable and therefore regulation in some form would be justified. But although Feinberg distinguishes offence and harm, the former might be construed as a type of harm, in the sense that the offence experienced can be construed as a form of suffering. Furthermore offensiveness may be the rationale for restrictions on environmental grounds where the harm is to the local area. It has proved easier to obtain regulation on grounds of offensiveness than on physical harm, but normally the appropriate form of regulation is restriction rather than prohibition.

The claims of harms arising from a free market in pornography have been challenged by opponents of regulation who have focused on the absence of proven or identifiable harm. Some have gone further and have stressed the positive benefits of pornography in educating and liberating citizens and in the enhancement of sexual pleasure. The involvement of the state and criminal or civil law in the enforcement of essentially private moral choices has also been subject to strong criticism.[3]

In unravelling these arguments we need to be clear on the type of harm we are dealing with and who is harmed: is it the user of the material, the community or particular sections of the community? These questions are not always sufficiently clearly distinguished in the pornography and censorship debate. In evaluating the validity of liberal and libertarian arguments against regulation, it is important to be clear on whether self-regarding or other-regarding action is at issue, although there will be difficult borderline cases. The location of pornography on either side of this distinction has been problematic. An examination of these issues entails consideration of key legal conceptions including causation, intention, remoteness and proximity, and raises questions regarding the boundaries of civil and criminal law. These arguments will now be considered in more detail.

IMITATIVE HARMS

The assertion of a link between pornography and sexual crime is one of the most controversial claims advanced by critics of pornography. Murder and rape trials in the United States and the United Kingdom have, in some cases, revealed instances of apparent imitation of particular practices found in literature on the accused's person at the time, or identical to those shown in films seen by the offender. The influence of pornography on sexual offences has been referred to in a number of English and American cases by judges, counsel, expert witnesses and defendants. The work of de Sade was referred to by the Moors murderers. Imitative crimes raise problems for the civil and criminal law. In the English case of *R. v. Taylor* (1987) 9 Cr App R (S) 198, a rapist lost his appeal against a nine-year sentence for an attack on two women in a beauty salon undertaken when he was 16. His psychiatrist had stated that he had acted on impulse while still affected by the effects of glue sniffing and in circumstances which recalled to his mind a similar situation described in pornographic books he had been given to read. This, the psychiatrist said, was consistent with what is known of the effects of solvents and pornography on immature and unstable persons. Lord Lane said that 'here is yet another example, if further example is required, of the effect of that type of literature or sometimes that type of video film on people of immature and unstable character' (at 200). The viewing of a violent video film was cited in 1993 at the trial of Thompson and Venables for the abduction and murder of two-year-old James Bulger. The same film was also implicated in the torture and murder of a Manchester schoolgirl.

In *R.* v. *Holloway* (1982) Cr App R (S) 128, for example, Lord Justice Lawton referred to the fact that

> in the course of our judicial experience we have dealt with cases of sexual offenders who have undoubtedly been incited to engage in criminal conduct by pornographic material. This is not an uncommon experience for judges dealing with sexual offenders. Pornography, and particularly the type known as 'hard porn' in our experience has a corrupting influence.
>
> (at 131)

He also cited examples of cases in the Family Division of marriage problems resulting from husbands who had been reading or seeing pornography and seeking 'to introduce in the matrimonial bed what they have read or seen' (at 131). Pornography may be shown to the victims of sexual offences, as in *R.* v. *Liddle* (1985) 7 Cr App R (S) 59, where the accused had a history of sexual offences which included showing the victims pornography. The judiciary may be more aware of the effects of pornography than the general public, which has implications for the use of the law. Relying on the judiciary to implement stronger measures to control pornography may be more promising than pessimistic critics of the use of law suggest.

In the United States, in *Hoggard* v. *State* 27 Ark 117 640 SW 2d 102 (1982), for example, which concerned the buggery of a 6-year-old boy, the court recognised that pornography could have an instrumental role: 'the pornography was used as the instrument by which the crime itself was solicited – the child was encouraged to look at the pictures and then encouraged to engage in it' (at 106).

Exotic practices found in unusual videos may be tried on sexual partners as well as strangers; the fact that the practice appears in the film may be used to demonstrate its normality and desirability. For example, MacKinnon (1984: 17–18) cites the example of hospital admissions of women unconscious or dead after being raped in the throat following the showing of *Deep Throat*. Although the practice was executed in the film by means of hypnosis, this was not made clear in the film itself.

A number of examples of harms inflicted following viewing of specific films may be found, among them self-inflicted harms including bizarre methods of suicide. Here one might argue that if the 'victims' are adults and knowingly accept the risk of a particular course of action, it will be difficult to say that the film caused the taking of that risk. This would seem to lie within the sphere of self-regarding action, and therefore fall outside the scope of Mill's principle; the only reason for intervention would be on paternalistic grounds which would be hard to defend. But we also find cases which are clearly other-regarding.

A useful analysis of imitative harms is given by Feinberg (1987b). He refers to a robbery in which the victims were made to drink bleach, an idea the attackers had taken from a Clint Eastwood film. An example particularly pertinent to the problem of pornography is the case of *Olivia N., a minor,* v. *National Broadcasting Co. Inc.* App 141 Cal Rptr 511. A 9-year-old girl was attacked by a gang of adolescents and penetrated by a bottle, which, the victim argued, imitated a virtually identical scene in a television film. She sued NBC for negligently creating the risk which resulted in her injury, and although she did not succeed, the case illustrates some of the issues which arise in dealing with imitative harms.

Prima facie the responsibility for the assault lies with the initiator of the direct harm, namely the gang members, who cannot evade their own responsibility by blaming the company. There might have been a prior disposition to harm others, but the responsibility of the perpetrator, as Feinberg says, does not prevent us from *also* imputing responsibility to the film company: 'there might be room on the hook for both A and B because there are some cases in which it is true both that A caused B's harmful action, and that B's action was fully voluntary' (Feinberg, 1987b: 237). It might be plausible to see the actor's responsibility cancelling out the company's where the action is entirely self-regarding and the risk is voluntarily assumed.

For criminal responsibility to be imputed one would need the mental element of evil intent, negligence or recklessness. One would also need to establish causation using a 'but for' test for the *actus reus* of such an offence to be made out: that without the company's action, the harm to the victim would not have occurred and that this made the vital difference. It might be argued that the film-maker should have known that this film might affect a disturbed person and lead him to harm others. But unless the negligence is really gross, in the sense of taking an obvious and substantial risk, then the use of the criminal law and penal sanctions would not be justified. Nonetheless Feinberg accepts that even where criminal sanctions would be inappropriate, we might still say that A did harm C and, in such cases, C should have access to a civil remedy, in the law of tort, to obtain damages or an injunction to prevent future showings of the film.

On this view, the civil Ordinances proposed by Dworkin and MacKinnon would seem to lie within the scope of intervention contemplated by Feinberg's argument. He is unwilling to include the suggestibility of films and the indirect causes within the criminal law but sees the case for permitting a remedy in damages for indirect causes of harm as more persuasive. These costs could be built into film budgets and could be spread quite widely, falling on commercial sponsors, advertisers and insurance companies, and on the ultimate consumers. They would be offset by the enormous profits made by producers of such films as there is currently a demand for increasingly violent feature films.[4] It would not constitute a form of prior restraint, so would not infringe the right to free speech. Fault would not be required, so predictability and foreseeability would not need to be established, but proof of causation would be required and, as this might be difficult, vexatious claims would be discouraged. Circumstantial evidence could be admitted to establish causation. Evidence of causation would be the close proximity in time between the viewing and the harm and the novelty of the crime. Feinberg does not refer to similar-fact evidentiary rules here, but the tests of 'striking similarity', 'unusual features' or 'underlying unity' already used in the law of evidence might be employed.

Similar fact evidence has to be connected with the accused and his or her participation in the crime under consideration. It is normally used to rebut a claim of accident or coincidence. In the notorious 'brides in the bath' case, credibility was strained when the accused lost a succession of his brides in the same circumstances. As Lord Maugham said in *R. v. Smith* (1914–15) All ER 262:

> No reasonable man would believe it possible that Smith had successively married three women, persuaded them to make wills in his favour, bought three suitable baths, placed them in rooms which could not be locked, taken each wife to a doctor and suggested to him that she suffered from epileptic fits, and had then been so unlucky that each of the three had some kind of fit in the bath and had been drowned.

In these types of cases, one would be looking at examples of past behaviour which display such strong similarity that they cannot reasonably be construed as accidental or coincidental.

The principle was elaborated in *Makin v. A-G for New South Wales* (1894) AC 57. Makin was tried for the murder of a child; he had cared for the child in exchange for a small payment from the child's mother. Subsequently, the child's skeleton had been found in his back garden. Evidence was admitted to show that babies' skeletons had been found at houses where the accused formerly lived. In the past the accused had 'fostered' children for a small payment of money, but those children had also disappeared. This evidence was admitted not to show intent, but rather to show that the child had actually been murdered in the current case. Similarly in *R. v. Straffen* (1952) 2 All ER 657, Straffen was charged with the murder of a young girl. Evidence was admitted of two previous murders committed by him on the grounds of the similarity of the deaths and circumstances surrounding them with the present case, including the fact that all the victims were killed by manual strangulation; there was no evidence of sexual assault, no apparent motive, no evidence of a struggle and no attempt to conceal the bodies. All the bodies had been left where they could easily be detected.

Similar fact evidence is now most likely to be admitted in cases involving unusual sexual proclivities and practices, so it would seem particularly relevant to imitative sexual crimes. It usually demands a degree of proximity in time. Since *D.P.P.* v. *Boardman* (1972) AC 241, it has been used mostly to challenge coincidence and the likelihood of a person possessing the same characteristics as the guilty person. The issue of likelihood is very important: the less common the behaviour, the more likely it is to be admitted. As Lord Hailsham said in *Boardman*:

> Whilst it would certainly not be enough to identify the culprit in a series of burglaries that he climbed in through a ground floor window, the fact that he left the same humorous limerick on the walls of the sitting room, or an esoteric symbol written in lipstick on the mirror, might well be enough. In a sex case ... whilst a repeated homosexual act by itself might be insufficient to admit the evidence as confirmatory of identity or design, the fact that it was alleged to have been performed wearing the ceremonial head-dress of a Red Indian chief or other eccentric garb might well in appropriate circumstances suffice.
>
> (at 454)

The test of striking similarity could be applied to imitative rapes. Although one could argue that the perpetrators of the direct harm would have harmed their victim in any case, there would be room also for an action for damages for the incremental harms, such as the effects of the drinking of the bleach or the assault with the bottle, referred to earlier.

Although in *Harm to Others* (1987b) Feinberg is sympathetic to the imposition of civil liability in certain cases, in *Offense to Others* (1987a), he seems more sceptical of feminist arguments for regulation based on the causal connection between pornography and violence against women. Although he accepts that there may be copy-cat crimes, it is difficult, he argues, to justify controls on pornography on that ground, otherwise few books would be left uncensored. The issue turns on the question of prior disposition:

> It is not likely that non-rapists are converted into rapists *simply* by reading and viewing pornography. If pornography has a serious causal bearing on the occurrence of rape, as opposed to the trivial copy-cat effect, it must be in virtue of its role (still to be established) in implanting the appropriate cruel dispositions in the first place.
>
> (1987a: 150)

It is curious that he sees the copy-cat effect as trivial, a view unlikely to be shared by victims of such crimes. No serious review of the evidence of harms is given by Feinberg. The question is not just one of implantation but rather a matter of reinforcement.

If harms are indirectly produced, it is not of itself enough to warrant regulation, argues Feinberg. We need further conditions, for example, the 'but for' test, discussed in *Harm to Others*: that is, he would not have done what he did but for what was communicated to him by the film. But sellers and writers of pornography may not advocate or solicit rape. For it to count as incitement, which warrants the intervention of the criminal law, there would have to be strong evidence of serious and likely harm which would not have occurred without incitement, and that it was unlikely more speech could have been used to prevent the harm.

HARMS IN THE PRODUCTION PROCESS

Harm may also be involved in the production of pornography if participants suffer bodily harm as part of the film-making process or are coerced into taking part. Once individuals have been persuaded to appear, the film itself may be used as proof of their participation to ensure further compliance or as the basis for threats to tell parents where minors are involved. Substantial evidence of coercion, including physical coercion and blackmail to ensure further cooperation in pornographic productions, was admitted at the Minneapolis Hearings (1983). The harms caused to the victims in these cases may be exacerbated by the repeated showings of the film. For this reason the use of injunctions where coercion has been proven was seen as a key component of the Indianapolis Ordinance. The experience of Linda Marchiano (Lovelace) was cited in submissions: her coerced involvement in pornography and the use of intimidation and violence, including death threats against other members of her family.

From a libertarian standpoint, consent is crucial: where agents freely consent to involvement in an activity, in full knowledge of what is involved, then normally those activities should be protected from regulation. But the existence of consent and coercion is problematic in the case of pornographic productions. For the consent of participants needs to be viewed in the context of the dynamics of the relationship between actors and producers, women's limited job opportunities and evidence of a prior history of abuse where appropriate.

Pornography may contain depictions of acts of violence which stop short of murder, but include mutilation and beatings. Given the poor technical quality of many films, sophisticated skills and techniques enabling the simulation of violence may not be available or seen as sufficiently titillating. The most extreme form would be snuff movies, in which women are filmed while allegedly being murdered, although the existence of such films has been hotly debated.[5] MacKinnon in her submission to the court in *American Booksellers* v. *Hudnut* referred to a case on this issue in California.[6] The enormous potential profits arising from the expansion of the market for home videos may encourage the investment in more 'exciting' materials with snuff movies being the logical end-point of the continuum, where characters are actually killed.

Raids in Britain in recent years have netted films of ritual sacrifices and the disembowelling of a foetus from a heavily pregnant woman, prompting debate on whether the events in these low-budget films can be simulated. Films of autopsies have also been circulating.

The question might be posed as to whether animation techniques might be used instead of real actors, to meet the objections of those who criticise pornography because of the harms entailed in production. The interaction of human actors with animated characters has been used successfully in the film industry in, for example, *Roger Rabbit*, and this might be deployed in pornographic productions. The expansion of computer pornography may well be the next 'advance' of the forces of the production of pornography, with the potential for the exploitation of virtual reality technology. If consumers were satisfied and found the products sufficiently stimulating and the harms of the production process were eliminated, would this rescue pornography from feminist criticism? The use of animation instead of real actors, a defender of animated pornography might argue, would satisfy free speech interests and protect potential participants. Animated child pornography on this argument would benefit children, if such material met a need which would otherwise be satisfied by the real abuse of children, as well as removing them from the production process. But this argument is unpersuasive, for if the cartoons depicted the torture and sexual abuse of childen as desirable practices, they might still be seen as harmful in encouraging and legitimating such practices. The sale of images of children being subjected to abuse may undermine the credibility of survivors of abuse. Children as a group already possess fewer rights and demand less respect than adults. The status of children clearly would not be enhanced by such material. The effect on the viewers and the culture in general also needs to be considered. Similarly, cartoons presenting violence against women as desirable and pleasurable for victims and perpetrators serve a legitimating function in validating violence against women. They may contribute to a process of desensitisation and have adverse implications for the credibility of the victims of sexual offences.

THE CREDIBILITY OF VICTIMS OF SEXUAL OFFENCES

The effect of a free market in pornography on particular groups, namely child and adult survivors of rape, abuse and violence, for whom a major problem is gaining credibility, also needs to be considered. The relationship between pornography and the credibility of survivors of sexual violence is complex. Although to defenders of free speech it might seem too remote to warrant intervention, the issue needs to be addressed. It is only relatively recently that the extent of child sexual abuse has been acknowledged. New doubts regarding the credibility of child witnesses have been expressed following the Cleveland and Orkney investigations. Numerous challenges to children's evidence have been mounted. Complaints of rape by adult women have for long been treated with suspicion by the police, judges, juries and the general public. Both children and women have been subject to corroboration warnings when giving evidence; juries have been warned of the dangers of convicting on their uncorroborated testimony. Proving absence of consent in rape cases has been a major problem for prosecutors which has resulted in a reluctance to proceed with complaints from certain categories of women, who are unlikely to be believed in the witness box.[7] Marital rape has only recently been criminalised in England. Similarly, domestic violence has been seen by the police and public as distinguishable from ordinary violent crime and, like sexual harassment at work, has been taken seriously only in the past decade. The awareness of complainants that they will not be believed is reflected in the under-reporting of a variety of offences including domestic violence, rape, sexual harassment and incest.[8] Interviews with adult survivors of child sexual abuse have confirmed the extent of this hidden abuse.

The problem for the victims is that they may not be believed, or may be seen as inviting the attack. If women and children are portrayed in pornography as acquiescing and enjoying violence and abuse, if these assaults are portrayed as normal sex, then it becomes harder for the survivors of sexual violence to establish their credibility and to be taken seriously. The desire to believe that participants in pornographic films and videos are willingly colluding mirrors the attitudes towards victims of sexual offences outside the context. Difficult as it is for victims of sexual offences to be believed, it may be even harder for those coerced into pornographic productions. As MacKinnon (1984) says, the description of sexual abuse will be construed as a description of a voluntary sexual act. This is predicated on assumptions about the nature of women contained in and perpetuated by pornography, as well as the strong presumption of consent between contracting partners in commercial enterprises. This is why consent and the existence of a contract were precluded as defences when drafting the Ordinances.

The legitimation of non-consensual violent sex is an important dimension of pornography. The problems victims experience can be seen as a manifestation of a deeper problem of women's 'silence', in the sense that women's views are seen generally as having less value and authority than men's. Pornography can therefore be seen as a way of silencing women by denying their value, depicting them simply as a means to an end, namely male pleasure, rather than being treated as having value in themselves, in the Kantian sense. Moreover, they are presented as enjoying and choosing this role, and their pleasure in subordination is portrayed as natural and normal.

A number of small-scale studies have been undertaken to ascertain the effects of exposure to pornography on tolerance of sexual crimes and the process of desensitisation.[9] If sex is defined in pornography as violence, then the tolerance of crimes of sexual violence may increase. This may be more pronounced as pornography becomes more violent. Some experimental studies have found that men exposed to pornography become more tolerant of rape and violence against women than men who have not. The former are more likely than the latter to accept rape myths, seeing rape victims as having less worth and suffering fewer injuries (Zillman and Bryant, 1982; Malamuth and Donnerstein, 1984). Social psychologists also gave evidence at the Minneapolis Hearings in 1983. Among the expert witnesses was Donnerstein, who argued that, on the basis of experimental studies he had conducted, desensitisation could result from viewing violent films, as measured by the degree of sympathy with rape victims. Laboratory experiments on 'normal' males have found that exposure to pornography increases acceptance of rape myths and of violence against women (Malamuth and Donnerstein, 1984). While these studies on their own might be seen as inconclusive, the impact of pornography may be further corroborated by the experience of victims on the 'receiving end' of pornography, although their experience has been under-researched.

Further evidence of the process of desensitisation may be found in the experience of Denmark, where changes in the subject-matter of pornography occurred following deregulation. In the mid–1960s the pictures of nude women changed to shots of women with their legs spread apart, holding their vulvas open. But as sales declined by 1967, as Barry points out, so the pictures became more explicit, depicting sexual activities stopping short of penetration (Barry, 1984). Within a year sales declined again, and hard-core magazines with no limits on the content were introduced and sales boomed and remained high, which would seem to support the satiation-desensitisation hypothesis.

Statistically significant correlations have been found between the circulation of pornographic magazines and rape. Baron and Straus (1984) found a significant positive correlation between variations in rates of reported rape between states and the aggregate rates of circulation in those states of popular magazines including *Playboy*. Although correlations clearly do not establish causation, the authors attempt to identify a possible explanation of these patterns in terms of their contribution to the legitimisation of violence. A longitudinal content analysis of sexual violence in the best-selling erotic magazines found increases in the amount of violent sex depicted (Malamuth and Spinner, 1980).

The link between pornography-as-fantasy and the reality of rape is complex. Rape trials themselves may be pornographic in the sense that media reports record the details in a voyeuristic fashion, describing the incidents in a way designed to titillate readers. Although cross-examination of the complainant on her sexual history with men other than the accused is usually prohibited, it may be permitted at the discretion of the trial judge, providing the basis for lascivious articles in the tabloids.[10] The issues of consent, respectability and ambivalence of women and the implication that female protest really means consent are routinely raised in rape trials and echo the familiar themes of pornography.

CHILD PORNOGRAPHY

It is often noted that children's involvement in pornography is irrelevant to the pornography and censorship debate because their participation is non-contentious. Most societies would condemn the use of children in pornography. Children occupy a privileged position within liberalism, because they are deemed to lack the capacity to make their own choices and decisions. Children are excluded from the realm of rational moral agents, and their consent is not relevant to participation in pornography.

But the participation of children is relevant to the pornography and censorship debate, and their position should not be excluded *a priori* from the discussion for three reasons: first, because the rationale underpinning their exclusion may throw light on the position of other participants, second, because of the close connections between child and adult pornography, and third, because of the implications for credibility discussed above.

If we consider the kinds of examples where Mill countenances intervention and denies individuals a free hand, for example, in child protection, what is his rationale for intervention, and can it be applied to the regulation of adult pornography? Mill advocated quite extensive intervention where children's interests are concerned: for example, he favoured laws forbidding marriage unless the parties can show they are capable of caring for children, which would seem to go a lot further than the regulation of pornography in limiting choice and discriminating against poorer individuals. He recognised that it is a restraint on liberty for people to control their own inclinations, but the alternative would be a life of misery and depravity for children. From this standpoint, one might argue that the restraints on producers of pornography are justified in order to protect all victims. There is clearly no difficulty on the Millian view with restraints on the use of children in pornography which are already in existence in the United States and Britain. The issue then is whether women as a social group also warrant protection. If one of the justifications for child protection is that children require special protection because they are liable to be exploited by more powerful individuals and groups, can the same appeal to disparities of power also be invoked as a reason for special protection of women's interests? Women are vulnerable to abuse and violence within the family and marginalised outside the domestic sphere. Historically both groups, women and children, have been seen as legitimate objects of violence; in society generally the physical punishment of children is still widely accepted; both have faced problems of credibility when trying to defend themselves against abuse and exploitation.

Women seem to possess a special status in so far as they may be portrayed as objects of domination, degradation, capture, genocide and mutilation with relatively few restraints. Attempts to control this market are usually met by a fierce defence of free speech rights. It is difficult to imagine a comparable group whose images of destruction and exploitation could be so freely distributed. A flourishing supply of materials on sale and display on corner bookstalls selling material celebrating Nazi attacks on Jewish people or acts of violence against black people would rightly be widely condemned. But if the object of assault and exploitation is female, this is frequently defended as protected speech and attempts to limit it attacked as censorship.

One might argue that children are irrelevant to the pornography and censorship debate as paternalistic policies for child protection are accepted even by libertarians, but this does not dispose of the issue, as the distinction between child and adult pornography is not so clear-cut in practice. Sentencers in England and the United States do take account of the content of materials when sentencing pornographers and would normally impose harsher penalties when children are involved. In England possession of child pornography constitutes an offence. Children may be shown pornography as part of the process of continuing sexual abuse. Evidence of this has been admitted in cases of sexual abuse in the United States and England.[11] The possession of pornographic materials *per se* may be seen as an indication of abuse and alert child-protection agencies to the likelihood of abuse. Adult pornography may be used to initiate children into taking part in pornographic films and photographs and to blackmail them into continued participation. It is questionable whether child pornography can be eliminated without also regulating adult pornography. Moreover, without restraints on adult pornography, one might argue that there will be fewer checks on the sexual abuse of children.

Child pornography may be significantly linked with the traffic in children. Barry (1984) reports that the Los Angeles Police Department Children's Unit for sexually exploited children found an international market in the late 1970s for blonde-haired, blue-eyed American children, both for use in pornography and for prostitution. In some cases photographs were taken by abusers, who after molesting and photographing the children, sold the pictures to professional pornographers or distributed them through mail-order networks. Sometimes they are sold through bookshops and larger mail-order operations. Paedophile groups may circulate and promote the use of such material.

Pornography constitutes an international market for buyers and suppliers, which raises problems for law enforcers and customs officials seeking to enforce domestic legislation. Given the high profits and size of the pornography industry, organised crime may be attracted to the industry, as has happened in the United States.

PORNOGRAPHY AND THE IDEOLOGY OF CULTURAL SADISM

Pornography has been seen by Barry (1984) as a significant component of a set of practices and ideas which encourage sexual violence by presenting it as normal behaviour. She defines this ideology as cultural sadism and describes pornography as the 'crystallisation of cultural sadism'. It is the major institution promoting the ideology of sexual violence, albeit wrapped up in concepts of sexual liberation. In its portrayal of women as forever sexually willing and unsatisfied, with the potential to undermine and destroy men, it provides a way of dealing with male hatred of and aggression towards women through fantasy, in which women are brought under men's control.

Cultural sadism is wider than pornography, and would include, for example, female circumcision, but it is an important means by which cultural sadism is translated into the sexual practices of consumers, given that the dominant theme is degradation, abuse and cruelty to women. Sadism and violent male aggression may be misrepresented in pornography as normal sexuality, love or romance, and a source of pleasure for women. This distortion of reality, argues Barry, is essentially a political act, as behaviour is labelled as normal by those with the power to label. While the use of pornography clearly cannot account for all acts of sexual violence or relations of servitude, nonetheless its impact extends beyond the direct effects on consumers.

Pornography diffuses the ideology of cultural sadism into the expectations of normal sexual behaviour, and into the practice of individuals. In the ideology of cultural sadism, argues Barry, it is taken for granted that men have whatever they wish to gratify their sexual needs, even if it means the annihilation or destruction of another person, typically a woman. In *The Story of O*, for example, the victim willingly consents to being repeatedly raped and assaulted and ultimately demands her own murder. The three principal themes of pornography Barry identifies are sexual sadism, presented as a source of sexual pleasure for women, the presentation of sadism as part of the sado-masochistic duality of human nature, into which both parties enter freely, and the presentation of beatings and violence in an unrealistic way, for example, the leaving of no marks on the victims' bodies and a denial of the reality of pain and suffering.

Pornography, Barry argues, is clearly intended for effect, to produce a sexual response in the consumer, through, for example, masturbation, rather than an aesthetic experience. Even if consumed in a public venue, it may be viewed in private booths, and if the experience is pleasurable, it is likely to be repeated. Because it occurs in private, it will not be subject to checks from reality and the line between reality and fantasy blurs. Given this isolation, the events depicted which cause sexual stimulation receive a powerful reinforcing stimulus. If held in the memory, they may be subsequently acted out. But even if the pornography leads to sexual fantasies which are not directly acted out, they are still retained in the mind as part of the individual's sexual experience and shape the individual's personality. If young males are among the consumers the effect is likely to be influential over a long period of time.

Barry's focus on pornography as fantasy offers one way of understanding its influence but important issues are overlooked in her analysis. Although she sees pornography as a key diffuser of the ideology of cultural sadism, she does not fully elucidate the mechanisms involved or specify their precise effects. It is also difficult to see pornography as fantasy when, for many readers, it constitutes 'reality', although she does acknowledge the blurring of the boundaries in the process of consumption. But as 'reality', its impact is likely to be more extensive, and an understanding of its effects is crucial. Her argument that pornography denies the experience of pain is also problematic: not least because violent pornography may be difficult to simulate and also because evidence of pain and suffering is precisely what many customers want. This would seem to be supported by evidence of desensitisation and of the increase in the violent content of materials with deregulation. It is also difficult to see pornography as a private mode of consumption in the sense she describes, as videos may be consumed in the home in the company of others.

Feinberg (1987a) examines the cultural links between violence and pornography in terms of 'a cult of machismo' constituted by the values of group loyalty, fighting, and the view of women as trophies. Pornography, he says, does not appeal to the psychologically normal male, only to those who have already embraced macho culture:

> Pornography does not cause normal decent chaps, through a single exposure, to metamorphose into rapists. Pornography-reading machos commit rape, but that is because they already have macho values, not because they read the violent pornography that panders to them.
>
> (Feinberg, 1987a: 153)

To challenge macho values, says Feinberg, we need to re-educate, using moral education rather than the criminal law. It is possible that *constant* exposure to violent material might affect a normal person, but even this, he says, is unlikely to occur, because violent material will probably not appeal to someone without the prior disposition. He argues that violent pornography is more a symptom of machismo than a cause of it, and merely treating symptoms is not the best way to offer protection to potential victims of rapists.

Feinberg sees the macho culture as the primary cause of existence of violent pornography in so far as it supplies the audience. The macho culture is also a cause of real-life violence, in that it provides the motive. So the most pornography may be responsible for is a small spillover effect, but pornography is not the prime cause of violence against women.

But Feinberg is too dismissive of the significance of pornography in explaining violence. He assumes too sharp a division between normal and abnormal males which is difficult to reconcile with the high levels of demand. Moreover, even if it is not the prime cause of violence, this does not mean regulation is unwarranted in view of the important role of pornography as a reinforcer of the macho or sadistic ideology. Even in non-violent or 'milder' material, the cultural climate is one in which women are portrayed in demeaning and degrading ways.

THE HARMFUL EFFECTS ON COMMUNITY MORALITY

Constraints on pornography might also be seen as a means of upholding a community's moral standards. The focus on using law to enforce a society's moral standards has its roots in the eighteenth century but is associated more recently with Lord Devlin in *The Enforcement of Morals* (1968).

Lord Devlin was addressing the issue in the context of the Wolfenden Report (1957), which reviewed the law governing homosexuality and prostitution. It generated a debate between Hart and Devlin on the relationship between law and morals and the question of whether state intervention in the enforcement of morality may be justified where physical harm to others is not in issue. Lord Devlin challenged the assumption that morality was a matter for private judgment. Society may pass judgment on moral issues and society may use the law to protect and preserve morality, to enforce its moral judgments. 'What makes a society of any sort is a community of ideas, not only political ideas but also ideas about the way its members should behave and govern their lives' (1968: 9). Without this morality, society could not survive but would disintegrate. A common morality is the price paid for social cohesion. If we accept society's right to make moral judgments and that common morality is necessary to society, then society may use the law to protect morality, just as it uses the law to safeguard other things which are essential to its survival. In practice the law should accord the maximum freedom to individuals which is compatible with the integrity of society. Privacy should be respected as far as possible, but the law may justifiably intervene to protect society.

On this argument, then, if a community decides that it does not wish to live in a culture where pornography freely flourishes, it will be legitimate to use the law to express this view. Here we are taking account of the effects on society as a whole as well as on participants. A similar argument was used by Justice Burger in *Paris Adult Theatre v. Slaton* 413 US 49 (1973), where he referred to the adverse effect of pornography on 'the mode ... the style and quality of life, now and in the future'.

At the time Lord Devlin's view seemed out of step with the mood of sexual liberation. Hart (1968) argued that the mere fact that the private behaviour of others may offend or distress us cannot justify intervention. Because sexual impulses are so important to individual development, heavy-handed intervention can undermine individual prospects of happiness. There is no evidence to suggest that sexual deviance threatens the survival of society, as deviation from orthodox sexual morality does not usually reflect a general hostility to society. Morality is not a 'seamless web' so that deviation on one aspect means a rejection of the whole morality. In any case, diversity of life-styles and experimentation may be of value. The fact that sexual morals change through time means that the law is too inflexible to capture these changes. In any event, use of the law may not be the best means of teaching morality. But, it will be argued, the argument from diversity does not undermine the case for the regulation of pornography but rather supports it. In recent years the right of society to intervene in the private sphere has gained more support. Where harms to others are in issue, the fact of consent cannot justify non-intervention by society in the private lives of individuals.[12]

ENVIRONMENTAL HARMS

Environmental harms have also been cited in support of the case for regulation. Various ways of dealing with the environmental effects of pornography have been proposed, including limiting the number of shops which sell pornography, dispersing them through the city, and confining them to particular streets or areas through planning controls. One form of regulation used in the United States is zoning, which is usually justified in terms of offensiveness. Because it restricts rather than prohibits access to pornography, it meets with more support from defenders of pornography and free speech. Pornographic bookshops have been subject to zoning laws in the United States.

The Supreme Court in 1976 upheld a Detroit Ordinance confining the bookshops to certain areas. Municipal zoning ordinances will be upheld if they permit them to survive, but not if access to them is significantly restricted.[13] In *Young v. American Mini-Theatres* 427 US 50 (1976), the court held by a bare majority that the Detroit Ordinance prohibiting the siting of adult cinemas and bookshops in certain locations was a valid means of regulation because of the city's interest in protecting the character of its neighbourhoods, and this interest supported its classification of films, although it included some films which might be constitutionally protected. In England a limited form of concentration has been deployed through planning regulations and controls on sex shops and cinemas. The Williams Report (1979) also favoured the use of restriction rather than prohibition.

Zoning does not necessarily solve the problem of environmental harms. Although the environmental effects of sex clubs, shows and shops may be contained by zoning, as in *Renton* v. *Playtime Theatres* 10 S Ct 925 (1986), this means that some neighbourhoods are protected at the expense of others, so that residents in the selected areas suffer loss of their property values as well as a poorer quality of life and a decline in their visual environment. Prostitutes may be drawn to the area because of its character, attracting kerb-crawlers. Nor does zoning of sex shops prohibit the routine sale of 'soft pornography' in high-street shops and corner shops, so that pornographic material remains visible. Even if public displays of material are prohibited, the sight of rows of shops with blank fronts is depressing and contributes to the atmosphere of decay of such areas; it would not be tolerated in middle-class residential districts, and zoning ordinances have met with opposition from some neighbourhood groups.

The justification for zoning and restrictions is normally in terms of offensiveness rather than direct physical or psychological harm, although offensiveness might still be construed as a harm. As restriction makes it harder for consumers to follow the activities they favour, particularly those who lack the resources to travel across the city, the borderline between restriction and prohibition may not be so clear-cut. It also would not satisfy those who object to pornography and related activities simply because they exist, rather than because of their appearance, but the offence resulting from bare knowledge would be difficult to justify on liberal principles.

If the goods of sex shops were dispersed into ordinary retail outlets, this would make it even harder to avoid the confrontation with offensive images. The inclusion of the depiction of violence and subordination in the context of 'normal shopping' might also further legitimise its place as part of everyday life. One solution might be to encourage the mail order of materials and to close down direct retail outlets. But zoning and mail order both fail to address the problem of displacement of consumption of pornography to the private sphere.

Although the harm-based argument for regulation is seen by Feinberg as weak, he accepts that there may be grounds for offence-based regulation, although this might best take the form of restriction rather than outright prohibition and the issue of avoidability is crucial. Erotic materials can be redirected or restricted to avoid a nuisance, and those who find them embarrassing or shocking can avoid them. But violent or degrading materials remain offensive whether in view or not. In the case of pornographic or racist films, one may experience profound offence whether or not one sees them. Nonetheless the offensiveness will carry relatively little weight if one can reasonably avoid them. 'The offense principle ... will not warrant legal prohibition of the films unless the offense they cause is not reasonably avoidable' (1987a: 159). Even if we experience moral outrage that is not reasonably avoidable, it is difficult to ban everything that causes moral outrage without relying on legal moralism.

If there is no convincing evidence of a causal link to social harms, argues Feinberg,

> pornography ought to be prohibited by law only when it is obscene and then precisely because it is obscene. But obscenity (extreme offensiveness) is only a necessary condition, not a sufficient condition, for rightful prohibition. In addition, the offending conduct must not be reasonably avoidable, and the risk of offense must not have been voluntarily assumed by the beholders.
>
> (1987a: 142)

A racist film shown in a private club to an audience of racists, he says may be insufficient to warrant intervention, but if there were racist signs in the city advertising it, which were not avoidable, then intervention might be justified.

PORNOGRAPHY AND THE PRIVATE SPHERE

As it is still relatively unusual for hard-core pornography to be read obtrusively in public places, the home remains the major site for the consumption of pornography, and this has been strengthened by the growth of the market in home videos. With technological advances, home videos have supplanted 'sex cinemas' as the principal venue for the enjoyment of pornography. But because the private sphere is the domain most revered by liberalism, regulation of pornography for home consumption is likely to be strongly resisted. At the same time women's exposure to pornography is intensified in a context where it may be hard for them to prevent men bringing pornography into the home. In *Stanley* v. *Georgia* 394 US 557 (1969) the possession of obscene material at home was held to be protected by the right to privacy. The home, construed by liberal legalism as the arena of personal choice, is seen as the legitimate zone for the viewing of pornography; but the private sphere of the home is marked by fundamental inequalities of power which are obscured by the notions of choice and privacy. Accounts of domination and exploitation in pornographic films and magazines may become part of everyday life, rather than something exotic. Degradation and domination are eroticised and made normal, which may increase pressures on women to emulate practices contained in the material. The tactic of avoidance which Mill recommends for dealing with disapproval of others' 'self-regarding' actions does not constitute a viable option for women confronted with pornography in the home.

When the environmental costs, the physical costs and the general climate of opinions and practices engendered by pornography in which individual spontaneity and originality are stifled and perpetuated are aggregated, it is difficult to defend the view of pornography as a purely self-regarding activity. From a Millian perspective, a liberal feminist could advocate regulation on the harm principle, on the ground that it is other-regarding and harmful to the interests of others. The libertarian defence of pornography has largely rested on the presumption that pornography consists for the most part of relatively benign material, when in fact images of violence, torture, mutilation and domination are commonplace. Consequently, Mill's examples of harmless actions wrongly criminalised by an over-zealous state, such as carving blasphemous comments on a gate, seem far removed from the celebration of sexual violence in the world of pornography.

But even if the link between pornography and physical harm were refuted, other arguments might be advanced on which to ground a claim for regulation, including the argument from autonomy, which builds on the perfectionist strand in liberalism. This will be considered following a discussion of the evidential problems which arise in claims of harm and which raise issues of causation, remoteness and proximity.

Chapter 3

Proving harm

The proponents of the regulation of pornography must establish that pornography causes harm in the face of the widespread presumption that pornography is harmless. Methodological and ethical problems face the researcher in establishing causation. Moreover, there is considerable disagreement over whether the studies which have been conducted confirm or challenge the hypothesis that pornography is harmful. The Williams Report (1979), the President's Commission (1970) and the report by Howitt and Cumberbatch (1990) found no conclusive evidence of a causal link between pornography and violence, while the Meese Commission (Attorney-General's Commission, 1986) and some experimental studies have suggested that pornography may be harmful. The question of who should determine the connection between pornography and the various types of harm, whether it should be the responsibility of the courts, Parliament, social scientists or lawyers, is also contentious. In England the jury will normally ascertain whether obscene material is likely to deprave and corrupt the consumer, and expert evidence on this is not admissible in most cases. This means that social scientific findings are not usually taken account of by the court. However, such research has been actively sought by the Home Office in the United Kingdom and by Commissions in the United States. These Commissions have made use of findings from experimental psychology as well as philosophical enquiry.[1]

In the United States constitutional issues may be at stake regarding who should be making the decisions on questions of causation, the legislature or the courts, and whether judges are competent to determine issues of harm. In *Paris Adult Theatre* v. *Slaton* 413 US 49 (1973), the court said 'It is not for us to resolve empirical uncertainties underlying state legislation, except in the exceptional case where that legislation plainly impinges upon rights protected by the Constitution itself' (at 60).

There are problems in isolating the precise causal link and key variables and in generalising from specific studies. There are also evidential problems regarding the standard and burden of proof. How many studies are needed to rebut the presumption of harmlessness and to persuade sceptics of the actual or potentially harmful effects of pornography? It is also difficult to ascertain what kind of test would satisfy those who reject a causal link between pornography and various types of harm. On whom should the burden lie to adduce evidence? In the debate so far the burden has rested on those wishing to argue that pornography is harmful to support their hypothesis, but the presumption of harmlessness has been taken for granted rather than vigorously tested.

The contrasting views of the connection between pornography and sexual violence may be understood in the context of the changing ideological climate. When sexual libertarian arguments were advanced in the 1960s, emphasis was placed on the use of pornography in sexual fantasy, as a way of relieving sexual tensions and removing sexual repressions. This libertarian view may be contrasted with the moral right perspective which gained more support in the 1970s and 1980s, which sees pornography as undermining the family and threatening conventional morality.

Scepticism regarding the link between pornography and harm is widespread and includes libertarian opposition to regulation as well as libertarian strands within feminism. Feminist philosophers of science, including Sandra Harding (1983) and Evelyn Fox Keller (1985), have also focused on the limitations of the positivist and masculinist methodology used in social science and which is used to acquire knowledge on the impact of pornography. But while social scientific methodology is susceptible to criticism, this does not mean that all social scientific studies lack value, any more than we would reject the value of all crime statistics because they do not accurately record the amount of criminal activity. Unpacking the way statistics are constructed is a valuable exercise which throws light on social and political processes. In any case, crime statistics may be supplemented by victim and self-report studies, so in studying pornography, a range of different techniques can be used, including interviews with participants, critical appraisals of existing studies and the testing of hypotheses with new experiments. The testimony of victims who have given their evidence at the various Hearings and Commissions on Obscenity and the findings of experimental studies may be used to supplement data on sexual offences and to test the harm hypothesis. Moreover, the critical appraisal of existing studies for their omissions and distortions presupposes that there is a truth to be revealed.

The standard and burden of proof, the quantity of evidence, and the relationship between causation and correlation, facts and values will be examined before looking at the specific problems with the major sources of evidence cited in the pornography and censorship debate.

THE STANDARD OF PROOF

In considering the causal links between pornography and anti-social behaviour, the courts have demanded a very high standard of proof. The debate has generally been conducted in terms of conclusive proof rather than the balance of probabilities, even when the regulation being sought is a civil remedy rather than criminalisation. Given the methodological difficulties in proving harm, it may be impossible to prove beyond reasonable doubt that pornography causes harm either generally or in a particular case.

This demands a very high standard if it means absolute or conclusive proof of causation. The possibility of absolute proof has been subject to vigorous criticism within the natural sciences and the social sciences because of the hermeneutic problems of meaning and interpretation. The difficulty of giving monocausal accounts of human behaviour, and the problems of uncertainty arising from the presence of the observer and the formulation of covering laws are even more formidable in the social sphere, where there are additional ethical and practical problems of experimentation. For example, it is difficult to use victims of pornography as part of feminist campaigns because of the salacious coverage they are likely to receive in the press. Moreover, this would also perpetuate the image of women as weak, passive victims, but if they are presented as 'strong' they are seen to be unharmed, and this may be reflected in a lighter sentence. In the Ealing vicarage rape case, the judge argued that the victim was not greatly affected by the rape. The question of causation is especially problematic in the pornography debate because it is hard to reach agreement on what would constitute a reliable test of the link between pornography and crime as well as on the weight of the evidence.

Schauer (1982) acknowledges the force of feminist critiques of pornography in relation to the violence and the degradation of women, but argues that given the wide range of communicative materials at which feminist criticism is directed, a high standard of proof would be required to justify regulation. Because of the strong presumption against regulation arising from the free speech principle, a high standard of proof is necessary which it is very difficult for advocates of change to meet.

Even with direct physical harms the amount of evidence required to justify any move towards regulation must be substantial. As MacKinnon observes, in *Memoirs* v. *Massachusetts* 383. US 413 (1966) Justice Douglas argued that 'The First Amendment demands more than a horrible example or two of the perpetrator of a crime of sexual violence, in whose pocket is found a pornographic book, before it allows the Nation to be saddled with a regime of censorship' (at 432). Yet in *Brown* v. *Board of Education* 349 US 294 (1955) the court did not require numerous studies to be convinced of the harmful effects of segregation on the self-perceptions of black children. One might argue, however, that the damage is so obvious by its very nature in the case of segregation. At the Minneapolis Hearings MacKinnon argued that evidence of damage caused by pornography is stronger than the correlation between smoking and cancer. Most of the discussion has focused on the impact of the violent content of pornography, but there may be problems in determining the amount of violence, depending on the selection of material. Feinberg estimates it to be as high as 10 per cent, while MacKinnon and others see violent material as the norm rather than the exception and a continuity has been observed between 'soft' and 'hard' pornography in terms of the common themes of subordination and bondage. However, most commentators agree that pornography has become more violent since the 1960s, even if they disagree on the exact proportions of violent material.

Simon Lee (1990) has argued that the standard of proof required will vary depending on the seriousness of the harm. If the cost to others from the free speech in question is high, society will be more willing to limit free speech, and less likely to demand conclusive proof. The problem here is that it may be difficult to separate the costs from the standard and burden of proof. In determining what counts as a cost, certain presumptions regarding the amount of evidence needed and the responsibility for adducing it may affect our evaluation: we cannot easily separate the issues of cost and proof. It may be easier when considering physical injury, but the types of harms arising from pornography may well be more complex. He does acknowledge that the effects may be problematic and subject to disagreement, so that some see pornography as a cause of violence and degradation while others might see it simply as a symptom of violence in society.

THE BURDEN OF PROOF

There is also the issue of who should carry the burden of proof, that is, whose case will fail if the burden is not discharged. The general principle of English and American law is that he who affirms must prove. In the context of the pornography debate, the burden of proof has been placed on those who assert that pornography is harmful. Failure to discharge that burden has meant the failure to achieve stronger regulation of pornography. In criminal law, the burden of proof is a fundamental principle designed to protect the accused and is strengthened by the requirement of a high standard of proof. But in academic debates, similar language and terminology has been used even where the liberty of the citizen is not in issue, but merely economic factors such as the loss of revenue from pornography or costs imposed through remedies, where the sharing of burdens might be more appropriate.

In the social sciences Popperian methodology has emphasised falsifiability rather than verifiability.[2] Instead of seeking to prove claims we should see them as tentative hypotheses, subject to constant testing. Yet the presumption of harmlessness has largely been just that: a presumption rather than a hypothesis subject to rigorous testing by those who hold it. It is not simply that the evidence to support harmlessness is unreliable or flawed but that defenders often have not felt obliged to provide evidence. The dogmatic claim that pornography is harmless and bears no relation to violence against women or to their general subordinate position is asserted rather than supported by evidence. In contrast, advocates of regulation have marshalled evidence and where possible conducted their own research.

Despite the presumption of harmlessness held by defenders of the pornography industry, the impact of pornography is already presupposed in many practices, including its use in behaviour modification and aversion therapy programmes, to resocialise offenders away from violent sex or child molestation towards more positive sexual behaviours.

A sexual response to an artefact may serve as a powerful reinforcer, which is likely to encourage the consumer to use that source of pleasure again, thereby strengthening its influence on behaviour. It is therefore curious that the dominant ideology of the post-war period has been to assert the claim that pornography has no influence on behaviour. As Barry observes: 'Social scientists have been so successful in convincing people that there is no relationship between pornography and sexual violence that behavioural scientists, while demonstrating that relationship, act as if there were none' (Barry, 1984: 248).

CAUSATION AND CORRELATION

One problem with the research on the impact of pornography is that much of the evidence takes the form of correlations rather than causal connections, for example, a positive correlation between increases in pornography consumption and increases in sexual offences. It is difficult to prove causation: even if we find societies with high levels of consumption and high levels of sexual violence, a 'co-relation' does not establish causation. But a strong correlation may suggest a problem worthy of further investigation in the course of which complex causal links may be revealed. For example, Max Weber (1965) noticed a strong correlation between holding Protestant beliefs and entrepreneurial economic activity. This generated a major study of the links between the Protestant Ethic and the ascetic rationality of capitalism. It led him to undertake qualitative research on the content and influence of the ideas and their effects on social practice. Similarly, in exploring causal links between pornography consumption and behavioural patterns, statistical correlations are insufficient to establish causation. But they may be a useful starting point to generate analysis and understanding of the images and meanings attached to the representation of women in pornography. Qualitative research will reveal whether the correlation is spurious and may unearth hidden variables. If a correlation could be found between a change in the quantity and quality of pornography and an increase or decrease in sexual offences, this would not of itself amount to a causal connection.

The prohibition on pornography in Muslim countries, such as Saudi Arabia, where we still find violence against women, including sexual offences, is often cited to refute the claim that pornography incites violence against women. Feinberg (1987a), for example, dismisses the causal connection between rape and pornography partly on this ground. But a formal prohibition on pornography accompanied by the existence of violence does not conclusively disprove the hypothesis, as there may well be a flourishing black market and it would be naive to assume a formal ban represents the reality. In fact critics of regulation often argue that there is no point in restricting sales or 'criminalising' pornography because this will create a black market and increase demand because it is forbidden. In the absence of pornography, it may be argued, men are quite capable of dreaming up their own fantasies and may contemplate and act out violence against women. Even if we had a totally pornography-free society and sexual offences persisted, this would not invalidate the case for regulation. For it does not rest on the claim that pornography is the only, or the sole, factor in violence against women. The feminist project is more modest, in recognising pornography as a significant factor contributing to a general cultural climate in which women are viewed negatively as well as triggering some acts of violence in specific cases, in which case legal redress should be permitted. As we saw earlier, this might be limited to obtaining a civil remedy in damages for aggravated torts – in the case of imitative harms, using a 'but for' test.

The relationship between relaxation of controls and changing crime patterns in Denmark is often cited in the debate, but caution needs to be exercised in examining the evidence. Legal controls were relaxed in Denmark in 1965. Reported cases of sexual offences of physical indecency, that is, sexual assaults other than rape and exhibitionism, declined during the 1960s. This decline was popularly attributed by commentators to the general liberalisation of sexuality, including the permissive approach to pornography. It was also cited as part of the evidence in the 1970 Report of the President's Commission (Ben-Veniste, 1970).

But the decline in the number of convictions may partly reflect the decline in reporting of offences rather than a decline in the amount of crime. Kutchinksy (1973) argued that while under-reporting was insufficient to account for the decline, the reluctance to report reflected a shift in public attitudes. It may be that in the context of this 'liberalisation' and the availability of pornography, survivors of sexual violence may well believe that less importance will be attached to such complaints. The evidence on the incidence of rape is also ambiguous. Official statistics indicated an increase in the reporting of rape following an initial decrease in 1967. But results vary depending on whether national statistics or those for Copenhagen are used.

THE LIMITS OF EXPERIMENTAL RESEARCH

Experimental research to measure desensitisation has shown that what is seen as violence changes with exposure to films. It may also be difficult to infer from laboratory experiments that a demand for more violent material resulted from exposure, or was already present prior to viewing. It is difficult to isolate and measure the causative force of a film whether in real life or in a laboratory experiment, to isolate the precise causal link. Even in carefully controlled experimental conditions, it may be hard to isolate the specific factor which leads to attitudinal changes when we are dealing with the whole context of the film. It may be even harder in real life to establish the causal significance of a particular film and to know whether a rapist would have raped in any case, even if he had not seen the film, when external factors are difficult to control. One possibility here is to use a 'but for' test, referred to earlier, when dealing with imitative crimes. This would be most useful in dealing with, for example, rapes where there is a distinctive *modus operandi*, but it would be harder to infer causation if we compared an 'ordinary rape' in the film with an 'ordinary rape' in real life, given the frequency of such incidents in popular films and everyday life.

Experiments have been conducted which show the effects of viewing pornography on students' attitudes, but there may be problems in generalising from them. A laboratory experiment tells us how subjects act in those experimental conditions, so it may be of limited generalisability. The respondents will be aware that they are 'on trial' and may be affected by the way the experiment is conducted and the presence of the observer, the fact that they know they are being observed, whereas the consumer of pornography may be enjoying and executing his fantasies without external observation. The importance of prior disposition in mediating the impact of pornography has been emphasised by commentators, including Feinberg (1987a), but if this is the key variable, it may be lacking in experimental subjects. Moreover, the experimental subject may be dragooned into participation, or take part for a small emolument, in contrast to the consumer who actively consumes pornography for its own sake. A further problem with laboratory research is that tests are constructed and conducted by social scientists and the views of the victims of violence may not be taken into account.

Some studies focus on the differential response of rapists and non-rapists to pornographic materials. Barry (1984) cites a study by Abel (1977) which played audio-tapes including both mutually enjoyable heterosexual intercourse and rape to two groups, rapists and non-rapists. The respondents were asked to visualise what was being described but not to masturbate, and their sexual responses were measured. He measured the degree to which aggressive force in the rape context evoked a sexual response. The non-rapists' sexual responses to descriptions of rape were significantly lower than those of the rapists. The inference here is that those who are already predisposed to commit acts of sexual violence will find that predisposition reinforced through pornography.

These studies may be problematic in presupposing a sharp distinction between rapists and non-rapists, when the line between them may be blurred, given the high incidence of rape and the fact that there may be a continuity of attitudes towards women held by rapists and 'normal' men. A defender of pornography might infer from this that if predisposition is a key factor in the response, then this reduces the causative significance of pornography. In other words, the man who has already raped, who also finds rape descriptions stimulating, may well have raped without the intervening variable of the pornography. But even if this could be conclusively established, it would not preclude a legal remedy for an aggravated rape as argued earlier.

FACTS AND VALUES

Because of the emotive nature of pornography, which arouses strong feelings in defence of free speech and revulsion at its content, it is particularly difficult to distinguish normative and descriptive dimensions of the debate. It has been argued that the selective use of sources and witnesses was crucial in determining the final findings of the President's Commission and the Meese Commission. The President's Commission was criticised for overlooking available evidence of harmful effects, while the Meese Commission, it has been argued, rested on a commitment to certain values.

The chair of the Meese Commission argued that harm must be evaluated using two further criteria in addition to social scientific findings: the totality of evidence and 'moral, ethical and cultural values'. The totality of evidence was construed as including expert opinion, common sense, anecdotal evidence, personal experience and victim testimony. The appeal to 'moral, ethical and cultural values' raised problems for those committed to value-free scientific research who would see such values as irrelevant to a determination of the fundamental question of causation.

The analysis of harm in the Commission's report was written by Frederick Schauer. His analysis is criticised by Carole Vance (1986) for exaggerating the evidence of harm, drawing conclusions without supporting evidence and misconstruing the meaning of causality in social science. She is particularly critical of the fact that he does not challenge the inclusion of moral and cultural values in the Commission's methodology. Vance challenges the conduct and procedure of the Commission in its selection of witnesses and the way it gathered the evidence to establish harm. She describes it as a 'show trial' in which pornography was found guilty. A large number of the witnesses interviewed were members of vice squads or of anti-pornography groups as well as victims who testified to the harms caused to them by pornography. But one might argue here that Vance's own positivistic conception of methodology is somewhat old-fashioned as positivism has been subjected to considerable criticism in the philosophy of the natural and the social sciences.[3] Even if an investigator is committed to certain values, this does not mean that we collapse into total relativism and that the studies have nothing of worth to say. Awareness of the influence and impact of values may encourage a more rigorous assessment of evidence and a willingness to consider a range of sources.

COSTS AND BENEFITS

If the perfect methodology could be devised which gave us information on the extent of harm, this would still not resolve the issue of regulation. For even if harm can be conclusively proven, a felicific calculus will usually be employed by the courts and academic commentators to balance the harm to women against the harm to pornographers and consumers resulting from restriction, prohibition or other forms of regulation. Where harm is proven, for example in terms of physical harm or the degrading depiction of women, these harms may be outweighed by the harms consequent on the suppression of the pornographers' free speech interests. The United States Appeals Court when considering the Indianapolis Ordinance took this approach, accepting harm and causation, but still seeing the fact of harm as insufficient to warrant a civil action against pornographers.[4] The acceptance by the Indianapolis legislature and others that such proof existed was insufficient to justify regulation. In the Canadian Supreme Court, however, it was accepted that the harms to women, children and society resulting from pornography were sufficient to justify obscenity legislation which *prima facie* infringed the right to free expression.[5]

If we could establish a causal connection between exposure and violent assaults and provided this only affected a small number of men, then defenders of free speech might argue that this would not warrant inter-ference with the right to view of the large numbers of law-abiding con-sumers who are unaffected by the material and who obtain considerable pleasure from it, nor justify the economic effects on the pornography industry. Instead we should shoulder the risk of exposure to the few individuals adversely affected by pornography. Similarly the right to pos-sess fire-arms has been strongly defended, despite high homicide rates involving the use of guns.

While there are substantial evidentiary and methodological problems in asserting harm, these are not necessarily insuperable. The court in *Paris Adult Theatre* v. *Slaton* 413 US 49 (1973) did say that 'although there was no conclusive proof of a connection between anti-social behaviour and obscene material, the legislature of Georgia could quite reasonably determine that such a connection does or might exist' (at 60–61). What is problematic, however, is that if the courts accept that proof is possible and that it has been established, new obstacles will be raised, namely the overwhelming or absolute protection afforded to free speech rights, and the claim that benefits are not sufficient to justify encroachment on those rights.

Chapter 4

Diversity and autonomy

The appeal to diversity and autonomy may be made by both sides of the pornography and censorship debate. The principle of autonomy may be used to defend free speech claims where the right is raised against the state.[1] Autonomy may be invoked in defence of pornography as part of the general defence of free speech, but it may also be used to justify state intervention to regulate speech. Although pornographers defend their practice by an appeal to the need for sexual diversity and choice, the development of a choice of options is a key element of the feminist critique of pornography, but given a quite distinct content. The concept of autonomy in the latter case bears little resemblance to the enfeebled and diluted version of this notion employed by pornographers in their celebration and defence of sexual freedom. The feminist concept of autonomy is arguably grounded in the heart of liberal theory, in Mill's work, including chapter 3 of *On Liberty* and in subsequent developments in liberal thinking, particularly the work of Joseph Raz.

MILL'S CONCEPT OF INDIVIDUALITY

The arguments for diversity, individuality and autonomy as a justification for non-intervention by governments and public opinion are an important aspect of Mill's analysis in *On Liberty*, where diversity is valued for its own sake as well as for endowing benefits on society.

In chapter 3 of that work Mill analyses the notion of individuality in terms of an autonomous individual capable of making choices and developing the more noble aspects of his character. His assertion of the desirability of individual autonomy is bound up with his fear of the majority. The danger of majoritarianism is precisely that it will 'fetter the development, and, if possible, prevent the formation, of any individuality not in harmony with its ways, and compels all characters to fashion themselves upon the model of its own' (Mill, 1970: 130), crushing individual spontaneity. For this reason Mill places great importance on experimentation and the exploration of a range of life-styles.

If we consider pornography from this standpoint we find a dominant recurring theme, namely a perception of women which stresses the characteristics of subordination, passivity and self-definition in terms of sexual subordination. This perception may be expressed in various genres, but we still find a limited number of images of women. Mill's model of human flourishing, construed in terms of choices, contrasts sharply with the homogeneity of pornography. This popular perception is so pervasive and so-called 'soft' pornography is so highly visible that it is difficult for women to avoid confrontations with that negative self-image.

Freedom to develop without impediment is essential to human flourishing, and part of the feminist argument for regulation is that pornography stifles women's development by expressing and perpetuating negative ideas and images and therefore does not deserve free speech protection. The focus on autonomy is also important to the feminist critique of pornography because of the difficulties of proving harm and causation of sexual and violent offences considered earlier. This perpetual confrontation with negative self-images arguably undermines women's development and awareness of their potential, regardless of whether a link between pornography and violent crime may be conclusively established.

Mill stresses the need for all people, not just the intellectual elite, to develop their capacities. He emphasises that human faculties and moral preferences can be exercised only in making choices:

> The human faculties of perception, judgment, discriminative feeling, mental activity, and even moral preference, are exercised only in making a choice. He who does anything because it is the custom makes no choice. He gains no practice either in discerning or in desiring what is best. The mental and moral, like the muscular powers, are improved only by being used ... He who lets the world, or his own portion of it, choose his plan of life for him, has no need of any other faculty than the ape-like one of imitation. He who chooses his plan for himself, employs all his faculties.

> (Mill, 1970: 187)

This presupposes that human development requires both the act of choosing and a range of options. For this reason he places great importance on experimentation and on the exploration of a range of life-styles. Mill's analysis rests on a dynamic conception of human nature:

> Human nature is not a machine to be built after a model, and set to do exactly the work prescribed for it, but a tree, which requires to grow and develop itself on all sides, according to the tendency of the inward forces which make it a living thing.

> (Mill, 1970: 198)

This analogy of the tree used by Mill, and his general concern to promote individuality, may be seen as providing a foundation for a theory of autonomy.

If we apply Mill's argument to pornography, one could argue that it is this truncation of other areas of lived experience which is one of the most pernicious features of pornography. Although it might be claimed that pornography could be retained alongside these other forms, the difficulty is how these other forms will ever develop if the depersonalised and reductionist view predominates. Mill was pessimistic about his own culture, in which society has 'fairly got the better of individuality' (Mill, 1970: 190) and his pessimism was justified if one considers the commercial success of the pornography industry now. He argued that the worst effect of the loss of individuality was the morbid concern with others' opinions, which extends from other-regarding to self-regarding actions, generating conformity. If this occurs, human faculties wither and die. When he addressed the issue of censorship in chapter 3, his concern was with the censorship imposed by popular opinion, or custom, rather than state interference: 'Thus the mind itself is bowed to the yoke: even in what people do for pleasure, conformity is the first thing thought of; they like in crowds' (Mill, 1970: 198). Choices and preferences are made only within the narrow bounds of the norm while eccentricities of taste are condemned:

> But the man, and still more the woman, who can be accused either of doing 'what nobody does', or of not doing 'what everybody does', is the subject of as much depreciatory remark as if he or she had committed some grave moral delinquency.
>
> (Mill, 1970: 198)

Self-development for Mill is construed in terms of the resistance to conformity and the development of individuality which enhance the quality of life:

> It is not by wearing down into uniformity all that is individual in themselves, but by cultivating it, and calling it forth, within the limits imposed by the rights and interests of others, that human beings become a noble and beautiful object of contemplation; and as the works partake the character of those who do them, by the same process human life also becomes rich, diversified, and animating, furnishing more abundant aliment to high thoughts and elevating feelings . . . In proportion to the development of his individuality, each person becomes more valuable to himself, and is therefore capable of being more valuable to others. There is a greater fulness of life about his own existence, and when there is more life in the units there is more in the mass which is composed of them.
>
> (Mill, 1970: 192)

The picture Mill paints is relevant to the effects of pornography in shaping the public view of women to a particular set of limited ideas, precluding other dimensions of women's behaviour and abilities, inhibiting the capacity for self-development. In Mill's conformist society, exceptional and ordinary individuals are inhibited from flourishing. Just as individuals need their boots individually made, he says, so individuals may all need different conditions for their spiritual development.

Yet far from promoting such spiritual development, pornography actually stifles it. It is intellectually undemanding, offering a repetition of images, and even the written material makes negligible demands on the reader. It might be argued that pornography should be seen simply as a sex aid or sex toy, designed to evoke a sexual response. As Schauer (1982) points out, it would be absurd to demand First Amendment protection for prostitutes or massage parlours, so it is questionable whether this protection should be given to pornography, just because it may achieve its effect through a written medium. Pornography contributes nothing to human flourishing or growth. It stunts and inhibits the development of aesthetic sensibilities and fosters the perception of women as irrational dehumanised objects.

Instead of generating new ideas or a range of choices, pornography rather reaffirms a view of women as irrational dehumanised objects. In pornography women are denied the capacity to struggle and hence denied full consciousness, and are reduced to the level of mere animal existence rather than self-consciousness. Their resistance to rape is depicted as feigned rather than genuine, for coerced sex is seen as awakening their true nature as sexual beings. Their ultimate objectification rests in their desire to become an object for others. This depersonalisation is also expressed in the terms used to describe them in pornography, as animals, or in terms which reduce them to parts of their bodies. This dehumanisation may be construed in terms of being reduced to an object of the male gaze in the Sartrean sense of being reduced to a thing in itself rather than the *pour-soi* (Sartre, 1943).

Pornography can be seen as constituting the triumph of the irrational, in its celebration of violence and its identification of women with the realm of the irrational rather than the realm of logic and rational reflection. Not only are women portrayed as irrational within pornography, but their efforts to challenge it have themselves been soundly criticised as irrational. Simpson (1983), for example, reviewing the work of the Williams Committee, on which he served, dismisses the work of Susan Brownmiller and Andrea Dworkin as political propaganda, rallying war cries rather than objective rational discussion. His comments on the feminist view of pornography seem out of touch with what was happening in England and the United States at the time. He argues that it is useless to look to Dworkin's work for any coherent legislative proposals or practical programmes as she is concerned only with consciousness raising, yet Dworkin was responsible, with MacKinnon, for the major legislative initiative in this area in the 1980s.

critique of pornography.[3] If it is so used, then the potential harm to the consumers of pornography would be a legitimate area of inquiry, which would otherwise be excluded by a narrow construction of the harm principle. Of course the consumers may include women, and this would entail consideration of the ways in which women's sexuality is constructed. More importantly, there would seem to be scope for regulation or intervention to discourage the consumption of pornography in favour of more edifying options as pornography is an option which undermines autonomy. On Raz's view it would be permissible for the state to take the initiative in promoting choices, and discouraging those which do not promote autonomy. He denies that this is necessarily incompatible with the harm principle because the latter principle only restricts the use of *coercion* and one can pursue perfectionist goals without coercion through the use of subsidies, such as taxation and education. One might, for example, seek to discourage pornography by imposing levies and using the money to subsidise feminist presses, women's aid refuges and various educational projects. However, it is debatable whether this does take us outside the realm of coercion, for taxation might be seen as effectively excluding poorer members of society from access to the customable goods.

A moral theory which values autonomy can justify restricting the autonomy of one person for the sake of greater autonomy of others or even of the person himself or herself in the future. The state has a duty to promote positive freedom by creating the conditions of autonomy which include promoting desirable options and discouraging repugnant ones, as well as preventing the denial of freedom in the negative sense.

Raz argues that his approach goes beyond the harm principle but is consistent with it, in the sense that a violation of autonomy is harmful, for if opportunities are not available, people are harmed by their absence. The demand of feminist campaigners for the regulation of pornography would therefore be justifiable within the terms of Raz's argument. It is not puritanical in the sense of being motivated by hostility to certain sources of pleasure, or based on arbitrary grounds, but is grounded in the recognition that pornography contributes to a climate in which women's capacity to develop their human faculties is undermined as images are conveyed which emphasise their subordination and unreflective nature.

Perfectionist policies, says Raz, are permitted if they do not rely on coercion, although coercion could be used in those extreme cases where the offence or harm to the feelings of others interferes with their abilities to lead normal autonomous lives in the community. Usually there would be other means available to control offensiveness, such as restriction, which do not invade freedom.

Because Raz's approach does not protect morally repugnant forms of life or acts, it can be usefully deployed in the feminist critique of pornography. In practice it involves a plurality of projects rather than a particular option and the exclusion of morally bad and repugnant options. Raz's approach might seem to be closer to a collectivist or communitarian model, but he rejects this charge on the ground that he does not advocate a strong centralist state or radical change through political means; rather he seeks a framework of conditions conducive to pluralism and autonomy. Although he emphasises the congruence of his approach with classical liberalism, it would not satisfy those who see the value of liberalism lying in the fact that it protects the *least* desirable options in society. For example, Ronald Dworkin argues that even if society as a whole is worse off through the presence of pornography, its publication should still be protected. The more unattractive the option, the greater is the need for a liberal or libertarian theory to protect it.

From a libertarian perspective, pornography would be seen as an option, whatever view one takes of its desirability, and a devotee might defend the celebration of sado-masochism in pornography as an exercise of freedom of choice.[4] Groups representing paedophiliacs, such as the Paedophile Information Exchange (PIE), have in the past defended their sexual interest in children in terms of the right to explore and express their own sexual preferences. But if autonomy, on Raz's argument, is valuable only if directed at good options, there is no reason for the state to provide or to protect worthless options. The state owes a duty to its citizens to create an environment in which these options can flourish. The presence of bad options contributes nothing to the value of autonomy and cannot help to satisfy it.

If we focus on the ways in which the state may promote the development of autonomy we are using a positive rather than a negative concept of freedom. If applied to freedom of speech it would entail, for example, the facilitation of access to the means of dissemination of ideas, and the provision of protection to speakers vulnerable to attack by hostile opponents. But the free speech right has for the most part been construed in a negative way, in terms of protection from the state rather than by considering how the state can intervene to enhance speech protection. As Lee (1990) says, this means creating a climate in which free speech can flourish, through compulsory education and other measures, rather than freedom from governmental regulation of free speech. While autonomy demands exposure to a variety of options, it competes with other values, and there might be cases where we accept restrictions on autonomy because of the implications for respect for the dignity of others, as in the case of racist speech. Here one might also consider the value of the speech in question, and this may be easy in relation to religious or political statements, but, he says, it may be harder to determine the grounds on which pornography is seen as non-valuable. Lee does not consider fully the implications for pornography as his prime concern is with racist speech, but if, as I have argued above, pornography lacks any redeeming value, then the costs of that speech may be outweighed by the need to respect the dignity of women. In any case, autonomy is compatible with restraints on pornography precisely because the latter is a morally repugnant option; autonomy is not undermined by the exclusion of a bad choice.

Raz explores the implications of a perfectionist approach by considering the problems raised by a religious sect which denies autonomy to its members and thereby harms its children. In such circumstances the case for toleration is weak, argues Raz, and on perfectionist principles, a society would be justified in taking action to assimilate a group, even when it means that the culture dies or is changed by that process. If the culture is broken up, or people are wrenched from it so sharply that they are unable to have a rewarding life, then we may have to tolerate it. But the danger, he argues, is that liberals and conservatives may join forces with members of the sect to preserve it, thereby condemning its children to an impoverished life when a better approach would be to use assimilationist policies, if necessary implementing them through the force of law.

If we apply this argument to pornography, the fact that we are dealing with mass culture rather than a minority sect would not prevent its use, for Raz extends his argument to the whole of an indigenous people. Pornography, as mass or popular culture, arguably denies autonomy to those immersed in the culture and therefore should be subject to regulation. One might reply that pornography could be assimilated into a higher cultural form, such as erotic art or literature, but it is difficult to see how this would be possible given the limited scope of pornography. If assimilation is not possible, because the values within the practice are so inimical to autonomy, then on the above argument prohibition would be justified.

Raz's perfectionism provides a useful liberal model on which to launch a feminist critique of pornography, which offers an alternative to either consequentialist or rights-based approaches and to theories of individual choice. But it also raises some difficulties. His account of moral pluralism would not satisfy those who see the incommensurability of moral and cultural values leading to a problem of relativism. If there are fundamental disagreements over what is morally repugnant or desirable, will they necessarily be tempered by the value of autonomy? In such situations, who is to decide which is the best value to pursue? Although in the pornography debate both defenders and critics may operate within the general constellation of liberal values, this may be a more serious problem when dealing with disagreements over fundamental religious beliefs.

The commitment to perfectionist goals is also problematic. Why should bad choices be denied any value? For example, one might see the bad choice as having educational value, for it is only through the experience of making a wrong decision that one learns how and when to make the right one. The right to make mistakes and to select the wrong choice might be seen as a cornerstone of liberal thought. The idea of a society in which they are excluded altogether may be highly virtuous but extremely dull. One justification of pornography is that while the darker side of the human character is repressed by the superego within everyday life, pornography enables it to be explored within the harmless bounds of fantasy, thereby containing these impulses within a safe environment. The pornographer might defend the the existence of the 'bad choice' here, possibly acknowledging feminist criticism, but arguing that only by confronting the most negative views of women does the consumer learn to distinguish these from more positive perceptions, perhaps pointing to the use of pornography in therapeutic programmes.

Problems also arise regarding the relation of harm and autonomy. If the threat to autonomy is itself construed as a harm, does the autonomy principle collapse into a form of the harm principle? Conversely, if it is wider in embracing self-regarding actions and perfectionist goals, does it negate the harm principle? It may be better to see autonomy as a distinct ground for regulation in view of the problems of proving harm. More importantly, even though harms to women arising from pornography have sometimes been acknowledged by the courts, measures to impose liability on pornographers have been struck down in the United States as unconstitutional.[5]

What is valuable in Raz's work is the idea that there are certain shared goods which are of value in themselves and which demand protection, expressed in his ends-paternalism. A focus on autonomy also offers an alternative to either utilitarian or rights-based approaches. The promotion of autonomy may well conflict with the maximisation of happiness of the majority of individuals engaged in the mass consumption of pornography. Autonomy may be a valuable dimension of the feminist critique of pornography. While the principle has also been used as a justification of free speech in First Amendment jurisprudence, it will be argued that it offers a weak basis for the protection of free speech.

Chapter 5

Feminism, truth and infallibility

FREE SPEECH AND THE PURSUIT OF TRUTH

The argument from truth is often invoked as a justification for free speech. The view that exposure to a range of ideas is essential to the discovery of the truth is found in First Amendment jurisprudence and also in the work of Mill (1970). He argues that the free circulation of a range of ideas facilitates the pursuit of the truth. Freedom of thought demands freedom to publish. Unless a culture can guarantee freedom of opinions and ideas, it does not deserve to be described as free. While intervention might be warranted in an undeveloped culture, the mark of a civilised society, he argues, is that it allows diverse ideas to flourish. Yet it is in this personal area that the 'engines of moral repression', as Mill describes them, are most active. While people are no longer executed for unorthodox thoughts, the law of blasphemy meets the same need to punish those with different ideas.

Although Mill does not specifically address the issue of pornography, he does refer to the efforts of the Puritans to crush public amusements of which they disapproved and to the 'moral police', a term also used to describe contemporary anti-pornography crusaders. He criticises the zeal of those 'professed philanthropists' such as sabbatarians who wish to control how individuals spend their leisure time:

> Though the feeling which breaks out in the repeated attempts to stop railway travelling on Sunday, in resistance to the opening of Museums, and the like, has not the cruelty of the old persecutors, the state of mind indicated by it is fundamentally the same. It is a determination not to tolerate others in doing what is permitted by their religion, because it is not permitted by the persecutor's religion.

(Mill, 1970: 223)

Mill's ideal society is one in which all individuals are free to pursue their own tastes, where they accept the consequences of their actions without being subject to censure by others, however unusual their tastes. The eccentric could not legitimately impose his tastes on society as a whole, and society could not justify silencing the eccentric.

His method of explanation is essentially a methodological individualist one: for in explaining morality, he sees moral life as consisting of an aggregate of individuals in which each individual counts as one and no more than one and is of equal value to others. It also rests on a conception of moral independence, that in the private sphere, the individual is sovereign and should not be restrained simply on the grounds of others' disapproval. He sees intolerance as close to the surface of middle-class life, a hangover from past religious persecution; little is needed to spark it off again. The weight of the 'do-gooder', for Mill, may be even more oppressive than legal sanctions in crushing unorthodox views, spontaneity and individuality, which are essential to a healthy society. If the crusades of the 'moral police' succeed, it will be a Pyrrhic victory, as a blanket ban means that a discussion of the crusaders' ideas is denied, so that their 'faith' ossifies, while for society as a whole prohibition of radical views means the potential loss of the truth.

Mill's attachment to truth is in part justified on grounds of utility, in providing knowledge which may be used to promote public welfare, but he also values truth as an independent good, in the sense that we should seek the truth even if it may not be attainable. For Mill, knowledge and wisdom may be acquired only by exposure to a range of opinions and ideas. Ideas should be constantly challenged, and ideas once held to be true are rejected in the light of new evidence.[1] Essential to the growth of knowledge are a clash of ideas and an open-minded rather than a dogmatic attitude, in which one subjects one's own ideas to constant testing and keeps one's mind open to the possibility that those ideas could be refuted:

> There is the greatest difference between presuming an opinion to be true, because, with every opportunity for contesting it, it has not been refuted, and assuming its truth for the purpose of not permitting its refutation. Complete liberty of contradicting and disproving our opinion is the very condition which justifies us in assuming its truth for purposes of action; and on no other terms can a being with human faculties have any rational assurance of being right.
>
> (Mill, 1970: 145)

We have confidence in our ideas only because our views have been challenged, but at the point we accept their truth as unchallengeable, our views crystallise into dogmatism.

The precondition for the pursuit of truth is a multiplicity of views, a market place of ideas, subject to critical validation by others rather than a single dominant paradigm. It is only when a conjecture has been subject to criticism and repeated testing that one could hold that view with confidence, but not with certainty. This approach, which we might describe as 'democratic pluralist', raises problems both as a scientific methodology and as a model of political practice. A common weakness in the notion of a search for truth is the assumption that all propositions or hypotheses have equal merit prior to testing. Yet in practice many ideas are repressed and denied any consideration. Scientists, for a variety of reasons, are reluctant to consider hypotheses which conflict with well-established theories. Hypotheses which conflict with energy-conservation laws, for example, are not even entertained. The same applies to political life. Data obtained from experiments which breach human rights and ethical principles might be ruled out as unusable without testing. Here truth may not be the most important issue when viewed in the context of values such as respect for life. Even if we accept, for the sake of argument, that discovery of the truth is possible, there might still be circumstances in which, if research might be illuminating, a group, society or government might be willing and justified in suppressing it because of the existence of a competing right or interest. Furthermore, the high premium required in the search for truth may actually inhibit rational inquiry. The philosopher C. S. Peirce warned how the pursuit of truth may block off the road to inquiry, and in practice scientists as well as political reformers seek more pragmatic solutions (Lamb, 1991).

The claims which compete with the search for the truth are usually justified by an appeal to utility, and Mill himself accepts restraints where incitement to immediate violence is possible. But if restraints may be legitimately justified on grounds of utility, then the case for doing so in terms of competing rights is even stronger. For example, sado-masochistic pornography might arguably give us insights into the nature of human cruelty which may be seen as of educational value, but restraints might still be justified if its effect is to inhibit the right to dignity, respect and self-realisation of the group depicted as the object of that sadism.

We could also point to examples where contributions might be excluded regardless of their contribution to the truth so that the truth is not the paramount consideration. Abusive expressions and hate speech, for example, might be excluded on policy grounds; or truths might be excluded because of the methods used to obtain them, as in the case of scientific knowledge gained through Nazi medical experiments. Barendt (1985) and Schauer (1982) give the example of literature which shows that a particular ethnic group has a lower IQ where the community might wish to restrict circulation of it because of its effects on racial harmony and offensiveness irrespective of whether it is true. But in this contentious area, methodology would also be crucial, so that the truth of the claim is hard to evaluate without a full consideration of the methodology used to achieve that result.

As well as the question of whether the pursuit of truth is the paramount value, there is also the question of whether the free market is the best means of reaching the truth. There are problems in attributing the greater truth to the ability to survive competition. In the 1930s, for example, theories of racial superiority achieved dominance in Nazi Germany and were viewed as representing the truth by supporters of the Party, notwithstanding the fact that those theories were seriously flawed.

Mill's appeal to truth as a justification of freedom of opinion and freedom to publish, his emphasis on the free market of ideas and of the dangers of assuming infallibility, has found expression in American jurisprudence. It is a view particularly associated with Oliver Wendell Holmes, in *Abrams* v. *United States* 250 US 616 (1919), where he refers to the importance of a free market of ideas.[2] It is a view influenced by American pragmatism. In *Abrams*, Justice Holmes argued that truths are not absolute but relative and can be judged only when freely competing in the market place of ideas and judged against other claims. He seems to accept verisimilitude as an ideal rather than reality: we subject claims to criticism in the hope of finding the truth but in practice can never be confident that we have found the truth. Because certainty can rarely, if ever, be attained, it would be presumptuous and arrogant for the state to intervene to inhibit discussion. To do so would presume that the state was correct and that truth was attainable.

As Schauer (1982) says, it is not clear why free discussion should be seen as the only means of finding the truth; the truth argument takes for granted that free rational discussion is best without explaining why this is the case. It may be that open discussion is the best way of finding the truth, but it is not explained by this model. Barendt (1985) finds the free-market argument implausible because the link between truth and the market is unclear, reflecting hostility to intervention for its own sake. Barendt argues that a number of areas which fall within protected speech may not be couched in a propositional form at all, so that it is hard to see how truth claims could figure in the argument. The example he cites is the case of *Cohen* v. *California* 403 US 15 (1971), where the slogan 'Fuck the draft' displayed on a jacket was held to be constitutionally protected speech. But of course the truth claim is not the only justification of the First Amendment, and in *Cohen* the slogan would still be seen as an expression of a political opinion, albeit in an inelegant form. Moreover, as he says, we can already find a number of areas of settled law where constraints on the truth prevail, for example, limits on the disclosure of information which is seen as a threat to national security precisely because it *is* accurate. Even the strongest critics of official secrecy would countenance restraints where real emergencies exist such as the location of strategic sites during wartime.

In the case of pornography, however, it might be argued that pornography stifles the truth. Given the quantity of pornographic material and its wide circulation, the pornography industry may actually prevent the discovery of the truth about women's nature and abilities. As Mill said in *The Subjection of Women*, it may be difficult to determine the character and potential of women because of the problem of abstracting them from a social context in which their servitude has a long history and deep foundation (Mill, 1984).

The inclusion of pornography in Mill's conception of the free market of political ideas is problematic. First it is difficult to include pornography within the ambit of political speech, which has always held a privileged position, partly because of the need for an educated citizenry and the need for control of potentially tyrannical governments. The extension of free speech protection to pornography is hard to justify on these grounds. Furthermore, the rise of mass society has, as Mill anticipated, allowed mass tastes and preferences to predominate. Pornography is part of the popular media rather than an eccentric taste or specialist market.

Although we can find evidence of a laissez-faire model of free speech in American jurisprudence, Mill's view of freedom of speech and the truth rests on a more complex and deeper classical liberal view which recognises the need for regulation in certain cases and is sensitive to the effects of customary restraints as well as governmental intervention.

Schauer (1982) argues that Mill is able to provide a causal link between free speech and the advancement of knowledge in *On Liberty* by reference to infallibility: we can never be sure of our fallibility; our beliefs might be wrong, but if we allow ideas to circulate which we believe to be false, we give them the benefit of the doubt that they could be true. Conversely any repression of those ideas could include repression of the truth. Mill's approach is useful because it draws our attention to the importance of comparing ideas and to the fact that the truth may lie in a suppressed view. Because Mill's *On Liberty* could be seen as arguing for an objective truth, even though we can never be absolutely sure that we have discovered the truth, it has been criticised by 'relativists' who reject the idea of an objective truth. But as Schauer says, this is to mistake truth for certainty and to focus on certainty rather than the advancement of knowledge. Popper's focus on falsifiability rather than verifiability is helpful here as the other side of the coin to Mill's argument for truth (Popper, 1963). Popper is not concerned with the search for certainty, but sees knowledge advancing through the constant search for error and rejection of falsified views. Both see the expression of opposing views as the only means of recognising our fallibility and of rejecting or revising mistaken beliefs. But they both fail to address the practical question of whether scientists or ordinary members of the community do actually think in this way, whether people are as rational as Mill and Popper assume. The assumption that scientific communities operate in such a rational way has been subject to criticism.[3] Apart from cases of extreme emergency where there is no opportunity for full rational discussion, in normal life within an 'open' system, some people may still be willing to embrace false theories, such as theories of racial superiority, leading to real problems of the persecution of ethnic minorities.

FEMINISM AND INFALLIBILITY

Mill's egalitarian moral theory, if applied to pornography, might seem to suggest that even if a large number of women object to the circulation of pornography, then they should not be able to impose restraints on producers and consumers, just as the pornographer should not be able to impose his view of appropriate sexual behaviour on the rest of society. But this argument fails to take account of the fact that at present the pornography industry does wield considerable power in terms of the size of the market and its links to mainstream publishing, so that the two parties to the debate are not of equal strength.

To the pornographer, the feminist critique of his livelihood as immoral could be seen as simply a new form of intolerance, and the comparison between feminist critics and the National Viewers' and Listeners' Association in the United Kingdom is often made. The pornographer might therefore argue that he defends the right of feminists to hold and propagate their opinions providing that they stop short of legal prohibition, but they do not reciprocate by permitting him the same freedom. Instead, on the basis of untested hypotheses, they wish to prohibit others from enjoying pornography in the firm belief that their view is right. Campaigners against pornography who assume that their views are correct and seek to impose them on others are ruling out the possibility that they could be wrong. Furthermore they seek to do so in the absence of convincing evidence of harm.

If we draw an analogy between the pursuit of knowledge in general and our understanding of sexuality, the pornographer could argue that pornography encourages sexual diversity and experimentation, encourages people to shed repressive ideas and taboos, and thereby adds to our understanding of a crucial dimension of human life. The problem with this argument, however, is that what actually emerges from the pornography industry is a very limited number of ideas about sexual behaviour which centre on domination and inequality.

Mill's argument for freedom of expression reflects his anxiety that a view which contains the truth may be stifled, denying society the *possibility* of knowing the truth. The pornographer might argue that feminists should concede the possibility that pornography is healthy and non-harmful and that they might be wrong, that there is room for both views and that the debate between feminists and pornographers can only enhance understanding. Similarly modern liberals such as Janet Radcliffe Richards (1982) have pointed to the dangers of feminism ignoring the need for the continual revision of beliefs, their own included, and the dangers of assuming infallibility. But it is feminist research and theory rather than liberalism which has extended the boundaries of inquiry and analysis to areas hitherto unexplored by liberal thought. Foremost here would be the scrutiny of the private sphere of the home and family which has revealed the extent of violence and sexual exploitation of women and children within the family. Moreover, feminism has broadened our understanding of methodology by recognising the value of human experience as a resource for the researcher. In the pornography and censorship debate, feminist thought has moved the debate beyond permissiveness and sexual libertarianism, to consider the potential and real harms which may arise from the production of pornography.

Essential to Mill's experimental approach is the need to explore different ways of living in order to develop our understanding of human relations. Consequently there would seem to be no *a priori* reason why a pornography-free society or one with low pornography consumption is not worthy of experiment. The difficulty with the pornographer's blanket defence of the industry is that it seems to preclude diversity or experiment. It constitutes a one-dimensional approach, defending the *status quo*, is hostile to alternatives and means that nothing ever changes. We know what a pornography-dependent society is like, but we have no experience as yet of the alternative, so at the end of the experimental period, we would be able to make a rational choice between the two modes of life.

Chapter 6

Free speech and majoritarianism

The relationship between free speech and majoritarianism is problematic for a number of reasons. First, it raises the issue of whether the demand for pornography should be construed as a minority taste and sexual preference, or an expression of mass culture. It is argued here that the latter more accurately characterises the current position. Second, there is the issue of how to deal with free speech rights when the majority opt to waive those rights to further community interests. On a Dworkinian argument the free speech right would trump the majority interest in most cases (Dworkin, 1977c). It would only be in exceptional cases, for example, when competing with other rights, that the right to free speech would be weighed in the balance. Both these issues will be considered.

THE DESPOTISM OF CUSTOM

The burden of proving the need for change has fallen, as we have seen, firmly on the shoulders of feminists campaigning against pornography. While any proponent of a different way of living should be able to give reasons why that path is preferable, existing practices should also be subjected to justification and to rigorous tests to see whether the assumptions, beliefs and arguments on which they rest are still valid. There have been few serious attempts by those directly involved in the pornography industry to justify the existing state of affairs.[1]

Usually the defence of pornography has been parasitic upon other types of protected speech, such as artistic works, sex education and political speech, rather than presented on its own terms. In the United States grandiloquent appeals have been made to First Amendment absolutism and to the liberating effects of pornographic material. It is therefore curious that accusations of infallibility have been directed at feminists rather than defenders of the industry.

Liberal philosophers, however, have been less reticent and marshalled arguments in defence of the right to use pornography. Foremost in these arguments is the defence of moral independence, the right of individuals to make their own consumption choices, and to pursue freely activities which meet with disapproval, provided that they affect only themselves. The taste for pornography is usually perceived as an eccentric foible rather than representing a degrading view of women. Although this defence has often relied on Millian arguments, Mill's anti-majoritarianism and his critique of the tyranny of custom are relevant to the feminist case for regulation and to the autonomy argument.

For Mill, the despotism of custom exerts the will of the majority and constitutes a barrier to social advancement. If homogenisation is not resisted, the prevailing cultural views come to be seen as 'natural' and any deviations are seen as unnatural. The alternative Mill advocated is diversity or heterogeneity. He stressed the need to challenge the deep slumber of decided opinion and pointed to the danger of assuming the infallibility of existing opinions. The yoke of public opinion may be heavier than the weight of the law in coercing individuals to conform to existing norms and could be as repressive as direct political oppression. He saw the constraint of custom as a particular problem in England compared to other European societies with more repressive laws.

The pornography industry is a major industry with a massive turnover and profits. As pornography constitutes a substantial area of consumption, it may be construed as part of the weight of custom. Protecting pornography means the protection of a set of power relations rooted in financial and patriarchal interests. While pornography is primarily consumed by men, women are still confronted with it as passive readers when it is displayed in high-street retailers, albeit on the top shelf. MacKinnon (1987) estimates the annual turnover of the American industry to be in the region of $8 billion. In the United Kingdom there is a substantial market in glossy magazines and videos.[2] In the United States the pornography industry has links with organised crime. In the United Kingdom the industry is more decentralised, with no evidence of organised crime, but rather a cottage industry. But the size of the market in both jurisdictions and the vast amount of material which has been seized, combined with the technical ease of duplication of video cassettes, suggest that a mass interest rather than a minority one is represented.

The profitability of the pornography industry and the fact that some material will be on the borderline of legality will mean that there are few restraints on pricing. In this respect the consumer may be in a weak position in relation to the seller compared to other markets, with little opportunity for redress if the contents are unsatisfactory. The fact that consumers are willing to run the risk of being exploited demonstrates how strong the demand is for the material and the attractiveness of the industry for producers.

Some of the difficulties the courts have faced in distinguishing the obscene from the non-obscene reflect the proximity of the content of pornography to mainstream attitudes towards women. For this reason the test of 'community standards' used in *Miller* v. *California* 381 US 479 (1965) raises problems in regulating pornography. Injunctions to prevent the showing of *Deep Throat*, for example, were granted in some American states but not others. In England the variability of jury verdicts between and within courts shows the extent to which the pornographic genre is interwoven with cultural norms of appropriate female behaviour.

In *1984* Orwell referred to the use of pornography to keep the masses happy and as a method of social control by allowing them to think that they were engaging in a daring activity while its production was controlled by the state. This equation of pornography with the unorthodox is still found in modern liberal writing. Defenders of the industry have contrasted the feminist view of pornography as a further expression of the 'moral majority', crushing the unorthodox and daring pornographer. But the protection of the pornography industry does not reflect the expression of a minority taste. Rather it is the massive weight of custom which is being shielded, and with it the central values governing women's subordination, while the feminist critique seeks to challenge orthodox ideas. This may account for the hostile and misogynous responses to feminism.

Although the right to use pornography has been construed by Ronald Dworkin (1986a) and others as a right of the individual against the moral majority, feminist campaigners do not constitute a powerful group capable of 'railroading' its ideas through Congress or Parliament, but rather a group seeking to obtain rights already enjoyed by others under the First Amendment and the European Convention on Human Rights.

The resistance to pornography, far from crushing sexual diversity, challenges the weight of custom. The reality of pornography is not a celebration of diversity but rather centres on one theme, namely inequality; although one finds distinct genres in pornography, what they share is the positive value of exploiting and controlling a subordinate group, which may include women from particular ethnic minorities, disabled individuals and animals. Racist stereotypes of passivity are frequently deployed, and the domination of black and Asian women by white males is eroticised.

One of the problems, as Mill perceived, is that when cultural attitudes crystallise to the point where they are seen as natural, even minor changes appear threatening. Coupled with this is the fact that the act of resistance itself conflicts with the images of female passivity found in the mass culture of pornography.

Because pornographic culture is popular culture, its pervasiveness, predicated on the equation of sexuality with subordination, makes it difficult for the critic to rely on the weapons of persuasion and avoidance recommended by liberal commentators. Stronger measures may be required, which could take the form of civil redress modelled on the Indianapolis

Ordinance, amended criminal laws and penal sanctions, or more carefully drafted directions to juries.

In place of the weight of custom, feminists have asserted the need for greater choice which would benefit society as a whole as well as women. If, as Mill argues, the power of custom is a barrier to advancement, then the feminist project can provide a basis for social improvement in facilitating the development of individuality and autonomy. The regulation of pornography may itself promote diversity and social improvement in freeing female talents from the yoke of stereotypical expectations and ideas. It might therefore seem odd that Mill's work has been used to champion the pornographer rather than as part of a critique of pornography.

WAIVING FREE SPEECH RIGHTS

The waiver of free speech rights has arisen principally in relation to the desire of communities to limit racist speech or the speech of those who attack democracy. As Alexander Meiklejohn (1960: 24) asks, 'Are we bound to grant freedom of speech to those who, if they had the power, would refuse it to us?' This issue has also arisen in the United States in the context of adjudication on the constitutionality of legislation where the community has elected to attempt to regulate pornography as in the Indianapolis case, where the majority on the city council have voted to waive free speech rights and introduce an Ordinance providing a remedy to victims of pornography. Here the legislature of the city of Indianapolis, its elected representatives and the Mayor, enacted a civil-rights Ordinance to provide remedies for those harmed by pornography. Before doing so, they heard a wide range of views, examined the available evidence on harm, and at the end of that process, took a rational decision to provide redress in order to pursue the goals of combating discrimination and so protecting victims. Ultimately the Ordinance was struck down by the Supreme Court as an unconstitutional infringement of the free speech rights of pornographers and publishers.[3]

The links between free speech and majoritarianism are complex. A key justification of free speech in English and American jurisprudence has been its importance to the workings of democratic government. Mill, for example, saw freedom of opinion and a diversity of ideas and opinions as a healthy check on governments to prevent abuses of power. The relationship between political freedom and free speech has also been emphasised by Meiklejohn (1960), who has argued that the most important justification for First Amendment speech rights is that all citizens need access to a range of political ideas if they are to participate in the process of government. Society as a whole can be improved and public welfare increased if all participate and exercise control over elected representatives. Of course this does not mean, he says, that everyone should take part in public debate on every issue, but it does mean that citizens should not be prevented from contributing 'because their views are thought to be false or dangerous' (Meiklejohn, 1960: 27). Unless citizens have free access to knowledge, information and ideas, they will be unable to evaluate or assess policies. Unless those with political views have a forum in which to express their ideas, they will be unable to influence the political process. In this sense the free speech interest belongs to both audience and speaker. The principle of freedom of speech, says Meiklejohn (1960: 27), 'is not a Law of Nature or of Reason in the abstract. It is a deduction from the basic American agreement that public issues shall be decided by universal suffrage.' The democracy justification, he argues, is more important than the argument from truth:

> The primary purpose of the First Amendment is, then, that all the citizens shall, so far as possible, understand the issues which bear upon our common life. That is why no idea, no opinion, no doubt, no belief, no counterbelief, no relevant information, may be kept from them.
>
> (1960: 75)

The gaining of truth is secondary to the placing of the truth in the hands of the people.

Political speech has therefore been given a privileged place in liberal democracies and received stronger legal and constitutional protection than other forms of speech such as commercial speech. Justice Brandeis in *Whitney v. California* 274 US 357 (1927) described the greatest menace to freedom as an inert people and argued that public discussion is a political duty. In England and the United States the claims of manufacturers and sellers about their products are subject to much greater control, through the laws governing misrepresentation, than claims regarding the merits or shortcomings of politicians, their parties and policies. Essential to the informing of voters would be a free press as a forum for political views and providing information on which to make rational choices. The focus then is on the public interest in free speech and the way in which it benefits the political community.

This view of free speech as an instrument of democracy is problematic. From a Dworkinian perspective, free speech is construed as a right to be upheld against majoritarian considerations (Dworkin, 1977c). This means that where the rights and the wishes of the majority conflict with the free speech right, for example, in a decision to limit free speech, then normally the free speech right should prevail. Constraints may need to be exerted on the majority and their representatives, to prevent them from limiting free speech, even where the ideas in question are inimical to the democracy. Similarly Schauer (1982) argues that the free speech principle can constitute an independent principle only if is protected from majoritarian wishes, in which case we need to be clear why it is given this protection. For this reason he finds the democracy justification of the First Amendment problematic because the idea of popular sovereignty seems to undermine the free speech principle; the stronger our commitment to democracy, the less we are likely to tolerate a right which undermines the power of that majority, and yet this is what the free speech right means in practice, by virtue of being a right.

This conflict becomes apparent on occasions when the majority, having heard a range of views, decide to restrict or waive their free speech rights. Although in the United States constitutional barriers will prevent the majority from enacting such legislation, the issue may not be so clear-cut if the ground for restraint reflects the rationale for the original right of free speech. If the case for regulation of pornography is based on creating a political climate in which women's voices can be heard and a range of views expressed, then this would be an example where the reasons for the original right and apparent infringement do coincide. Given the effects of pornography on women's autonomy and self-realisation, their participation in public life is arguably undermined by the free market in pornography. In pornographic videos and magazines, women are located firmly within the sphere of sexuality, conceptualised here as 'private', in the sense of being excluded from the arena of civil rights. Moreover, that confinement is seen as resulting from their essential nature. The goal of participation, on which the defence of free speech rests, can be achieved only by accepting some constraints on certain groups and activities which are committed to excluding the participation of sectors of society from political life. The purpose of the free speech right and the aim of the regulation may coincide in that case. The majority may also choose to limit free speech in the interests of the democracy, for example, to suppress the speech or demonstrations of fascist groups, which are committed to the rejection of democratic institutions and principles. Here one might argue that the long-term interest in free speech must be protected against the short-term interest in free speech.

The regulation of pornography might be defended on the ground that the democracy justification of free speech is irrelevant to pornography because pornography makes no contribution to representative government or the political process in general. But there are problems with this argument if applied to pornography. Because we are not dealing here with political speech, political freedom is not adversely affected by constraints such as the Ordinances, and participation in political life cannot be undermined.

Chapter 7

The slippery slope

The slippery slope argument is often used by opponents of the regulation of pornography. It has been deployed by liberals and feminist writers who are fearful that once regulation of pornography is in place, it may be used against other materials, notably artistic, literary and political works and gay and lesbian literature. The slippery slope has been seen as particularly acute when applied to pornography, because there may be a greater tendency to make mistakes here than in other areas of speech. A minimalist approach, using the least possible regulation, risks failing to control hard-core pornography; a zealous approach runs the risk of inclusion of literary works and the erosion of the free speech principle. Striking the optimum point is difficult, and this problem has exercised academic commentators and the courts in interpreting the law, and legislatures drafting obscenity legislation in England and the United States. In the context of free speech concerns, over-regulation has been seen as more dangerous than under-regulation. As Schauer (1982) says, society may impose a lower level of regulation when drafting legal rules, to protect artistic works in order to set up a 'buffer zone' in which the free speech right is given priority. But this emphasis is now shifting under the impact of campaigns against pornography.

DOWN THE SLIPPERY SLOPE

The slippery slope argument has been advanced by the American Civil Liberties Union, which has consistently opposed censorship of literary and visual works on the grounds that valuable material will be suppressed along with the trivial and pornographic. In the United States the slippery slope argument has often been advanced because of the experience of McCarthyism and its impact on cinema and other cultural forms. Because constraints on speech have in the past adversely affected the Left rather than the Right, liberal opinion has tended to dominate the defence of free speech, which has made it difficult for feminism to gain a hearing on the pornography issue. Fears of descending the slippery slope may be grounded in examples of literary, artistic and educational texts which have been suppressed but have later been recognised as valuable. The risk of suppression is that unconventional political thinking and artistic expression will be crushed. The only ground on which this risk might justifiably be overridden is where there is a clear and present danger of obscene material causing serious harm. But unless evidence of harm is convincing, which is challenged by opponents of regulation, there can be no ground for intervention. If tangible harms are not in question, then offensiveness alone will be insufficient to justify the prohibition of such material. Once on the 'slippery slope' of regulation, legislation could be used against unorthodox ideas, including gay, lesbian and radical feminist materials. Such prohibitions on pornography, it is feared, may extend to radical political ideas in a repressive political climate.

Schauer (1982) identifies two types of slippery slope arguments. The first concerns the problem of 'over-inclusiveness', that too much may be included when drafting a regulating rule, which arises from the vagueness of human speech. This is a linguistic problem. It raises the question of how we can draft statutes sufficiently narrowly to avoid catching certain works. But there is also the problem, he says, of 'limited learnability', that is, the limits on the complexity of conceptions which people can reasonably be expected to grasp. Even if we draw up a rigorous code using skilled lawyers, it still needs to be taught to judges and juries, and at each stage the information is passed on, there is a danger of sliding down the slope.

The weapon of legislation, it is feared, may be used arbitrarily against particular groups. Historically it is true that the effects of state censorship have been to stifle radical thinking. Primarily, censorship has been used to crush religious and political dissent; conversely freedom of speech has been developed to protect religious and political freedom, rather than the freedom of the pornographer. Works critical of prevailing sexual morality such as Joyce's *Ulysses* have been subject to censorship. The history of obscenity legislation demonstrates many examples of literary works caught by over-regulation. Prior to the 1959 Obscene Publications Act, there was a series of notorious trials of literary and sex education works. In the past, destruction orders have been served on booksellers. In the 1970s there were a number of prosecutions, including those leading to the *Oz* trial and *The Little Red School Book*, which many saw as an attack on alternative lifestyles and a backlash against 1960s sexual freedom. In Britain in the early 1980s a series of raids by Customs and Excise officers were made on Gay's the Word bookshop, and a number of imports of American feminist titles were seized under the Customs Consolidation Act 1876. By being charged under this Act, the defendants were precluded from using the public good defence available under the 1959 Obscene Publications Act, to protect works of literary, scientific, artistic or educational importance. Censorship has also been used in the United Kingdom, in the form of control of political speech by the use of broadcasting restrictions.[1]

If it is not known in advance whether a particular book is obscene until the law has been tested in relation to that particular text, there will be problems of predictability and uncertainty. In a homophobic or anti-feminist atmosphere, it is feared that legislation may be deployed against homosexuals and feminists. Once the law is in place, it may not be easy to ensure these groups are protected if the political climate changes. These fears may be especially pertinent in the 1990s, when attacks have been successfully launched on abortion provisions and the treatment of homosexuality in teaching materials in schools. A civil or criminal law may be used to undermine feminist objectives and to push sexuality back into the private arena, out of the sphere of public discussion. The laws could be captured by the moral right to assert a particular ideology of the family.

In such a political climate, distributors and booksellers may err on the side of conservatism and become more apprehensive about handling material which may attract the attention of the police or moral entrepreneurs, so that there will be a chilling effect on the publishing and distribution industry generally, not just on those who have actually been convicted. Each time a publisher is prosecuted, others will be deterred from taking risks. Given that the harms deemed to arise from pornography are debatable, the risk of a slippery slope may be seen as too high a price to pay when balancing harms. This approach is taken by both Feinberg (1987a) and Barendt (1985). For the presumption of free speech to be rebutted, a proven link to sexual offences would need to be established.

Precise drafting is essential to exclude political or literary works from the ambit of legislation and to counteract its potentially chilling effect. If legislation is based on offensiveness, then the risk of descending the slope may seem greater; but we may invoke criteria to prevent a speedy descent, for example, questions of avoidability and the seriousness of the offence.

Censorship has been seen as harmful by Mill and others because a diversity of ideas is essential for the truth to emerge. The truth argument is bound up with the slippery slope argument in the sense that if all views are given a hearing, then the view which holds the truth will not be put at risk. In contrast, an indiscriminate form of censorship cannot distinguish between speech which contributes to the truth and that which does not. But if pornography contributes nothing to the pursuit of the truth, it would not fall within this justification of free speech. Instead it celebrates the subordination of women, using the depiction of subordination as a means of sexual arousal.

The slippery slope argument usually focuses on the threat to artistic works and those lying in the 'grey area' between soft pornography and erotic literature. The relationship between works of art and pornography has been open to discussion, with some commentators arguing that pornographic works can be artistic while others see them as mutually exclusive.[2] But while there may be difficult borderline cases, these are more likely to fall within the category of erotica rather than pornography. The distinction between pornographic and literary works may be sufficiently clear in most cases for them not to be caught by carefully drafted legislation. The two should be distinguishable in terms of their aims and content. It is difficult to argue that pornography has any literary merit. Apart from the differences in the content of artistic and pornographic work, a distinction might be drawn in terms of the profitability of the pornography industry and the fact that the purpose of producers is to make money. Traditionally commercial speech has ranked fairly low when considering First Amendment protection, compared to political speech, for example.

The fact that serious literature has been prohibited in the past under obscenity provisions may seem to provide support for the slippery slope argument. For this reason the Williams Report (1979) favoured a relaxation of controls on all literary works. But in practice the materials subject to control here and in the United States are largely pictorial texts rather than written ones, which means genuine literary works are likely to escape because they take the written form. In England there are various devices built into the legislation which acknowledge the slippery slope problem, such as the public good defence in the Obscene Publications Act 1959. While writers and publishers have to establish the literary or other benefits, the use of expert evidence is admissible. Once the defence has been made out, the text can be published even if it is obscene, provided that it has that quality. Similarly in the United States, using the test formulated in *Miller* v. *California* 413 US 15 (1973), the court will consider whether a work has any serious literary, artistic or political value.

What is interesting is the appeal of the *sorites* argument to some feminist critics of pornography as well as its defenders. This has had the effect of dividing feminists on the pornography issue. Smart (1989), for example, is critical of the use of legal constraints on pornography as a feminist strategy. Her critique rests in part on a slippery slope argument. She argues that because the moral right is a major force in the movement against pornography, once censorship is in place it may well be used to constrain feminism rather than to enhance it. This argument is problematic as we cannot know in advance what the effect of regulation would be, and it is by no means certain that it would necessarily lead to greater regulation of women's lives. On the contrary, if it encouraged the promotion of autonomy, it is possible that it would strengthen the protection of women's rights and interests. Even if we can never precisely determine their impact, to reject legal measures will mean stagnation rather than change in the absence of viable alternatives. Advocates of regulation have been careful to distinguish themselves from the moral right by placing their analysis of pornography within the context of a critique of the family. Part of the argument for regulation is precisely that it may strengthen women's position within the private sphere and the credibility of victims of sexual violence.

Prohibition is a blunt instrument, and for this reason Mill was cautious about using cumbersome legislation to prohibit potentially risky activities. But the problem could be solved in formulating the mental element of the offence, namely by relying on intentionality, to distinguish pornography from works with a redeeming value. If intent to sexually arouse the audience is combined with the *actus reus* of degrading or dehumanising depictions of women, this would rescue educational and medical materials or critiques of pornography describing pornographic materials which unwittingly have the effect of sexually arousing some consumers.

A well-defined programme of regulation may have benefits for publishers. For where there is a climate of uncertainty, with some works prosecuted and others untouched, and when the law is selectively enforced, uncertainty itself can have a chilling effect. If publishers do not want to risk being caught by an uncertain or unevenly enforced law, they may well censor themselves, perhaps more rigorously than the law would demand, so that a clear-cut system of regulation would be preferable.

In any case the distinction between prior restraint and subsequent regulation may be tenuous. The American courts have been much more critical of prior restraint than the English courts, and have favoured subsequent sanctions over prior restraint because of the latter's chilling effect on publishers and film-makers. Yet the key issue may not be the timing of the restraint but, as Schauer (1982) says, the composition of the body which restrains and the breadth of its discretion, whether proceedings are held in public and the standards which are used. The possibility of punishment, he says, may deter film-makers more effectively than a system of prior restraint, because of the massive costs of investment in film productions. This may mean that publishers and film-makers are unwilling to take risks. A system of prior restraint where films are reviewed by a censorship board before distribution, on clearly ascertainable criteria with rights of appeal and representation, might be better for producers. They would know that once granted approval, they are protected from subsequent protracted and expensive litigation.

This would also avoid the problem of wasteful duplication of litigation and burden on the courts' time, when the same film is challenged in a number of different cities in the United States, while in England a publication may meet with a different response from juries or magistrates in different cities.

The slippery slope argument is also unconvincing in so far as we already have a number of well-established restraints on free speech, which are accepted as legitimate and which have not generated further censorship. As Lee (1990) says, the slippery slope argument favoured by defenders of free speech mistakenly presupposes that we are not yet on the slope rather than already on it, as if we commence from an absolutist position, when we already find acceptance of constraints on free speech in English and American law. So the choice is not between complete freedom of speech and total censorship.

Limits to free speech have already been accepted in the laws governing misrepresentation, breaches of confidentiality, official secrecy, protection of copyright and protection of reputation. Yet these have received far less critical attention for their free speech implications than the possibility of laws regulating pornography, which has stimulated a strong counter-offensive from civil libertarian pressure groups such as the American Civil Liberties Union.

Moreover, the fact that we are on the slope does not mean that future extensions of the law are in any sense inevitable or likely. In some areas we may find a move back up the slope or at least no evidence of encroachment on further areas. Limited resources will inevitably restrain an over-zealous prosecutor or law enforcer. The focus of regulation in London has shifted away from adult to child pornography because of the lack of resources and the relative importance attached to the two types of material. Bookshops are now unlikely to be subject to scrutiny, and literary texts unlikely to be forfeited. In 1992 efforts to raise a prosecution against texts by the Marquis de Sade failed because of the possibility of a public-good defence being invoked. The very fact that this defence may be raised may be sufficient to deter 'literary' prosecutions combined with the surfeit of material available to prosecute. So in practice this issue will rarely arise and the defence will rarely be invoked. We therefore need to get the slippery slope argument in perspective.

Although it may sometimes be difficult to know where to draw the line, it does not follow that restrictions should never be drawn. Of course it may be difficult, and which side of the line a particular work will fall will have to be thoroughly considered in each case. But this does not invalidate the claim that some speech may be harmful. The slippery slope argument thus tends to exaggerate, in suggesting that our descent is so rapid that it is not possible to apply brakes, when we have already stopped ourselves falling down the slope.

PORNOGRAPHY AND CENSORSHIP

Feminist campaigners have taken a number of positions on the question of whether a commitment to the regulation of pornography necessarily entails a commitment to censorship. The hostility to the legal regulation of pornography from liberal feminism has largely reflected a rejection of censorship, which is construed as repressive in itself, but is also likely to affect women and sexual minorities adversely. When the Indianapolis

Ordinance was enacted in the United States it mobilised feminists against censorship. For example, the Feminists Anti-Censorship Task Force (FACT) argued that the Ordinances did amount to a form of censorship (Duggan, 1985). Although the Ordinances were civil rather than criminal laws, their impact, it was argued, could be as strong as criminal laws of obscenity, because they would have the effect of removing materials from booksellers by means of injunctions, or the threat of injunctions. This seems to suggest that entirely innocent parties are having materials seized, but if we look at the wording of the Ordinance, it demands evidence of proven as well as anticipated harm, and has to be seen in that light.[3]

It has also been argued that suppression may make the forbidden idea more attractive. Annette Kuhn (1985) sees the attraction of pornography to consumers as lying in the fact that it is forbidden, so that censorship could actually increase its attractiveness. The greater the regulation and control, the more desirable it becomes and the greater the importance it assumes as a defence of sexual freedom. But if this is so, if restraint increases its commercial and consumer value, as the price increases on the black market, it is difficult to see why censorship is so strongly resisted by producers and consumers. It is in any case difficult to test this hypo-thesis, as adult pornography appears to be relatively freely available. Con-sumption has increased with new technologies and in the absence of constraint.

'Censorship' is a blanket term which glosses over relationships of power and inequality, which may be used by powerful groups to perpetuate their dominance. It is also a 'boo' word having negative connotations. The issue of censorship needs to be confronted because if women are deterred from campaigning against pornography by the fear of censorship, then the *status quo* will remain unchallenged.

Self-regulation has been proposed as an alternative to either formal censorship or non-intervention. Simon Lee (1990), for example, argues that voluntary censorship is preferable. In everyday life, he says, we exercise self-restraint or self-censorship in dealing sensitively with other people, avoiding topics which might offend them. Of course we have a right not to do so; but respect for others' feelings means that we voluntarily choose not to exercise that right. Demands for censorship will usually come, he says, from a group under threat, such as Muslims or women, so it is necessary to enhance their sense of security, in which case they can feel more confident.

But even if women felt more confident, would they construe pornogra-phy in a positive way? One could imagine engaging in a debate on Salman Rushdie's *The Satanic Verses* as a critique and reflection on Islam, but pornography does not aspire to or reach the level of a critique or reflection on women or their sexuality. Lee hypothesises a society in which women's speech is encouraged and women are accorded greater respect, but in that case, we would be unlikely to find a mass market in pornography, as the problem would already have been solved. While self-censorship may be desirable, it is unlikely to occur in the case of pornography, as a dilution of the content may mean that the materials are no longer in demand.

An alternative approach would challenge both censorship and pornography. Although this might seem, *prima facie*, a contradictory position, various arguments have been advanced within feminism which seek to reconcile demands for regulation of pornography with opposition to censorship, by arguing that pornography itself constitutes a form of censorship. The Campaign against Pornography and Censorship (CPC) was set up by women's rights campaigners, journalists and lawyers to disseminate information about pornography, compiling evidence of harms, to pursue the goal of legislation against pornography as a form of sex discrimination and incitement to sexual hatred, as well as other strategies, such as boycotts. Because pornography contributes to sex discrimination, sexual inequality, violence and sexism, the CPC argued, it should be eliminated through a variety of means including information, education, persuasion, legislation and lawful direct action on the grounds that it harms women. Its Policy Statement declares that:

> We believe that the portrayal of women as sex objects [in pin-ups, car and other advertisements, 'Miss World Competitions', page three] is one of the most powerful and visible expressions of the negative attitudes of sexism and is central to the sex objectification, and therefore dehumanisation and degradation, of women. We believe that pornography is the most extreme portrayal of women as less than human and less than equal. We believe that pornography reinforces women's unequal status by presenting them only as sexual and 'sexualized' objects for men's titillation and gratification and perpetuates their unequal status ... We believe therefore that pornography is propaganda against women which perpetuates sexism, sex discrimination and sexual violence.
>
> (1988)

It also challenges the representation of women in sexually stereotyped ways in children's books and advertising as well as pornography. At the same time, the Policy Statement affirms a commitment to freedom of expression and freedom of information and opposes censorship of any kind. Censorship is construed as a limitation of freedom, whereas the elimination of pornography is seen as contributing to women's freedom. Pornography *per se* is seen as a form of censorship, silencing and constraining women.

Many of the liberal defences of pornography have concentrated on state control of ideas and published works, but censorship needs to be construed more broadly. It may be carried out by a number of agencies outside the formal state apparatus. It may be undertaken voluntarily, through codes of ethics, or enforced by means of formal sanctions. We also need to consider the forms of restraint which already prevail in society and which are accepted within liberal democratic society, to see whether there is scope for the inclusion of pornography within these limits.

While the regulation of pornography may be seen as a restraint on the 'freedom' of manufacturers, distributors and consumers, this restraint may be seen as comparable to other areas where society accepts limits, for example, on the freedom to engage in dangerous sports, to carry offensive weapons, to drive motor vehicles at great speed, to consent to work in a hazardous environment, and to damage the environment through industrial pollution. An analogy might be drawn between restraints on the freedom to publish pornography and laws which aim to protect the environment. Certain constraints may be necessary for human and environmental flourishing. The recognition of the need to respect the rights and freedoms of others underpins much modern civil and criminal law and is the basis of restraints on freedom of action as well as limits on free speech.

To protect their civil liberties, the CPC argues, women should have a right to pursue a civil action against the manufacturers and distributors of pornography for the damage and harm arising from it. It is also critical of existing legislation which, it argues, has failed to control the circulation of pornography. The Obscene Publications Act 1959 defines obscenity subjectively in terms of what is 'likely to deprave and corrupt', but the CPC argues that pornography can be described objectively, using the definition of pornography from the Indianapolis Ordinance as the graphic, sexually explicit subordination of women through pictures and/or words that also includes one or more of the following: women portrayed as sexual objects, things or commodities, enjoying pain, reduced to body parts, penetrated by objects or animals etc. The existing legislation, it is argued, does not protect women from harm or take account of the impact of consumption of pornography on the creation and perpetuation of 'negative' attitudes and certain forms of behaviour.

The CPC therefore argues that the existing obscenity legislation, which has been used repressively as a means of censoring art and literature, should be repealed. It should be replaced by new legislation using the Ordinance definition and which starts from the recognition of pornography as contributing to the perpetuation of sex discrimination and sexual hatred and violence.

Appeals to the threat of censorship, made by some liberals and feminist groups, can serve, albeit unwittingly, as a smokescreen to divert attention away from the harms caused by pornography. Moreover, the fear of censorship is at variance with the acceptance of limits on free speech in other areas of law such as defamation and in criminal procedure, in restrictions on court reporting in certain cases. This raises the question of whether pornography could be seen as a form of group libel or defamation in which false claims are made about women as a social group, with adverse effects on their reputations. Limitations on racist speech have already been accepted, so the fears of censorship in relation to sexual hatred would seem to be due to the specific status of women as a social group rather than the inviolability of free speech.

The existing constraints on free speech are both wide-ranging and, in some cases, draconian, including prior restraints, such as the use of injunctions to restrain publication of official secrets or breaches of confidence. They also go much further than the civil redress proposed by the Ordinance, in the case of official secrecy, for example, using the criminal law to control the flow of information. Yet criticism of these restraints has focused less on the free speech implications than on questions of government accountability. Moreover, notwithstanding the criticisms of the Official Secrets Act, it has been retained by successive governments from both major political parties. The acceptance of censorship in areas like national security cuts across party boundaries. The Labour Party, while favouring freedom of information when in opposition, once in power has used this legislation and other methods to limit information and has allowed national security considerations to prevail over the right to information. Less concern has been expressed over the issue of sex and violence in the media, where the ground has been occupied principally by the Conservative Party, although the sponsor of the Page Three Bill was a Labour MP, Clare Short.

Both parties accept censorship in certain areas, and yet are hostile to the regulation of pornography, arguably reflecting the lack of importance attached to women's claims. The fact that campaigns and pressure groups against censorship such as Article 19 and the Campaign for Press and Broadcasting Freedom have been launched in the United Kingdom testify to the wide-ranging limits on free speech already in place. We need to consider what limitations on speech are acceptable and whether an absolutist approach to speech rights is compatible with respect for the freedom and dignity of other groups.

The focus on free speech and freedom of the press in the pornography and censorship debate also fails to acknowledge the strong power of the press and particularly the concentration of ownership. The image of a free market of ideas in liberal theory is hard to reconcile with the hard reality of the increasing monopolisation of the means of dissemination of ideas, and the uniformity of content in the media in the late twentieth century. This is not to suggest that a simple conspiracy theory may account for the content. While a crude identity of the economic interests of capital and the production of news may be appropriate in considering reporting of, for example, industrial disputes, more subtle processes may operate in the representation of women. The extent to which women and other groups are already censored by the media therefore needs to be taken into account when considering the regulation of pornography, which might then be defended as removing this form of censorship from women. Apart from the concentration of ownership, everyday editorial control may mean women's voices are excluded or marginalised. Editors act as gatekeepers, deciding which particular forms of speech may be published. Although women are organising for better access and promotion, equal opportunities have still not been achieved. The concern of employers and governments to break the power of trade unions in the 1980s was not matched by a concern with monopolisation of ownership, although the potential for dominance of the market was increasing with cable and satellite television. Censorship may be achieved in a variety of ways through budgetary controls of state-financed broadcasting as well as strategic use of key appointments to ensure that senior executives are sympathetic to a particular approach.

Censorship should not be construed simply as state repression and regulation: it may be exerted through a number of agencies. Changes of editorial direction may be controlled by advertisers and by the fear of losing out in circulation wars. Advertisers may also exert pressure directly in certain cases. When attempts were made to popularise the *Star* by increasing its pornographic content, this was halted not by the objections of feminist critics or the journalists employed on it, but by pressure from major advertisers threatening to withdraw their advertising.

In recessionary times, the need for profitability of publishers may discourage them from publishing new writers instead of relying on safe established ones, leading to further homogeneity and conformity. Instead of the free market of ideas we find a market structured through the weight of the powerful, and a variety of forces discouraging diversity. A chilling effect may follow even without legal regulation, for example, in the case of the *fatwa* on Salman Rushdie. For this reason Lee is sceptical of a simple appeal to free speech rights. Instead he favours a consideration of the power of speech and its effects and of the specific costs of free speech, of whether those costs are worth it in particular cases, or whether it might be better to limit the right to free speech in certain circumstances, and this will involve consideration of competing rights and interests. 'It is possible', he says, 'to be passionately committed to a limited but realistic concept of free speech' (Lee, 1990: 25). The costs will depend on the circumstances, but the examples he gives include the denial of personal freedom in the Rushdie case, the effects on the Muslim community and its relationship to non-Muslims in Britain, and the huge costs in a libel action if one insists on exercising one's right. Clearly there will be disagreement on the extent of the costs and their justifiability. Conversely, the cost of free speech for distributors selling soft pornography through retail outlets is the risk of loss of goodwill from customers, if they insist on stocking pornography. The right to free speech, he argues, also needs to be construed more broadly in terms of achieving universal literacy and investment in education in order to develop critical faculties.

Pornography might be seen as already subject to censorship, in the sense that women are not permitted to see it. This point is made by Jeffreys (1988), who describes her treatment as a University summer-school tutor when she showed a selection of slides as part of a discussion of pornography. Following this she was not considered for reappointment. She argues that while it is acceptable for pornography to be shown to men in public or private and to women in the private sphere by men, this does not extend to showings by women to other women in a political context. Similarly, in the United States, the FACT campaigners would take part in debates with feminist campaigners against pornography only if the latter excluded slides and displays of pornography from their presentations. One reason for this, she argues, is that if pornography were shown to women, to reveal its full horror, there would be increased pressure for its prohibition. Women would become so angry that they would not be fobbed off by appeals to liberal arguments or theories of representation. Jeffreys' argument is also pertinent in view of the tendency of the general public, including women, to misconstrue the content of pornography. However, we also need to take account of the fact that they are regularly confronted with 'soft' pornography in high-street shops and news-stands.

Although groups such as Article 19 and Index on Censorship are opposed to any further increases in censorship, other civil libertarian groups, such as Liberty and the Campaign for Press and Broadcasting Freedom, recognise that women are exploited in pornography and that the civil liberties of different groups may conflict. Given this, an absolutist position on freedom of expression cannot be defended where restrictions are necessary in order to prevent harm. The Campaign for Press and Broadcasting Freedom addresses the apparent conflict between regulation and censorship. This group is committed to freedom of expression but does not see this as absolute: rights of individuals or groups may outweigh free speech rights. Press freedom has to be accompanied by responsibilities, for example, in reporting restrictions when dealing with victims, or limits on the publication of racist material. The Campaign is also critical of the monopolisation of the media, which it sees as undermining the diversity of opinions and ideas. An important aspect of its work would be to promote opportunities for weaker groups to disseminate their ideas and beliefs, to ensure maximum diversity of ideas as well as democratisation. The Campaign has backed a code of conduct on media sexism which is intended as a guide for media workers as well as a consciousness-raising mechanism. It has also undertaken research to assess attitudes towards sexism in the media and consider possible ways of eliminating it.

While free speech has been construed negatively in the censorship debate in terms of freedom from government control, a range of factors may limit the exercise of free speech, including economic constraints, for example, whether funds are available to publish, and spatial constraints, whether newspaper space or airtime is available, which in turn may depend on the price consumers and advertisers are willing to pay.

When Mill criticised censorship and intolerance, he was referring to the social condemnation of individuals because of their ideas, but the case of an editor deciding whether to print a particular contribution would be seen as an exercise of choice and of press freedom. Free speech may also be constrained by an act of communication by another person rather than the state.

But even if free speech is construed primarily in terms of protection from state regulation, there is still the problem that we do not all have equal access to the means of dissemination. While constraints of space and time may pose problems, some steps towards a free market can be achieved by preventing concentration of ownership, providing grants for minority newspapers and guaranteeing minority groups access to airtime.

Isaiah Berlin's distinction between positive and negative freedom has also been seen as relevant to the nature of free speech by a number of commentators (Berlin, 1967). Barendt (1985) questions whether free speech should be construed simply as a negative freedom, freedom from state interference, or as a positive freedom, which cannot be realised without the opportunity to exercise positive rights. We might distinguish between the right to free speech, which imposes a duty on the state to ensure those opportunities are available, and a liberty, where there is a right to exercise free speech without a correlative duty. Which is more appropriate may depend on whether we are referring to the speaker's or recipient's interest in having access to ideas. He sees the latter as a mere liberty, while finding the case for a claim right stronger in the speaker's case, where the state has discriminated against certain groups in denying access to the media or where a newspaper denies access to those groups.

On a positive conception of free speech, a duty could be construed in terms of rights of access to air waves and print media. Claim rights against the state to hold meetings and demonstrations using public places, notes Barendt, have found more favour in the United States than in the United Kingdom. Some legal duties to provide equal opportunities for speech by different groups have been imposed on the IBA and the BBC, but these are not rights of access for individuals. Otherwise the emphasis has been on self-regulation by the industry, although this has been increasingly under attack.

Although much of the pornography and censorship debate has rested on a negative concept of freedom, as a mere liberty, there is a broader conception of positive freedom implicit in feminist demands for regulation. The demand for restitution for unjust enrichment arising from the exploitation of women in pornography may be seen as part of a wider perfectionist goal of facilitating the entry of women's voices into the public debate. The simple view of feminist critics of pornography as censors, as we have seen, fails to take account of the complexity of the 'problem of censorship'.

On this broader model of censorship advanced here, the state might be construed in a positive way as the least repressive of all the potentially censoring bodies. Strengthening speech rights for women and other groups denied a voice may involve state subsidies and grants to them for minority publications or guaranteed airtime and newspaper space. This would be consistent with a perfectionist model which focuses on the promotion of autonomy.

Most of the discussion of censorship has occurred within the context of the conflict between the state and the individual, but this overlooks the power of the private censors. This broader approach is consistent with Mill's concept of free speech, for he construed censorship and constraint much more widely than state regulation, and focused particularly on the power of custom and society. Mill saw the tyranny of public opinion as more repressive in some cases than state controls on free speech.

There is no necessary contradiction between hostility to censorship and demands for regulation of pornography if, as has been argued, the freedom to produce and consume pornography means the silencing or repression of women as a social group and if the pornographer's freedom is bound up with the denial of women's freedom. Moreover, because censorship principally refers to censorship of political ideas, the twin goals of political freedom and the regulation of pornography may be construed as promoting women's autonomy, citizenship and participation.

Chapter 8

Feminism and puritanism

To the pornographer, the feminist critique of his livelihood as immoral could be seen as simply a new form of intolerance, and the comparison between feminist criticism and the views of the National Viewers' and Listeners' Association is often drawn. The feminist critique of pornography has been interpreted as a new form of puritanism, seeking to impose its values on others, and to encroach gradually on more and more areas of people's private lives. Underlying the liberal rejection of the case against pornography is the fear of state intervention in the private sphere to protect public morality.

Jeffreys (1988) describes how she has been subjected to verbal attacks by sexual libertarians who have compared her to born-again Christian zealots such as Jerry Falwell. In fact the feminist campaigners against pornography may be seen sometimes as more repressive, because they engage in direct action and confrontation with consumers, for example, picketing sex shops and high-street retailers.

Radical feminist critiques of the sex industry have also been subject to criticism from those liberals sympathetic to feminism, including Radcliffe Richards (1982) who argues that one reason for the unpopularity of feminism is its dreary attitude towards private pleasure, redolent of puritanism, which, she argues, repels men and women alike. By focusing on non-essential issues, feminism may, she says, lose sight of its principal role, namely to fight social injustice which discriminates against women. She cites the example of feminist criticism of beauty contests. Radcliffe Richards depicts them as harmless fun, freely engaged in by consenting adults. By 'taking on' such issues, she says, feminists may give rise to the impression that they are actually hostile to sex itself. She questions whether it is consistent to see sexual behaviour as degrading simply because it is the subject of a commercial contract. Other activities, such as nursing the sick, are not seen as degrading because people receive payment for them, so it is difficult to see what is special about sex. The degradation cannot be attributed to the uniqueness of sex, unless one wants to say that sex should occur only within strict marital boundaries, which is not part of the feminist argument. If a woman has sexual skills, she should be free to market them in the same way as any other skills she possesses. We would not condemn a concert pianist for pleasing men through the exercise of her talents, and likewise we should not condemn a striptease artist or prostitute for pleasing men through the use of her talents.

She identifies a puritan strand within feminism in its rejection of the sensual and its failure to appreciate the importance of sex, beauty and sensuality in people's lives. It is found in feminist hostility to women who deliberately dress in a way which invites the attention of men. 'A man who would not change his woman for any other in the world', she says, 'might still know that she would please him even more if she looked like the centre fold from the latest *Playboy*' (Radcliffe Richards, 1982: 232).

The risk of the association of feminism with puritanism has been raised by Smart (1989), who points to the danger of feminism sharing a platform with the moral right and of being incorporated into the law and order rhetoric. If this happened, she argues, it would expose feminism to the risk of increasing the power of law, which might then be used against feminism itself. She is particularly critical of MacKinnon's analysis of pornography in terms of coercion, which, she argues, ultimately construes coercion as essential to (hetero) sexuality. This view is so broad that it moves danger-ously close to the moral right's view of all representations of sex as degrad-ing: 'Ultimately it becomes a position virtually indistinguishable from the moral right in terms of its antithesis to sexuality and its reliance on blunt modes of legal censorship' (Smart, 1989: 123). While Radcliffe Richards sees modern feminism as a new form of puritanism, Smart is concerned with the possibility of feminism being manipulated by moral crusaders in a way which will ultimately work against the interests of feminism. Focusing on pornography as violence, she says, runs the risk of becoming part of the law and order campaign, which is antithetical to feminist goals.

Of course we can find instances where women have suffered as a result of campaigns by moral crusaders and where feminist campaigns have been commandeered by the moral right, for example, the treatment of prostitutes in the nineteenth century. But, whilst caution is necessary, to avoid cam-paigns because of the presence of the moral right on the same terrain would allow the moral right to define the terms of the debate.

While there is widespread concern on crime prevention and law and order, it is arguably preferable for feminism to exploit this opportunity to obtain a hearing, particularly given the fact that women's voices have so often been silenced in the past. In any case, anxieties over law and order reflect real fears on the part of communities. It is important for feminism to enter the discussion to see if it can recapture the ground of the law and order debate, and also to avoid strategies which rely on the confinement of women rather than combating the causes of aggression.

To equate feminism with puritanism is misleading because the feminist critique of pornography rests on fundamentally different perceptions of the distinction between the public and private spheres. Feminism is constructed on a critique of the patriarchal family and society, while puritanism aims at conserving the existing family structure rather than challenging it. The prohibition of pornography for the moral right is part of a package of reforms including limits on abortion and restrictions on sex education in schools. Moreover, the feminist critique of pornography would not be accompanied by a rejection of the use of sexually explicit materials as part of sex education or of erotica. Nor would it preclude material on a range of sexual orientations and alternative life-styles. The pressure groups campaigning for regulation of pornography, the Campaign against Pornography and the Campaign against Pornography and Censorship, have made it clear that that they are not opposed to sex education or discussions of sexuality, but are instead challenging the fusion of sex with violence found in pornography, and the depiction of abuse as pleasurable for women. Degradation for the moral right includes images of extra-marital sex, but what feminists find degrading in pornography is the portrayal in a sexual context of women's subordination to men.

Radcliffe Richards' equation of feminism with puritanism is hard to justify in so far as her criticism is based on a small number of texts which, even at the time, were not representative of the broad spectrum of feminist thought. Her defence of sensuality also seems at odds with her argument that feminism has failed to develop a rigorous use of rational argument and relies on feelings rather than logic.

When feminists criticise the sexual dimension of pornography, they are objecting to the definition of sex as the subordination of women and the depiction of their alleged enjoyment of that subordination. For this reason, feminists would see pornography as itself essential to an understanding of sex discrimination and as a form of sexual discrimination rather than as a merely tangential issue. The campaign against pornography does not constitute a rejection of sex *per se*, but rather the toppling of sexuality from the pinnacle of female existence, to make room for other dimensions of social life including the development of women's rational faculties and the promotion of autonomy.

Taking a strong moral position will inevitably prove unpopular. But adopting any moral position, including the view that pornography should be controlled, commits one to defending the rightness of that position. Although this approach conflicts with the relativism of laissez-faire liberalism, in which choice is paramount, it finds less support in other strands of liberalism. Of relevance here are Ronald Dworkin's defence of objectivism in moral thinking and his critique of scepticism in *Law's Empire*. The condition of having a moral belief, he says, is that one thinks that it is right and not just one view among others. It cannot be construed simply as a preference, comparable to a preference for a particular type of ice-cream (Dworkin, 1986b). While the feminist and moral right critiques may be distinguished, what they share is a strong commitment to their respective moral positions in contrast to what has been described as 'valueless individualism'.[1] Valueless individualism construes society as discrete individuals with their own views and beliefs; in this assembly of individuals there are no objective standards of right or wrong. Instead individuals are concerned with their own needs and desires. Examples here would be choice and contract theory. On this approach there is no possibility of mounting a critique of patriarchal societies. This individualism, she argues, runs through academic arguments for cultural diversity and value freedom. It might be seen as a reaction to traditional morality which embraces values, albeit predominantly heterosexual ones, so that homosexuality is condemned as perverse, and sexual perversion defined in terms of the non-heterosexual while heterosexual violence and exploitation pass unchallenged. Neither approach can successfully challenge sexual slavery and exploitation. What is needed is a new set of values. Feminist moral philosophers have therefore sought to expound systems of ethics based on feminine values of caring and cooperation.[2]

WOMEN AND PORNOGRAPHY

Although a recurring theme in the pornography and censorship debate has been the degrading and oppressive nature of pornography, some have argued that the view of women as passive victims of pornography represents only one interpretation. Attention should be given to meanings attached to it by women who use pornography and who would be adversely affected by puritanical demands for regulation. Women's enjoyment of pornography raises issues which are difficult to address from a harm-based standpoint. Among the most vociferous critics of the Dworkin–MacKinnon Ordinances have been women who enjoy pornography. Attention has also been drawn to the fact that gay and lesbian pornography, found in some feminist and gay bookshops, challenges the dominant heterosexual cultural form and the puritanism of the moral right and feminist campaigners.

On this argument, the use of pornography encompasses a number of perspectives on sexuality. Some women would see their consumption of pornography as both a source of sexual pleasure and affirmation of their sexual identities, as well as an exercise of freedom of choice. Instead of seeing women simply as victims, we should recognise that women are capable of placing their own meanings on pornographic material. Arguments drawn from liberal choice theory have been applied to the use and production of sado-masochistic material, provided the parties freely consent. 'Sadeian' women could be seen as epitomising the ultimate freedom, consenting to their subjection, as in *The Story of O*. If women enjoy s/m films and literature, on this argument, there are no reasonable grounds to deny them access to it.

But the sexual libertarian defence of pornography, with its focus on consumer sovereignty, is problematic whether the consumers are male or female, for it ignores the social context in which pornography is produced and consumed. Feminist defences of pornography grounded in contractual doctrine fail to take account of the structural constraints influencing choices. Of course we should recognise women's involvement in the pornography industry as actors and active consumers who enjoy using such material, but we should also recognise the contradictions in their use of pornography. What is pernicious in pornography is precisely that the celebration of male power in pornography is accepted by women themselves, and therefore some women's passive acceptance of pornography and opposition to regulation need to be understood from this standpoint. But even if such magazines are bought and enjoyed by women, they constitute only a small part of the market, and their existence does not negate the case for regulation.

As Jeffreys (1988) argues, the fact that women respond sexually to pornography does not mean we should abandon the quest for regulation and focus our hostility towards feminists trying to control and confront it. If our deepest emotions and sexual responses have been so controlled that we comply with our own oppression and even take pleasure in it, this should enrage us rather than disarm us. Women's sexual response to pornographic material reflects the fact that women's sexuality has been moulded within a hetero-patriarchal culture. The fact that women defend the right to pornography might be seen as the ultimate success of patriarchal power.

Treating lesbian pornography as a critique of reactionary morality is problematic, as it may still rest on an exploitative view of women's sexuality and the eroticisation of dominance and submission. The typical pornographic theme of a woman submitting to her 'true nature' is represented in lesbian pornography in her subordination to a surrogate male. Lesbianism may be defused and the threat to male hegemony neutralised by its construction in pornography as ancillary to heterosexuality. Lesbian pornography, much of which is produced by and for heterosexual men, argues Smith (1988: 179), 'is not for or about lesbians and lesbian sexuality, just as black pornography is not for black people and child pornography is not for children'. She contrasts lesbian pornography constructed through this hetero-patriarchal model with lesbian erotica, written and consumed by lesbians, where female sexuality and autonomy are celebrated and women are portrayed as strong and assertive.

The arguments over pornography reflect deeper divisions within feminism on the relative importance of sexual freedom and fundamental material conditions and issues. Attempts to regulate pornography reflect not just a concern with the immediate and dramatic consequences for sexual violence but a recognition that pornography contributes to a pervasive and well-established pattern of sex discrimination.

Chapter 9

The protection of free speech

In determining the scope of free speech protection, there are a number of difficult issues to consider, including the boundary between speech and conduct, the source of speech and the type of speech, as well as the relationship between the definition of speech and the harm principle. These issues will now be considered, followed by an examination of the interpretation of the First Amendment and its application to obscene materials.

SPEECH AND CONDUCT

Most philosophers and most legal systems would see speech as including written materials and the spoken word, but would find more difficulty in dealing with activities such as participation in a demonstration, the wearing of para-military uniforms, or the carrying or destruction of a flag. Here we find variations between the attitudes of the courts in England and the United States towards such conduct.

Problems arise in deciding where the boundaries of free speech lie and which particular forms of communication fall within it. Some symbols, such as a clenched fist, are used ostensively instead of words. Other symbols cannot be clearly equated with a particular word yet may fall within the principle, for example, waving a flag to indicate loyalty or patriotism, which shows intent to communicate a specific idea.

Schauer (1982) argues that the most difficult problems arise where communication is combined with non-communicative conduct. He gives the examples of a picket, which carries a particular message but also counts as an obstruction, and amplified speech where the noise is painful. This raises the question of how to balance the free speech interest against public interests in traffic control. We might not construe an action by the state to deal with the traffic control as a direct constraint on free speech, even though this might be a by-product of it. But if the action is directed specifically at control of marches by communists, he said, we would see it as a free speech issue, because it is aimed directly at the communicative aspect of the conduct. When examining constraints we need to be clear on the aims of the restriction, whether the means are proportional to the goals and whether the restriction is content-based.

If we formulate our definition of speech too widely, we lose the point of the free speech principle. Most performative uses of language, such as the making of contracts, he says, can be excluded from the principle and the law will intervene to regulate them. Propositional wrongs, for example, perjury and fraud, may seem harder to exclude, but still fall outside the scope of the principle; it would be impossible to defend a fraudulent misrepresentation by appealing to free speech rights.

Speech might be seen as a spectrum, ranging from words with no element of conduct, but which express feelings, through speech which proposes a particular form of conduct, to performative words which constitute conduct. However, the fact that a word or practice is construed as speech is a necessary but not a sufficient condition of free speech protection.

For conduct to be included within the scope of the First Amendment, it must have a communicative content. This clearly includes speech, but it is well established that it extends beyond spoken and written speech. The problem is that if the definition of speech is drawn too narrowly, then it would seem to limit the scope for political demonstrations and marches; if it is drawn too broadly, to include various forms of conduct on the borderline, then the state's interest in maintaining order may be undermined. Nonetheless, in the United States the courts have been willing to include borderline cases as speech, especially where the infringement appears to be content-based, for example, if a ban on a march is aimed at a particular group. If an activity is clearly conduct rather than speech and the restriction is not content-based, it is likely to be excluded from free speech protection. Even if a particular act falls the right side of the borderline, and is included within the scope of the First Amendment, rival considerations such as the state's interest in public order may be given more weight.

In the United States the wearing of certain forms of clothing to express political beliefs and the burning of the flag have been held to be protected by the First Amendment. In *Tinker* v. *Des Moines School District* 394 US 503 (1969) the Supreme Court held that students who wore black armbands to school in order to protest against the Vietnam war were protected by First Amendment speech rights. The wearing of the bands was sufficiently close to 'pure' speech to warrant inclusion within the scope of the clause. The wearing of political uniforms and the carrying of banners with swastikas have also been protected as political speech in *Skokie* v. *National Socialist Party* 373 NE 2d 21 (1978). In many cases the political demonstrations or the wearing of uniforms may also be accompanied by the distribution of political pamphlets so that the communicative intent is reinforced.

In the United Kingdom, prohibitions on political uniforms were imposed by the Public Order Act 1936 in response to disturbances in the East End of London and have also been used against members of para-military groups in Northern Ireland. Section 1 made it an offence to wear a uniform which signifies association with any political organisation or the promotion of any political object in any public place or at any public meeting. In *O'Moran* v. *D.P.P.* (1975) QB 864, a conviction under section 1 of the 1936 Public Order Act of a man wearing an IRA beret at a funeral was upheld by the Divisional Court. Lord Widgery said in that case that the solitary man wearing a black beret walking down Whitehall would not be seen as wearing a uniform unless evidence were adduced to show that the black beret, in conjunction with other items, had been used and recognised as the uniform of a particular political group. So it would be necessary for the prosecution to prove the association with the political organisation. The provision was retained in the 1986 Act and the wearing of uniforms is also covered by the Emergency Provisions Act and the Prevention of Terrorism Act. It is an offence to dress, wear or display any article in a public place in such a way or in such circumstances as to arouse reasonable apprehension that the individual is a member or supporter of a proscribed organisation. Flying flags associated with proscribed political organisations is also covered by these provisions.

Destruction of the American flag as a protest may also be seen as an expression of free speech in the United States. Attempts by state legislatures to prohibit it have been held to be unconstitutional.[1] Just as waving the flag might be seen as an expression of beliefs and ideas, so burning it could be seen as a communication of political ideas, reflecting the democratic justification of the First Amendment. Although the Supreme Court in *Texas* v. *Johnson* 109 S Ct 2533 (1989) did conclude that freedom of expression under the Constitution extended to flag-burning, the decision was split 5:4, and was criticised by both the President and Congress. This disapproval shows the concern with the symbolic and real harms of flag-desecration, even though we are dealing with an inanimate object. The reverence for the flag and the respect for the feelings and sensibilities of those who would be offended by its desecration contrast markedly with the indifference to the feelings of Jewish residents in the Skokie case, even though the residents of Skokie included a survivor who had seen his mother buried alive in a concentration camp. Here the Illinois Supreme Court refused an injunction preventing the display of swastikas by Nazi demonstrators marching in a Jewish community. Although the flag-burning ultimately did receive protection, the legislation to prohibit it received considerably more support than attempts to enact constraints on racist speech or on pornography.

Inclusion within the scope of the free speech clause will not guarantee protection in all circumstances, as the court will balance the free speech right against other interests such as public order. Lee (1990) argues that if we construct the problem in terms of speech versus conduct, then our perceptions will be guided by the final result we want, and this will determine where we locate it. He therefore favours an alternative two-stage test to bring out the relevant issues, first, asking why this kind of speech is valuable and second, considering how strong are the countervailing costs of this free speech. This, he argues, will give us a clearer picture of the values involved.

FREE SPEECH AND THE HARM PRINCIPLE

The harm principle becomes more important as the speech moves closer to conduct and as questions of balancing arise. Balancing may involve competing rights as well as public interests. Although there may be certain cases where words may be more hurtful than deeds and where the adverse effects last longer, for example, in the case of racist speech or psychological abuse, actions are likely to be other-regarding.

Mill made clear that when he advocated freedom of opinions he thought that people should be able to act on those opinions, unfettered by others, provided that it is at their own risk. But opinions are not immune from intervention if expressed in order to incite harmful acts, and in such cases intervention might be justified. He distinguishes between an attack on corn-dealers as starvers of the poor in the press, which should be protected, and moving among a vociferous mob outside a corn-dealer's premises, sporting a placard to that effect:

> Acts, of whatever kind, which, without justifiable cause, do harm to others, may be, and in the more important cases absolutely require to be, controlled by the unfavourable sentiments, and, when needful, by the active interference of mankind.
>
> (Mill, 1970: 184)

In limiting free speech in this context, Mill clearly has in mind instances of incitement. Modern examples might include incitement to racial hatred or an attack on meat-eating outside McDonalds to a group of animal liberationists. Although we are dealing with the spoken word, the act of speaking in that context, together with the content, takes the exhortation out of the realm of protected speech, because harmful actions are likely to be the immediate result of such speech and intended to have that effect.

In the modern context, then, speech may be restrained because it is harmful, and many of the exceptions to First Amendment protection and efforts to make individuals and corporations accountable for their speech reflect the other-regarding nature of speech.

Although the Supreme Court has broadened the scope of the First Amendment, a number of areas still remain outside the scope of the free speech clause, including many forms of commercial speech such as advertising, most areas of libel, and abusive speech. The fact that an activity constitutes speech in the ordinary sense of making a physical utterance by no means includes it within the scope of the free speech principle. Various forms of speech, including perjury and fraudulent speech, do not fall within it, but they would still be seen as speech in everyday discourse. Conversely, many kinds of conduct would not be seen as speech in ordinary language, such as wearing certain items of clothing, yet they are protected by the free speech principle.

The various limitations and qualifications on the exercise of the right to free speech take account of harms to others and the source of speech. These include libel, misrepresentation, perjury, false advertising, solicitation of crime, conspiracy, bribery, blackmail and treason. The law of libel limits free speech in making individuals accountable for the exercise of their right to free speech. Their right is subordinated to the effects on others. Public figures may be expected to be more resilient to attacks on their character and reputation, in part reflecting the democracy justification of free speech.[2] It is difficult to imagine anyone arguing that the law of libel should be abandoned, although laws governing group libel have received less support.

As most speech is other-regarding, affecting the interests of others, it is difficult to account for these exceptions on the grounds of the harm principle. Certainly in many cases, damages may be awarded on a grand scale for relatively minor harms, and the level of awards for libel has been strongly criticised when compared, for example, to the quantum paid for personal injuries of a physical nature.

'Fighting words', that is, personal insults, verbal abuse and provocative speech, it was held in *Chaplinsky* v. *New Hampshire* 315 US 568 (1942), do not fall within the scope of the clause because of their marginal social value and the fact that they do not express or communicate ideas. The public order interest prevails as such outbursts are likely to incite an immediate breach of the peace, causing injury. Although this has been narrowed subsequently, it has not been over-ruled. The court has limited the *Chaplinsky* doctrine, so that it may be applied only if the words are likely to incite the audience to physical violence.[3] It might be argued that incitement to sexual hatred could be taken out of the scope of the First Amendment, by seeing it as analogous to the fighting words exception.

In some areas of gender inequality, such as job advertisements, the court has been prepared to limit its protection of speech. In *Roberts* v. *United States Jaycees* 468 US 609 (1984), the Supreme Court held that the state's interest in removing sex discrimination could justify the impact of Minnesota's Human Rights Act on First Amendment rights of expressive association. The Court stated that like other forms of potentially expressive activities which 'produce special harms distinct from their communicative impact, such practices are entitled to no constitutional protection' (at 628). Limitations have been accepted on aesthetic grounds, as MacKinnon points out. In *Los Angeles* v. *Taxpayers for Vincent* 466 US 789 (1984) the court held that the city's aesthetic interests counted for more than a political candidate's speech right to paste signs on public property.

The importance of countervailing considerations where the presumption of free speech is rebuttable is reflected in international conventions, to take account of respect for the rights and reputations of others, the protection of national security, public order, public health or morals and the general welfare in a democratic society.[4]

THE SOURCE OF SPEECH

In determining the scope of free speech, the source of speech may be significant. Distinctions have been drawn between corporate speech and the speech of ordinary citizens. The question of harmful speech is clearly relevant here, but the distinction also reflects the inequality between consumer and corporation. In England, as well as the United States, constraints have been placed on unbridled representations which go beyond mere sales puffs, in the law of contract. Speech is rendered accountable in commercial contexts by means of the law of misrepresentation and mistake as well as statutory protections; in addition professional persons making statements in a professional context may be held liable in negligent misstatement in the law of tort since *Hedley Byrne & Co. Ltd* v. *Heller* (1964) AC 465.

When dealing with commercial interests, the courts and legislature in both England and the United States have been more willing to impose restrictions and liabilities on statements and to construe commercial claims, such as advertising, as excluded from free speech protection because the aim of the company is primarily to maximise profitability rather than to communicate ideas. Commercial speech has been seen as less valuable than political speech or the communication of religious beliefs and ideas. This may raise problems where the medium used incorporates a commercial interest, as in the press and commercial television. Press freedom in England and the United States has been seen as comparable to the ordinary individual's right to freedom of speech rather than entitling the press to greater privileges than an ordinary individual would possess. The press is seen as having a crucial political role as a restraint on the executive and in safeguarding the public interest, but this does not render it immune from the law of libel or from public interest and national security considerations. Therefore it may lawfully be restrained by the law of defamation, official secrecy legislation, and its own regulatory Codes and bodies.[5]

PORNOGRAPHY AND THE PROTECTION OF FREE SPEECH

In considering where pornography fits into the existing framework of free speech protection, the harm principle is relevant for the reasons given earlier. But should pornography be seen as mere speech, as conduct, or as a form of speech which has a harmful effect on others? If we draw an analogy with incitement, which criminal acts are being incited? One could point to the links with violent attacks on women, where acts of violence in pornographic material of a striking kind are acted out in reality. Rape and sexual offences would be the obvious examples, but, as we have seen, these raise problems of proximity and remoteness of causation as well as problems of intention. If the harm is implicit in the material itself, in the case of child abuse or an assault necessary to the making of the film, then the substantive offence of assault rather than the inchoate offence of incitement would be more appropriate if a prosecution is considered. One might also point to the implications of pornography for the attitudes and practices which shape women's lives. Whether the harms to women are sufficient to justify the regulation of pornographers' freedom of speech or outweighed by First Amendment speech rights is crucial.

Two issues are relevant here: whether pornography should be construed as speech, in the sense of incorporating a communicative intent, and whether the free speech interests of pornographers should be weighed against other rights and interests.

One might defend regulation by denying that pornography is speech. If the defining feature of speech for First Amendment purposes is communicative content, then one might claim that pornography is primarily a sex aid rather than a form of communicating ideas. Schauer (1982) argues that the regulation of hard-core pornography does not constitute a free speech issue and it is confusing to view it as such. He gives the example of a filmed close-up of the sexual activities and organs of participants where there is no dialogue, music or artistic elements, but the aim of the film is simply sexual stimulation. It would, he says, be a 'bizarrely literal or formalistic definition of speech' which sees this as speech. This is not to say that there is anything wrong with such a film, but the question is whether or not it is closer to activity or conduct than communication. As Schauer (1982: 181) says:

> There are virtually no differences in intent and effect from the sale of a plastic or vibrating sex aid, the sale of a body through prostitution or the sex act itself. At its most extreme, hard core pornography is a sex aid, no more and no less, and the fact that there is no physical contact is only fortuitous.

Pornography does not involve communication in the sense that we normally associate with language or great works of art. Although mental elements may be present in the physical response to viewing pornography, they are not, he argues, sufficient to render it communicative. Of course some great literary works may arouse the reader, but they are not intended to have that effect and possess additional qualities. Literary works frame the erotic within an aesthetic discourse. Pornography contains none of the features which would normally justify inclusion within First Amendment speech protection.

The view that pornography is closer to a sex aid than literature is also held by Feinberg (1987a: 169), who argues that:

> while the line between erotic realism in drama or literature, on the one hand, and pure pornography on the other, is obscure, at least the clear cases of pornography are easily distinguishable from any kind of express-ive art. So called 'filthy pictures' and hard-core pornographic 'tales' are simply devices meant to titillate the sex organs *via* the mediation of symbols.

Although this view has some plausibility, it could be argued that what is pernicious in pornography is precisely its communication of powerful ideas and statements about the nature of women and the legitimisation of their degradation and abuse. This argument has the merit of dispensing with the free speech implications of pornography at a stroke, but it underestimates the communicative content of pornography and the powerful nature of its message regarding the nature and position of women, which is conveyed at the same time as achieving sexual arousal. Without the communication of ideas, it would be less powerful and of less concern. The fact that those ideas may lead to a strong sexual response provides a powerful reinforce-ment mechanism. Once it is seen as communicative, then it is more likely to be included within the First Amendment, but this is not dispositive of the issue of regulation, as questions of balancing and protection need to be considered.

Pornography is important because of its sexual effect, which serves as a powerful reinforcer of a dehumanising form of sexuality. As MacKinnon argues:

> Unlike the 'literatures' of other inequalities, pornography works as a behavioural conditioner, reinforcer and stimulus, not as idea or advocacy. It is more like saying 'kill' to a trained guard dog – and also the training process itself.
>
> (1984: 28)

Even if pornography is seen as speech within our everyday sense of speech, it may not warrant First Amendment protection because many forms of speech may be excluded, including certain forms of commercial speech and defamatory statements. Whether or not it is seen as speech, the problem of regulation remains. If it is seen as speech it might still be controlled where competing interests are present, although if it is not seen as speech it might be protected on other grounds such as privacy. When pornography is considered as a practice, rather than as mere speech, this means that it is grounded in certain ways of treating women, in structured social relationships, and that it reconstitutes the world in which women live, both in the sense that it may affect the attitudes and treatment of women by men, but also in conveying to women a particular self-image. The analogy might be drawn with a sign saying 'Whites Only' in an apartheid system. At one level this is mere speech, but it also expresses and reinforces a system of structured inequality and lies on the same continuum as constructing a fence to keep blacks out. Anglo-American philosophers including Austin and Searle have long recognised the performative nature of words in speech acts, such as 'I do' in a marriage ceremony, or 'I accept' in agreeing to the terms of a contract, that the speaking itself constitutes an act. It is not only philosophers who recognise that mere words can have harmful effects. The civil and criminal law already recognise the power of words to harm. Similarly the depiction of women in pornography enjoying subordination or violence crystallises attitudes and is in itself a way of excluding women from the sphere of the rational life by defining them as subrational, defined through body parts and functions rather than intellectual capacities. Pornography also goes beyond mere speech in the sense that it constitutes an act of legitimation of male violence by presenting it as normal, attractive and pleasurable. Moreover, the written word and celluloid achieve a permanence which is lacking in ordinary language.[6] As it would be difficult to see pornography as a form of political speech, the fact that it constitutes a form of commercial speech which contributes to sex discrimination might be seen as justifying a low weighting.

The uncritical appeal to freedom of speech used to defend pornography does not take account of distinctions already drawn in classifying types of speech and conduct and defining the limits of protected speech. In some cases the fact of harm is sufficient to limit free speech, for example, where the speech itself may amount to a criminal act, as in the case of incitement, or incur civil sanctions in the tort of defamation. Conversely there may be some forms of speech, such as criticism of politicians, which although harmful are exempt from regulation. The status accorded to the harm will reflect the weight given to the competing right or interest. Even if the material falls clearly within the scope of the free speech principle, it may in practice be justifiably subject to regulation if it is outweighed by other interests. A framework of exclusions and exceptions already exists into which instruments designed to regulate pornography such as the Indianapolis Ordinance may be fitted, without making new rights. But although the Supreme Court has been opposed to giving constitutional protection to hard-core pornography, problems have arisen in defining obscenity and in applying the appropriate test established in *Miller* v. *California* 413 US 15 (1973). Attempts to provide redress for victims of pornography have been strongly resisted.

Chapter 10

Interpreting the First Amendment

The First Amendment to the Constitution of the United States stipulates that 'Congress shall make no law ... abridging the freedom of speech, or of the press, or of the right of people peaceably to assemble and petition the Government for a redress of grievances'. The right will be upheld against state legislatures and Congress, which may raise potential conflicts between the legislature and judiciary,[1] as illustrated by the treatment of the Indianapolis Ordinance in *American Booksellers* v. *Hudnut* 475 US 1001 (1986). The First Amendment has been so frequently cited by pornographers in American debates that it has been dubbed 'the pornographers' charter'.[2]

The First Amendment has been subject to considerable debate and interpretation on its scope, meaning and purpose. A number of justifications of the principle have been advanced by the courts and academic commentators. Fears of a slippery slope if the regulation of pornography is granted, expressed by liberals and some feminists, may be assuaged by a clearer understanding of the justifications of the First Amendment.

Although embodied in a written constitution, the scope and meaning of free speech rights has been subject to considerable debate. However, we can identify certain core elements, principally communication, used in interpreting the First Amendment. Even those justices who wish to maintain an absolutist position have faced problems in defining what counts as speech and where the boundaries should be drawn, for example, in borderline cases of symbolic speech.

We therefore need to be clear on the various distinctions the court will draw. First, there will be areas where the material clearly falls within the scope of the free speech principle, but in the case before the court the free speech interest is deemed to be outweighed by other interests. Second, some communications, such as defamatory remarks, which most people would see as speech, may be excluded from the principle. These issues are relevant to the pornography and censorship debate, raising the questions of whether pornography constitutes speech and if so, whether it should be protected or fall within the forms of speech excluded from the Amendment.

If it is included, then the issue arises of whether the free speech interest of pornographers should take precedence over the interests of those individuals and groups affected by pornography. The courts will reject content-based restrictions on speech which seem to limit the speech of particular groups or individuals.

Because the First Amendment requires interpretation, justices may draw on the various justifications or underlying principles when dealing with specific problems, some of which have their roots in classical liberal theory, principally in Mill's *On Liberty*. The justifications given by Mill, in chapter 2 of that work, include the importance of free speech to the discovery of the truth and the problems of presuming infallibility, the need for diversity of opinions, and the importance of moral independence as part of a general principle of liberty. Although Mill sought to assert the individual's right to moral independence and to hold unorthodox views without being stigmatised, he also saw this as beneficial to society as a whole. These concerns find expression in First Amendment jurisprudence, particularly in the significance of free and open discussion in preparing the citizenry to participate in the process of government; but the truth argument and the appeal to moral independence and autonomy may also be found. Furthermore, Mill's harm principle has been used in determining exceptions and restraints on free speech.

ABSOLUTISM AND BALANCING

An absolutist approach has been taken by some judges which permits no exceptions to the protection of free speech. Pornography, taking this view, should be entitled to the same protection as political speech, as any attempt to suppress it exposes the people to further governmental control of other forms of speech, such as political or literary works. Conversely a vigorous commitment to the right to publish pornography strengthens the protection of free speech. The risk of suppression, then, is that unconventional political thinking and artistic expression will be crushed.

Absolutism has been principally associated with Justices Black and Douglas,[3] who have tried to resist any legislation which could be seen as curtailing freedom of speech. Those who hold an absolutist position tend to define the scope of free speech as narrowly as possible. It is clearly harder to defend absolutism if the boundaries are widely drawn.

This absolutism has competed with and often conflicted with a 'balancing' approach in which the court is prepared to consider other interests and competing rights when determining what degree of protection to afford to free speech rights. It has been associated with Justice Frankfurter.[4] The balancing approach has been used since the 1930s. The competing rights and interests would include, for example, the right to privacy, individual reputation and national security. Balancing also raises the question of who should determine the weight to be accorded to each claim and the factors to be taken into account, whether this should be left, for example, to judicial discretion or juries, or formulated into clear rules. Inevitably, conflicts will arise between free speech and competing rights and interests, including national security, individual reputation and privacy. There are also contexts where constraints on the free speech of some groups or individuals may be necessary to protect the free speech of others. The balancing approach was clearly stated in *Paris Adult Theatre* v. *Slaton*, 413 US 49 (1973), where the court held that there were legitimate state interests at stake, including the public interest in the quality of life.

Absolutists would reject any form of prior restraint, but the moderates on the Supreme Court have accepted some restraint in exceptional circumstances where there is an immediate risk of harm, for example, to public order or national security, but the risk needs to be substantial, not merely speculative.

In order to maintain an absolutist position, it is necessary to construe speech narrowly, so that absolutists are more likely to construe symbolic speech as conduct. Non-absolutists, on the other hand, accept a softer boundary between speech and conduct. Absolutists are more likely to see pickets and demonstrations as forms of conduct rather than speech, which fall outside the scope of the Amendment, making it easier to defend their position. Absolutist judges are also likely to be more critical of permitting a heckler's veto. In *Feiner* v. *New York* 340 US 315 (1951) the Supreme Court upheld the conviction of a speaker for inciting a riot where there was a clear and present danger of disorder, while Justices Black and Douglas dissented, arguing that he had not intended to cause disorder and that the police should have protected the speaker by arresting unruly members of the crowd rather than him.

Balancing does not resolve the problems of interpretation. Rather it raises problems of proof, causation and the calculation of costs and benefits. If there is a presumption in favour of free speech, then the burden of proof will lie on those pointing to the social costs of unrestrained speech and arguing for regulation. Balancing may extend beyond public interest considerations to competing rights; although even here this conflict may ultimately be determined by the consequences of prioritising the two conflicting rights, in which case, as Schauer (1982: 134) says, the presumption in favour of free speech would be weaker as 'Free speech is not and cannot be an absolute right'. But in relation to public interest considerations, he argues, free speech should be given more weight. The harms arising from underprotection of that right will exceed those resulting from overprotection. In balancing the free speech principle against other interests, he says, we should ask the following four questions: what is the relative priority between free speech and the competing interests? Should the priority be determined by a fixed rule or a case-by-case approach?

Who should decide where the balance should be struck? In what types of rules should that balance be formulated? The relative weightings will also be affected by the type of speech. Political speech is given greater weight than literary speech in Supreme Court jurisprudence, and literary speech more than commercial speech. So how the speech is defined will affect the outcome of the balancing process. With competing rights the problem of balancing will be much harder.

These questions raise particular difficulties in relation to pornography, as the effects of the free market in pornography and the unrestrained free speech of pornographers may well be underestimated if victims are reluctant to report incidents and given the problems of proving imitative crimes and crimes in production. Consequently pornography may be given too much weight in the balancing process. Proving links with rape may be difficult if rape itself is under-reported. Deeper analysis will be required before the effects of free speech become clear. Coverage and protection of speech may also be distinguished, as part of the balancing process. A particular statement or form of speech may be covered by the free speech principle, but this does not entail that it will necessarily be protected on all occasions. While acknowledging the existence of a free speech interest, the court will be willing to limit it if, in the circumstances, other interests, such as national security or an immediate threat to disorder, should be considered. Schauer sees the distinction between coverage and protection as raising the difference between the strength and scope of the right. The strength refers to the capacity of the right to prevail over opposing rights and interests; but the wider the scope, he argues, the weaker the right will be, for if the scope is increased, the likelihood of conflict with a wider range of interests is increased. The strength of the right will thus correlate with the narrowness of its scope and make an absolutist position easier to defend. He cites the example of Meiklejohn's restriction of free speech protection to political speech: 'Freedom of speech as freedom of political deliberation gains simple absolutism at the cost of excluding much that a deep theory of the Free Speech Principle would argue for including' (1982: 135).

One could argue that the pornographer's claim of a free speech right is not, and should not be, sufficient to warrant protection in all circumstances. The right clearly does not embrace a right to commit perjury or extortion, for example, or to defame others. Schauer likens the free speech right to wearing a suit of armour, which may not protect one against all weapons, but this does not mean that the armour is of no value at all. Similarly the free speech right may afford considerable protection, but in certain cases, there may be arguments sufficiently powerful to justify overriding that right. The Supreme Court has been more willing to broaden the scope of the principle and to include a range of types of speech and borderline areas: for example some forms of commercial speech relating to political campaigns. He also argues that if we accept the free speech principle, this does not necessarily mean that speech should be free, but it does mean that speech restrictions do require a stronger justification than a simple appeal to the general principle of liberty. Free speech should be seen as an independent principle from liberty, so that it is more likely to withstand efforts to restrict it.

THE CLEAR AND PRESENT DANGER TEST

The Court has developed various rules, such as the clear and present danger test formulated in *Schenck* v. *United States* 249 US 47 (1919) to determine the appropriate issues to consider, and the relative weight to be given to free speech and competing interests, when engaging in the balancing process. As Justice Holmes said in that case: 'The most stringent protection of free speech would not protect a man in falsely shouting fire in a theatre and causing a panic.' Abridgement of free speech might be justified in such cases:

> The question in every case is whether the words are used in such circumstances and are of such a nature as to create a clear and present danger that they will bring about the substantive evils that Congress has a right to prevent.

> (at 252)

This case concerned the prosecution of opponents of the war who distributed leaflets opposing the draft amongst conscripts. Their conviction was upheld, although the effect might here seem to fall far short of the effects of shouting 'fire'. 'When a nation is at war', he observed, 'many things that might be said in time of peace are such a hindrance to its effort that their utterance will not be endured as long as men fight, and that no court could regard them as protected by any constitutional right' (at 252). The political climate will affect the use of the clear and present danger test. In the 1950s the courts were more inclined to accept national security claims when considering communist literature, and more willing to impose limitations on free speech. Today the courts are less tolerant of governmental claims and more wary of the dangers of suppression.

The test has been criticised by absolutist justices as incompatible with the First Amendment. Meiklejohn (1960: 30) is also highly critical of the use of this test to limit the First Amendment generally, and its application to the facts in *Schenck*, as it 'annuls the most significant purpose of the First Amendment', which he sees as the facilitation of self-government. It illegitimately shifts power on to the legislature to proceed whenever it perceives a threat to society. Immediately following the judgment the lower courts began using the test freely in relation to public safety, so that in *Abrams* v. *United States* 250 US 616 (1919) Justice Holmes emphasised that the danger had to be not only clear and present but extremely serious:

I think we should be eternally vigilant against attempts to check the expression of opinions that we loathe and think to be fraught with death unless they so imminently threaten interference with the lawful and pressing purposes of the law that an immediate check is required to save the country.

But this situation hardly prevailed in *Schenck*. In *Whitney* v. *California* 274 US 357 (1927) it was emphasised that the mere fact of destruction of property was not sufficient to justify speech suppression; nor was imminent danger, unless the evil was 'relatively serious'. Trivial harms are insufficient to warrant restraint. It would need a public emergency to justify the suppression of free speech, in which case public discussion and debate would already be impossible, says Meiklejohn. But in all other circumstances it should be possible to prevent the evil in question by more speech and public discussion. Certainly the threat to public safety alone should not justify speech suppression, he says, 'as it is precisely the appeal to public safety by legislatures which the First Amendment intended and intends to outlaw' (1960: 112).

Difficulties arise in determining the likelihood of danger and the type of evidence the court should consider. Where this is a danger of disorder it might be argued that allowing full speech expression will, in the long run, be less threatening than suppression because of the cathartic effects of speech. Certainly where the executive is acting unlawfully, public order arguments will not warrant restraint, even if there is a likelihood of disorder.

The clear and present danger test may be problematic because of the methodological problems of establishing harm considered earlier, but nonetheless it does show that the courts recognise the necessity of constraint. There may also be situations in which constraints on the free speech of some groups or individuals may be necessary, to protect the free speech of others. The court will consider the relative priority of free speech and competing rights or interests. The weight given to the various types of speech may depend on the justification used. Schauer (1982) argues that the clear and present danger rule demands considerable harm to the public interest before restraint can justifiably be imposed. If this were construed numerically, he says, we might see it as a 90 per cent standard, so dangers falling below that level would not warrant state intervention even though there are risks and dangers. This is a cost we must bear if we are committed to a free speech principle.

THE DEMOCRACY JUSTIFICATION

The special place of political speech has been recognised by the Supreme Court, which has been much more reluctant to limit speech in the political sphere than in other areas such as commercial speech, and tolerates verbal attacks on politicians. In *New York Times Co.* v. *Sullivan* 376 US 254 (1964) Justice Brennan referred to 'a profound national commitment to the principle that debate on public issues should be uninhibited, robust and wide open, and that it may well include vehement, caustic and sometimes unpleasantly sharp attacks on government and public officials' (at 270). The case concerned an action brought by a public official against the newspaper, and it was held that it could only be brought if the statement had been made maliciously, where the defendant knew it was untrue or was reckless regarding its truth. If the defence is couched in terms of a 'democracy' justification, this may mean that more protection is given to political speech than to literary works.

In Meiklejohn's analysis free speech is seen as essential to the performance of the duties of a citizen (Meiklejohn, 1960). But while he favours an absolutist approach, he limits free speech to freedom of political speech where there is no profit motive. Freedom of political speech is essential to a healthy democracy. Citizens need access to a range of ideas.

The democracy justification would seem to be potentially compatible with a limitation on pornography because pornography does not constitute political speech. The rejection of the regulation of pornography cannot be justified by an appeal to the democratic rationale of free speech because it would not fall within the realm of political speech. If the Court had upheld the Indianapolis Ordinance, it would not have encroached on the realm of political speech, for it is hard to see pornography as falling within that category.

One might argue that pornography contains a political element in the sense that it explores sexual politics. But it would be a feeble argument, as its conception of sexuality rests on a narrow view, namely, the presumption of female subordination. The most important justification for free speech in the United States, the democracy argument, cannot provide a basis for the protection of pornography, as it is hard to mount a defence of pornography in political terms. Opposition to the regulation of pornography cannot be justified by an appeal to the democratic rationale of free speech rights. This point was made forcefully by Justice Stevens in *Young* v. *American Mini-Theatres* 427 US 50 (1976):

> even though we recognize that the First Amendment will not tolerate the total suppression of erotic materials that have some arguably artistic value, it is manifest that society's interest in protecting this type of expression is of a wholly different, and lesser, magnitude than the interest inspired by Voltaire's immortal comment ['I disapprove of what you say, but I will defend to the death your right to say it']. Whether political oratory or philosophical discussion moves us to applaud or to despise what is said, every schoolchild can understand why our duty to defend the right to speak remains the same. But few of us would march our

sons and daughters off to war to preserve the citizen's right to see 'Specified Sexual Activities' exhibited in the theater of our choice.

(at 70)

Barendt (1985) attributes the special status of political speech to the powerful hold of the democracy justification and the need for the electorate to be fully informed in order to participate in decision-making and to evaluate government actions. He refers to the case of *Whitney* v. *California* 274 US 357 (1927), where Justice Brandeis emphasised the importance of free speech; if political debates were suppressed, society would run the risk of a threat to social order and revolution would be more likely. Barendt points to the existence of a similar balancing approach within the jurisprudence of the European Court of Human Rights on Article 10, for example, in the *Handyside* and *Sunday Times* cases and the greater weight placed on political speech. Generally the Court has been more willing to accept constraints on commercial speech than on political speech.

FREE SPEECH AND AUTONOMY

One also finds within First Amendment jurisprudence and free speech debates in the United States a defence of free speech in terms of its contribution to autonomy. On this principle even less protection may be given to commercial speech. Autonomy may be used not only to justify free speech claims where the right is raised against the state, but also to justify state intervention intended to promote autonomy which entails restraints on others' speech.

Scanlon (1972) sees free speech as essential to living an autonomous life. He constructs his theory of freedom of expression on a Millian Principle which he sees as being compatible with the exceptions and restraints on free speech we already accept, but which also acts as a brake on further constraints on freedom of expression. The principle, based on chapter 2 of Mill's *On Liberty*, identifies certain harms which, although they would not arise but for acts of expression, nonetheless cannot constitute justifications for legal restraints on those acts of expression. These include harms to individuals which result from their holding false beliefs arising from exposure to those acts of expression. The second example includes harmful consequences of acts which are carried out as a result of those acts of expression, where the link between the speech and the subsequent act consists only in the fact that the speech leads the agent to believe the act is worth doing. The individual, Scanlon argues, should be able to hear those views even if they are likely to foster beliefs which are undesirable or harmful to others, or lead to harmful actions. He sees this principle as a way of explaining the special protection given to speech as well as constraints found within the case law:

The Millian Principle, as a general principle about how governmental restrictions on the liberty of citizens may be justified, is a consequence of the view, coming down to us from Kant and others, that a legitimate government is one whose authority citizens can recognize while still regarding themselves as equal, autonomous, rational agents. Thus, while it is not a principle about legal responsibility, the Millian Principle has its origins in a certain view of human agency from which many of our ideas about responsibility also derive.

(1972: 214)

The advantage of this principle is that it gives a coherent rational basis to the existing restraints on free speech. For individuals to see themselves as autonomous they must first see themselves as sovereign in evaluating reasons for actions, using their own standards of rationality. Even if they decide that others' arguments are convincing, the decision must be based on their own independent reasons for approving their judgment as correct. Underpinning Scanlon's argument, then, is the view that the state's powers are confined to those which citizens may accept as legitimate, while still seeing themselves as autonomous.

Scanlon thus constructs his analysis of free speech on individual sovereignty. If citizens are equal, rational and autonomous agents, then individuals must be sovereign in determining what to believe and formulating reasons for actions. In order to exercise their autonomy and make a rational choice, individuals' decisions on a particular matter must be fully informed. It therefore follows that *access* to ideas and information must also be free as far as possible. The state should not enter into the area of individual choice by denying access to others' views.

On the Millian Principle there are two ways in which the state's right to decide whether to impose legal constraints on free expression must be limited for it to retain legitimacy. First, an autonomous individual would not accede to the state the power to protect him or her against false beliefs and would not defer to its judgment in such a matter. Second, where the state has prohibited certain conduct and defined it as illegal, the autonomous individual could not accept the right of the state to prevent that conduct by prohibiting advocacy of it. This is a matter to be determined by the rational agent. The focus of this argument, then, is on the limits to the state's authority rather than on individual rights.

Scanlon's defence of freedom of expression consists of the following components: first, the Millian Principle, which functions to exclude certain justifications for regulation of expression; second, further criteria within the limits bounded by that principle which may be considered, namely the balancing of the value of certain forms of expression relative to other social goods, the issue of equal access to the means of expression and the compatibility of the principle with competing rights. Taken together, he says, these criteria can account for those examples which our intuitions tell us violate free speech.

Although Scanlon emphasises the importance of access to unlimited speech for the benefits it will afford the speaker and audience, in the recent debate on pornography, the free market in pornography has been defended primarily in terms of the self-fulfilment of the audience to whom it is addressed – the consumers of pornography – rather than the producers, whose goal is pecuniary. But, as argued earlier, pornography contributes little to the self-fulfilment of the consumer or to the promotion of autonomy. While pornographers may appeal to the need for sexual diversity it is difficult to sustain this argument, given the actual uniformity in the content of the material. Although the First Amendment is predicated on the notion of the free autonomous individual, if it is construed to protect pornography, it facilitates the circulation of a medium which denies autonomy to women. The democracy and truth justifications of the First Amendment are also difficult to apply to the protection of pornography, as a free market in pornography makes no obvious contribution to truth, or to the democratic process.

THE SUPREME COURT'S TREATMENT OF OBSCENITY

The Supreme Court's analysis of obscenity has been developed in the context of assessing legal challenges to the constitutionality of laws passed by state legislatures to control obscenity. Prior to 1957 the Court paid little attention to the relationship between obscenity and the First Amendment. It used the *Hicklin* test, the tendency to deprave and corrupt, when considering obscene materials.

In *Roth* v. *United States* 354 US 476 (1957) the Supreme Court excluded obscene material from the protection of the free-speech principle; subsequently the Court has had difficulties in defining what constitutes obscenity. The majority of the Court found that it was not necessary to consider the empirical evidence of the likelihood of harms arising from pornography. The majority opinion was given by Justice Brennan. He criticised the *Hicklin* test, because it allowed books to be judged as obscene on the basis of isolated passages, and to be determined by the likely effects on unusually susceptible consumers. It assumed fixed standards regardless of time, place or circumstances. Instead, he argued, a book should be deemed obscene only if the dominant theme of the material taken as a whole is so judged, and the effect on the average person taken into account, applying contemporary community standards to the work. Obscenity was defined as material produced solely to arouse lustful thoughts. If the obscene material was utterly without redeeming social importance, it was excluded from First Amendment protection. The test of whether material was obscene was whether a court which applies prevailing community standards to the average person finds that the dominant theme of the materials taken as a whole appeals to a prurient interest. Problems have arisen in interpreting these concepts.

Feinberg (1987a) describes the court's approach as a mixture of moralism and paternalism, the aim being to protect individuals from themselves, seeing lustful states of mind as evil in themselves regardless of harm or offence.

Most of the material subsequently excluded from speech protection by the court has been pictorial, but written materials may also be excluded. Although hard-core pornography is not constitutionally protected, this has not resolved the problem of regulation of pornography. American jurisprudence has focused on the definition of obscenity, the appropriate community standard and on borderline cases of speech and conduct, such as nude dancing, and the problems of the value of the work taken as a whole.[5]

In *Manual Enterprises* v. *Day* 370 US 478 (1962) it was held that patent offensiveness and the appeal to prurient interest are both necessary for the materials in question to be judged obscene. Offensiveness rather than tangible harm has become a key ingredient in the control of obscenity. The importance of offensiveness is also reflected in the court's acceptance of restrictions on pornography through zoning ordinances. In *Paris Adult Theatre* v. *Slaton* 413 US 49 (1973) Justice Burger did refer to harm, noting that while no conclusive proof could be found of the connection between pornography and anti-social behaviour, it was reasonable for a state legislature to assume such a link. But the empirical evidence was not reviewed here, because it was already established that obscene material did not fall within the First Amendment.

In *Mishkin* v. *U.S.* 383 US 502 (1966) the court held that hard-core pornography which is offensive to the community lies outside the area of constitutionally protected speech. Mishkin appealed against his sentence for violation of a New York criminal statute prohibiting the dissemination of obscene materials. The books he disseminated included material on sado-masochism, homosexuality and lesbianism. The court said that the prurient interest applies to members of group at which they were aimed, that is, the specialist group, although patent offensiveness is determined by reference to the average person. The court also argued that Mishkin 'was not prosecuted for anything he said or believed but for what he did, for his dominant role in several enterprises engaged in producing and selling allegedly obscene books' (at 504).

The test of obscenity was reviewed in *Miller* v. *California* 413 US 15 (1973). The court defined obscenity to mean works which appeal to a prurient interest in sex, which portray sexual conduct in a patently offensive way, and which, taken as a whole, do not have serious literary, artistic, political or scientific value (at 24). Following *Miller*, the work has to be considered as a whole, and obscenity requires not that materials be utterly without redeeming social value, only that they lack serious literary, artistic, political or scientific value. The court affirmed that prohibitions on obscenity do have constitutional validity but did not rely on the harms resulting from pornography. Subsequent attempts to ground regulation in harm, such as the Indianapolis Ordinance, have received little support from the court.

The test in *Miller* was threefold: the court considers first whether the material in question appeals to a prurient interest; second, whether it portrays sexual conduct in a patently offensive way, the yardstick being whether the average person would find it offensive, using ordinary community standards; and third, whether the work has any serious literary, artistic or political value. 'Prurient interest' suggests a preoccupation with lascivious thoughts. This demands a subjective judgment, whereas the definitions of pornography favoured by most feminist critics and used in the Ordinance are more more clear-cut, descriptive and objective, referring to sexually explicit subordination rather than feelings or offensiveness. The test of feelings in *Miller*, as MacKinnon (1984: 31) observes, raises the problem that 'juries have often been the least likely to admit sexual arousal when the materials are the most openly abusive and violent'. There may also be examples of pornography which do not appeal to the prurient interest in sex but focus on violence against other parts of the body, or solely on violence. 'Patently offensive' would include descriptions of excretory functions, masturbation and the lewd exhibition of genitals, so an erect penis would be prohibited but a flaccid one permissible.

By the early 1970s when *Miller* and *Slaton* were decided, the Supreme Court had become more conservative and there was, as in the United Kingdom, a reaction to the permissiveness of the 1960s. Problems have arisen with the *Miller* test in subsequent cases, in relation to the definition of community standards, as the law has struggled to keep pace with the expansion of the pornography industry on the one hand and the demands of feminist groups for a consideration of the political implications of a free market in pornography on the other. In American jurisprudence, the yardstick is the average person, not the hypersensitive or blasé individual. In *Miller* itself, the standards were local, of the particular community where the film or book was being disseminated, rather than a national standard. Since then juries have not been confined to local standards but allowed to select the appropriate reference community, but they have not been allowed to use their own subjective responses to the material. The state may submit evidence of local community standards. But the results of prosecutions of similar publications elsewhere are not admissible. This raises problems of unpredictability as some films may be found obscene in some states, but not in others. Attempts have been made to argue that the fact that there is a huge demand for a particular film itself indicates acceptance by the community.[6] Although this is a particularly difficult problem, given the constitutional framework of the United States, similar problems have been found in the United Kingdom in variations between the levels of sophistication and tolerance of juries in different areas.

In *Stanley* v. *Georgia* 394 US 557 (1969) the court held that private possession of obscene material was constitutionally protected; the right to privacy includes the right to read pornography at home. One cannot be subject to prosecution in the absence of any attempt to sell or distribute the material. Justice Marshall said that: 'if the First Amendment means anything it means that a State has no business telling a man, sitting alone *in his own house*, what books he may read or what films he may watch'. This reflects the liberal view that the private sphere is sacrosanct, in which individuals are seen atomistically, rather than an arena of political relationships and inequalities of power. But the right to privacy does not cover the right to import pornography for personal use[7] or the right to receive pornographic material by post.[8] The consumption of pornography at home may be seen as part of a general right to privacy, implicitly guaranteed by the First and Fourteenth Amendments following *Griswold* v. *Connecticut* 381 US 479 (1965).

What is interesting in the *Stanley* v. *Georgia* case is the court's willingness to include private possession of pornography within the right to privacy, but to exclude the right to engage in homosexual behaviour.[9]

In *New York* v. *Ferber* 458 US 747 (1982) the court held that a criminal statute which prohibited distribution of material showing children engaged in sexual activities was constitutional. Here the film in question consisted principally of two boys masturbating. It constituted a permanent record of children's participation, and the harm to the children was exacerbated by its circulation. Although the act of masturbation itself was not illegal, and there was no evidence of coercion, the fact of the film's existence could encourage abuse if it were used to initiate children into sexual activity. Criminalisation of child pornography was important, because the literary and artistic value exception in the law of obscenity would mean that works embodying child pornography could be protected if they had such literary or artistic value. The appeal to the prurient interest test would not address the harm to the child in making the film. *Ferber* was important, both in terms of child protection and also in broadening the issues beyond those contained in obscenity law, providing a possible analogy to adult pornography. It recognised the aggravated harm of repeated showings of the films and it acknowledged harm even where there was no evidence of coercion, and identified the weaknesses of the law of obscenity. In a sense it moved some way towards the thinking behind the Minneapolis and Indianapolis Ordinances, even though the court later stopped short of following through the potential of *Ferber* by extending protection from children to women.

The statute in question in *Ferber* was challenged by the American Civil Liberties Union and an association of booksellers as a First Amendment violation. They argued that it did not fall within existing exceptions to the First Amendment; the state's interest in protecting children's welfare did not justify denial of First Amendment speech rights of publishers and distributors, and that it was overbroad and unconstitutional.[10] The court, however, accepted that the state did have a legitimate interest in protecting the children, and that if it was permitted to proceed against traffickers this would undermine the profitability of the market in child pornography, thereby attacking the incentive for producers and distributors.

In both *Miller* and *Ferber* the court accepted that the sexual exploitation of children was a legitimate ground for the imposition of criminal sanctions. While the court has been willing to deny speech protection where the interests of children are concerned, the need for protection of women's interests has not been developed because of the presumption of voluntariness and consent. In *Miller* the court also criticised the thrusting of pornography on to an unwilling audience or on to juveniles. This was especially pertinent as the Ordinance includes a provision dealing with the forcing of pornography on unwilling individuals in the home and school. Here, again, one can see a framework within which feminist arguments could be accommodated.

Some of these issues came to a head in the court's consideration of the constitutionality of the Indianapolis Ordinance. In *American Booksellers* v. *Hudnut* 771 F 2d 323 7th Circuit (1985) the Court of Appeals acknowledged the harms caused to women by pornography. This was summarily affirmed by the Supreme Court in *American Booksellers* v. *Hudnut* 475 US 1001 (1986). However, the harms were seen as being outweighed by the need to protect free speech rights, and the ordinance was seen as a content-based restriction.

Although the court has been unadventurous in interpreting the First Amendment, there are arguably problems with the Amendment itself. It rests on an abstract concept of free speech for all, assumes all speech is of equal value, and presupposes equal access to the means of expression and dissemination without taking account of substantive systematic inequalities which make it difficult for all individuals to express their right to free speech in practice. Although the laissez-faire model of knowledge seems attractive, it can only function in a society of perfect competition. However, if the speech of the powerful group dominates, the market is distorted. Moreover, even if women's speech is heard, this does not vitiate the original abuse to which participants are subject. In other words, speech is insufficient to compensate for coercion or assault, so further remedies are required.

Regulation of pornography as a feminist strategy might be construed as ensuring the First Amendment fulfils its promise by changing the social and political context within which it operates. In a non-hierarchical society, it might be possible for the First Amendment to protect all forms of speech. But as society is presently constituted, it may be that a breathing space or interim period is necessary where restraints are imposed temporarily to encourage the expression of alternative views.

The pornographers' free speech means in reality the loss of speech for others. The First Amendment and pornography have quite distinct aims. The aim of the former is to promote freedom of expression, while the latter silences women. By perpetuating myths of consent and acquiescence to abuse, it sustains the silence on violence against women in a number of forms, including rape and domestic violence, incest, forced prostitution and sexual harassment. Sexual offences are among the most difficult offences to prosecute because they usually occur in private, and raise particular problems of corroboration and scepticism regarding the credibility of child and female witnesses. Consequently, it may be that the most damaging effects of pornography lie in its impact on the credibility of the victims of such offences.

Chapter 11

The civil rights Ordinances

The civil rights Ordinances drafted in the United States in the 1980s are of interest because they afford an example of specific restitution for the harms arising from pornography. They are based on the harm principle rather than the offence principle, in contrast to many past regulatory measures. Although the Ordinances did not survive, their reception provides insights into the use of the law as a feminist strategy.

The City Councils in Minneapolis and Indianapolis had the power to pass legislation relating to the local area, but if it raised a matter of law, this could be referred to the District Court to consider its constitutionality. The court's ruling is then appealable up to the Supreme Court. The Indianapolis Ordinance was struck down, because the harms arising from pornography were seen as being less important than the right to publish those materials guaranteed by the First Amendment.

THE MINNEAPOLIS ORDINANCE

In 1983 the City Council was considering a new zoning law to limit pornography, confining adults-only bookshops, and cinemas and massage parlours to eight commercial districts within Minneapolis.[1] The proposal was approved by the Planning Commission but met with opposition from neighbourhood groups at a public hearing. Catherine MacKinnon and Andrea Dworkin, who were teaching at the University of Minnesota Law School at the time, testified at the zoning hearing.[2] They argued against the proposed zoning law because it failed to address the harmful effects of pornography; it also ignored the fact that pornography was widely available in ordinary supermarkets and stores regularly visited by women and children. They proposed instead that the City Council should tackle the problem of pornography as sex discrimination, by initially conducting hearings on its effects. They also proposed enacting an Ordinance specifically designed to regulate pornography, using an alternative civil-rights-based approach. The City Council had already approved an Ordinance prohibiting sex-based discrimination which could be amended, or a new

Ordinance could be drawn up, dealing, *inter alia*, with the coercion involved in pornography and providing injunctive relief.

MacKinnon and Dworkin were then requested to design a local Human Rights Ordinance to deal with pornography within the City Council's jurisdiction. Pornography was an important local issue, and there was concern about the impact of the zoning law on those neighbourhoods affected.

Hearings were subsequently conducted in Minneapolis to discuss the proposed civil rights Ordinance at which evidence was submitted by experts, victims and others on this issue.[3] Local experts on sexual abuse gave evidence relating to their work with victims of sexual assaults involving the use of pornography. Some witnesses testified that they had been coerced into participation in pornographic films. Psychologists and therapists gave evidence on the impact of pornography uncovered in work with sex offenders. Social workers and therapists working with child victims also testified to the use of adult pornography in the sexual abuse of children. Therapists from men's groups spoke of the effects of pornography on men's perception of women. Expert witnesses included Edward Donnerstein, who had conducted research on the effects of pornography on perceptions of rape victims and acceptance of rape myths, and Pauline Bart, who studied the use of pornography in medical school to desensitise medical students. MacKinnon and Dworkin also submitted closing statements summing up the research and findings.

The Council found that pornography was a key factor in creating and maintaining sexual inequality. In Minneapolis the Ordinance was passed by the City Council but vetoed by the Mayor, reintroduced, passed again and vetoed again in 1984. However, it was used as the basis of the Indianapolis Ordinance.

In the Ordinance, pornography is construed as a civil rights violation and a practice of sex discrimination; without the 'teeth' provided by the Ordinance, MacKinnon and Dworkin argued, the Council's commitment to gender equality was meaningless. The aim of the Ordinance was to hold those who benefit from injury to others' civil rights accountable to them. Women's pain, injury and suffering, as well as their enforced inferiority, were seen as more significant than the pleasure and profits afforded to pornographers and consumers or the effects on free speech rights. The production and use of pornography is construed as a form of sex discrimination which can affect the lives of all women even though they are not directly involved in production, by limiting the freedom of women and by perpetuating and maintaining inequality, constituting a systematic practice of exploitation and subordination based on sex which differentially harms women, by promoting bigotry and contempt and fostering acts of aggression, and hence undermining their participation in public life. It was envisaged that enforcement would be through a civil rights commission or, where appropriate, through judicial review.

The framers of the Ordinance emphasised that it was not a prior restraint, it was not aimed at the possession of pornography, and it did not rely on a test of offensiveness or on speculation. Rather its aim was restitution, to provide a remedy for proven injury and to prevent unjust enrichment from that injury. It was constructed on the basis of the harm principle, recognising the harms caused by production, distribution and consumption.

Pornography was defined as the sexually explicit subordination of women, graphically depicted through pictures and words which increase their dehumanisation. It may include one or more of the following: the presentation of women as dehumanised sex objects, things or commodities, the presentation of women as whores by nature, in scenarios of degradation, injury, abasement and torture, the presentation of women as filthy and inferior, in a context which makes these conditions sexual. It would include material on rape and the infliction of pain and mutilation, in which women are presented as enjoying pain and humiliation. The Ordinance allowed for the use of men, children, or transsexuals in the place of women for the purposes of the statute. It would also be open to a man or transsexual who alleges injury by pornography in the way in which women are injured by it to bring a civil action.

The Ordinance addressed a number of issues, including trafficking, assault, coercion and the forced consumption of pornography. It provided remedies, including injunctions. The production, sale, exhibition or distribution of pornography constituted discrimination against women by means of trafficking in pornography. The Ordinance also dealt with coercion: a person who is coerced, intimidated or fraudulently induced into performing for pornography shall have a cause of action against the maker, seller, exhibitor or distributor of the said pornography for damages and elimination of products of the performance from the public view. The limitation period for the action would be five years from the date of the coerced performance or the last appearance or sale of the product, whichever date is later.

The Ordinance ruled out a defence of *volenti*, making clear that proof of the following facts shall not negate a finding of coercion:

that the person is a woman, prostitute, over the age of majority, connected by blood or marriage to a person involved in the making of the pornography, or had sexual relations with anyone related to the making of the pornography, posed for sexually explicit pictures with them, that anyone else, including a spouse or other relative, has given permission on that person's behalf, or consented to the use of the performance, had knowledge of the operation, showed no resistance or appeared to cooperate actively, signed a contract, asserting a willingness to cooperate and the fact that no threats were used or the person was paid.

Clearly these broad stipulations would have greatly strengthened the power of the legislation had it been successful.

The Ordinance also addressed the problem of forcing pornography on individuals:

> Any woman, man, child or transsexual who has pornography forced on them in any place of employment, in education, in a home, or in a public place has a cause of action against the perpetrator and/or institution.

The Ordinance included redress for assault:

> Any woman, man, child or transsexual who is assaulted, physically attacked or injured in way directly caused by specific pornography has a claim for damages against the perpetrator, maker, distributor, the seller and/or exhibitor. She/he may also be granted an injunction against the specific pornography's further exhibition, distribution or sale.

THE INDIANAPOLIS ORDINANCE

A similar Ordinance was passed by the City Council in Indianapolis. This time it received mayoral support, but the Ordinance was subsequently struck down as unconstitutional by the Supreme Court. Attempts were also made to introduce Ordinances in Massachusetts and Suffolk County. President Reagan also set up a Commission to examine pornography which reported in 1986.[4] Under the provisions of the Ordinance, victims would be permitted to initiate a civil action against those who harm them in four areas:

(1) Where victims had been coerced into becoming models for pornographic material, they would be able to obtain injunctive relief from the court to remove the pornography from public circulation. The Supreme Court in *New York* v. *Ferber* 458 US 747 (1982) had recognised that the harm to a child appearing in a pornographic film was intensified by its circulation. MacKinnon argued that a similar intensification of harm occurred in relation to adult pornography, and the remedy offered by the Ordinance sought to limit the harm.

(2) It would be an actionable tort to force pornography on to a person at work or at home, in a public place, place of education or neighbourhood. Here the claim would lie directly against the perpetrator rather than the publisher. Forcing pornography is comparable to sexual harassment, which is already established as the basis for sex-discriminatory conduct.

(3) Trafficking in pornography, production, distribution and sale would also be actionable. The formation of private clubs or associations for the

purpose of trafficking would be made illegal and considered as a conspiracy to violate the civil rights of women. It would be open to any woman to file a complaint as an action against the subordination of women. This action received most criticism, although, as MacKinnon argues, the Supreme Court had already recognised the importance of trafficking in *Ferber*, in relation to child pornography, and in *Mishkin* v. *U.S.* 383 US 502 (1966), in relation to obscenity.

(4) Victims of assault, if they could establish a link between the attack and a pornographic work, would also have grounds for an action.

Apart from the forcing of pornography, the other activities of coercion, assault and trafficking were criminal acts rather than 'mere speech'. As in Minneapolis, pornography was defined as the sexually explicit subordination of women through pictures and/or words which also includes one of the following: (1) the presentation of women as dehumanised sex objects, things or commodities; (2) their presentation as sex objects who enjoy pain or humiliation; (3) the presentation of women as sex objects who experience sexual pleasure in being raped; (4) their presentation as sex objects tied up, cut up, bruised or mutilated; (5) their presentation in positions of sexual submission, servility or display; (6) presentation of women's body parts in such a way that they are reduced to those parts; (7) their presentation as whores by nature; (8) the presentation of women being penetrated by objects or animals; (9) women presented in scenes of degradation, injury or torture, shown as filthy, bleeding, bruised or hurt in a context which make these conditions sexual.

The individual, or in limited circumstances a group of women, could initiate an action against distributors or procurers, provided that it could be shown that the material is subordinating and falls within the definition of pornography and that the complainant was directly harmed, forced into participation or viewing of pornography, or assaulted as a direct consequence of pornography. The pornography in question must be specifically identified. An action on behalf of women as a group could be brought in relation to the trafficking count, and the group must show that dissemination of pornography violates women's civil rights. Defences of consent, contractual agreement and consideration were precluded. Remedies following a successful action consisted of damages and injunctions. The complainant could file a complaint with the City's Equal Opportunities Commission. If it was satisfied that there had been a violation, it could initiate an action.

THE DEFEAT OF THE ORDINANCE

The Ordinance met with an immediate challenge from an alliance of publishers and distributors, with the support of some feminist groups against censorship, who successfully applied for an injunction to prevent the operation of the law pending the hearing.

The Court of Appeals ruled the Ordinance unconstitutional, and this was upheld on a further appeal to the Supreme Court, who struck down the Ordinance in 1986 as a violation of the First Amendment in *American Booksellers* v. *Hudnut* 475 US 1001 (1986). It summarily affirmed the decision of the Court of Appeals in *American Booksellers* v. *Hudnut* 771 F 2d 323 7th Circuit (1985) and did not rehear the evidence. It implicitly accepted the Court of Appeals' recognition that pornography did violate women's rights in the ways identified by the Indianapolis Ordinance and which formed the basis for the Indianapolis legislation. What is significant is that the harmful effects of pornography were accepted. As Easterbrook J. observed:

> Depictions of subordination tend to perpetuate subordination. The subordinate status of women in turn leads to affront and lower pay at work, insult and injury at home, battery and rape on the streets, but this simply demonstrates the power of pornography as speech.

However, these harms were outweighed by the harmful effects on free speech. The Ordinance was held to be content-based, and seen as discriminating on the basis of viewpoint. It amounted to 'thought control' in defining an approved view of women. It was stressed that the feminist view of pornography was only one view among others. Perceptions of pornography may vary according to standpoint, and intervention could not therefore be justified. The following day the Supreme Court upheld the use of zoning as an alternative means of restricting pornography.

The Supreme Court thus lost an opportunity to develop the law in a way which could have protected women. Yet if the Court had upheld the Ordinance it would not have required the making of new law or a fundamental attack on the First Amendment, because there was already sufficient scope within existing exceptions to the First Amendment to allow for some forms of regulation.

The case for the Ordinance was submitted by MacKinnon, who argued that controls on pornography based on harm could be construed within existing exceptions to the First Amendment. She pointed to the various harm-based qualifications of free speech already recognised by the Supreme Court, including libel, misrepresentation and fighting words, considered above. The Court had also in the past, in *Pittsburgh Press* v. *Pittsburgh Human Rights Commission* 413 US 376 (1973), upheld an Ordinance prohibiting sex discrimination, in the form of sex-segregated advertising, which it said outweighed the free speech interest. She stressed that as a civil rights law, the Ordinance focuses on a 'civil conflict between *some* individuals who are harmed on the basis of their sex, principally women, and *other* individuals who do that harm, principally pornographers/pimps and their customers' (1984: ii) rather than on a conflict between state and individual

liberties. The Ordinance had been drafted, she said, to 'further the legitimate governmental interest in civil equality consistent with First Amendment guarantees'. The aim was to protect women's rights consistent with
the First Amendment, by balancing the rights of women against the rights
of pornographers and their customers to have access to such material.

She also argued that the publishers' claim was injusticiable. As they had
suffered no injury, they could not claim an injury simply from the existence
of the law.[5] The plaintiffs had no standing, as no action or threat of action
had been initiated against them. The existence of a chilling effect, even in
relation to First Amendment rights, was insufficient to prohibit legitimate
state action to prevent harms and to prevent discrimination, which is a
legitimate state interest. Discrimination is not constitutionally protected.
She questioned whether the fact that words and pictures are central to the
abuse should mean that pornography was immune from legislative action.
She argued that pornography can increase violence against women and
affect attitudes so that it is a fundamental factor in sex discrimination. She
also compared the position of women and children, referring to *Ferber* 458
US 747 (1982), where the court criminalised child pornography to further
the state interest in protecting children, and saw this as outweighing the
free speech interest. Here the court recognised that the state interest could
be advanced only by dealing with the incentive for profit for that exploitation. Where harms have been established and the state has a legitimate
interest such as the promotion of sex equality, then there is authority to
suggest that the court should not challenge such legislation.

The content of pornography not only implies that the participants consent but also has implications for the credibility of victims of violence
against women outside the context of pornography, for example, in 'everyday' contexts of rape and domestic violence. The credibility of victims of
sexual abuse including those coerced into production is undermined
because of the way pornography defines women as freely consenting to
their participation in abuse. Trafficking is seen as directly producing harms
where the coerced participant is seen as worthless. By giving such victims
a remedy in removing the film from public view, the Ordinance would
have directly empowered victims and struck at the producers' profits.
MacKinnon relied on Justice Stewart's opinion in *Roth* v. *United States*,
354 US 476 at 514 (1957) that free speech could be suppressed 'when
expression occurs in a setting where the capacity to make a choice is
absent', and where its expression is so closely bound up with illegal action
as to be inseparable from it.

THE REACTION TO THE ORDINANCE

A number of objections were raised to the Ordinance, encompassing many
of the arguments we have already encountered against regulation, including

the slippery slope argument and accusations of puritanism. The question of censorship dominated the debate. Lee (1990) is sceptical regarding the use of law as the first resort when the answer might lie in more speech from women giving alternative messages, such as the equal dignity of men and women, the devaluation of women by pornography and the nature and problems of male domination. But the expansion of the pornography market has paralleled the increase in feminist writings, and the latter seem to have had no dampening effect on demand. Even if women have greater access to the means of dissemination, they are unlikely to persuade those engaged in consumption.

Lee favours voluntary restraints rather than legal restrictions on free speech. But it is unlikely that pornographers would voluntarily restrain themselves given the huge profits realisable in the industry. To do so would presuppose a respect for women, yet the denigration of women is a defining feature of pornography. If the stage of self-restraint had been reached, we would already be in a pornography-free society. The 'more speech' argument presupposes the existence of the state of affairs which is being sought, when the key question is how it can be achieved. However, Lee does support the idea of an experimental pornography-free period. This would provide a breathing space for alternative publishing ventures to develop.

Rejections of the Ordinance based on appeals to free speech are unconvincing given the range of limits and exceptions to the First Amendment as well as the difficulties of construing pornography as speech considered earlier. In any event, if *Miller* and *Roth* have clearly excluded hard-core pornography as obscenity from First Amendment protection, why should free speech claims be readmitted when questions of restitution are raised?

Criticism of the Ordinance also came from women's groups concerned over the effectiveness of the procedures and whether they would meet the purposes for which they were designed. It was feared that the procedures would be too lengthy and cumbersome to provide speedy relief. The level of damages would need to be set very high to be a real deterrent given the profitability of the industry. There are also problems of enforcement.

A formal legal procedure may not be used by vulnerable individuals who are coerced into the production of pornography. If a support agency handled claims this could make the legislation more accessible, and this has proved to be the case in other areas of anti-discrimination law. However, the complainant would then be further removed from the procedure.

The drafting of the Ordinance was criticised for its vagueness. Terms such as 'sexual objectification', 'degradation' and 'subordination' used in the Ordinance, it was argued, leave too much scope for judicial interpretation which could be exploited by the moral right and could be used against feminist and gay writers and publishers, and artistic and educational materials. Clearly vagueness in drafting needs to be addressed carefully, but this is not an insuperable problem. It can be taken account of in considering similar legislation in the future. Moreover, if existing methods used to regulate pornography in England and the United States are beset by problems of variability between courts and states, and vagueness, a fresh approach may provide an opportunity to clarify the purpose of the law and its effectiveness. A further problem is whether the Ordinance could have been invoked in dealing with violent material which is not overtly sexual.

The slippery slope objections could be addressed by careful drafting and more finely drafted legislation, focusing on subordination, which may give greater protection than the current law to literary work and to feminist publications. The definition used by MacKinnon and Dworkin is directed much more specifically at pornography, while the English law of obscenity extends beyond pornography. Fears that feminist texts on pornography would be caught by the Ordinance are exaggerated, as they simply describe the way in which pornography depicts or encourages subordination and would not fall within the Ordinance definition of 'sexually explicit subordination of women'.

The floodgates problem, which was raised by some critics, is also met by imposing the burden of proof on the complainant and demanding a high standard of proof. Proof of harm is required, which, as we have seen, may be a difficult burden to meet and would deter vexatious and frivolous claims. It is more likely that the Ordinance will be under-effective in view of the difficulty of establishing harm. Similar fears were raised in Britain in relation to restrictions on racist speech, but the legislation is under-used rather than over-used.

An alliance of liberal and socialist feminists and libertarians, the Feminist Anti-Censorship Task Force (FACT), was formed to fight the Ordinance. They aligned themselves with the Association of American Publishers, the ACLU and the American Booksellers Association. They submitted a statement to the Court setting out their grounds for opposing the Ordinance. The group was suspicious of the support the Ordinance received from the moral right, including the Citizens for Decency through Law. The Mayor of Indianapolis, William Hudnut, was a Republican Presbyterian minister, who was opposed to pornography on religious and moral grounds, because he saw it as encouraging promiscuity. The support of the City Council for the Ordinance also met with some scepticism at a time when other inequalities, for example, discrimination against the black community, were not being addressed by political leaders. The Equal Opportunities Commission in Indianapolis, which would have been responsible for dealing with complaints, was already overwhelmed by claims of racial discrimination.

The centrality of pornography in perpetuating women's oppression was also questioned by FACT. Duggan (1985) argued that the Ordinance did not get to grips with the more fundamental causes of inequality and coercion and with acts of rape and assault rather than mere speech. As the existing criminal law can already deal adequately with them as well as with coercion into participation in pornography, she says, the Ordinance is superfluous. But the ability of the criminal law to deal with coercion in production is questionable in view of the problems of credibility of victims of abuse generally, and of complainants in relation to problems of pornography. The criminal law offers little restitution to the victims of pornography, in contrast to the Ordinance. It has proved ineffective in deterring or punishing those who harm women precisely because of the need to establish absence of consent in rape cases, for example. The 'presumption of consent' lies at the heart of the treatment of rape complaints and of the pornographic *genre*. The production of pornography is itself an act, and consumption of pornography constitutes an activity rather than mere 'thoughts'. Thoughts and actions cannot be so easily distinguished in everyday life when practices reflect attitudes and vice versa. The act of rape within and outside the pornographic context is surrounded by ideas, beliefs and myths which are central to its legitimation.

The perception of women underpinning the Ordinance was also criticised for treating women as victims requiring protection and as persons who do not enjoy sex and as unable to enter into legally binding contractual agreements, in effect treating women like children, as illustrated by the absence of a consent defence and the denial of contractual capacity. But the Ordinance provisions recognise the weight of constraints on women which affect their capacity to make free choices. Once the consent defence is permitted, it would be difficult in many cases to obtain a remedy, as the economic and psychological pressures on participants would be ignored in favour of the fact of formal consent and contractual obligations. It would be unrealistic to deny the vulnerability of women in the sex industry under the existing laws relating to pornography, and the opportunities for abuse and victimisation in a free market in pornography. This vulnerability is not a fixed quality, but rather a product of existing patriarchal structures and attitudes. The merit of the Ordinance is precisely that it seeks to empower women.

The Ordinance was also criticised by FACT for accepting too readily the role of pornography in causing violence, when violence predates pornography and other causes should be considered. But the Ordinance was not designed to remedy all forms of oppression of women, and it is hardly to be expected that a single legal instrument could achieve this. Of course pornography is not the only cause of violence against women, but this does not mean that pornography is insignificant.

It is also difficult to see how the Ordinance strengthens the censoring powers of the state, if actions are brought by individual women and the beneficiaries of the remedies are women rather than the state. As Kelly (1988) points out, if the effect of these civil actions is to force some pornographers out of business, this results from individual decisions to proceed and not state initiatives. The liberal concerns of FACT members, she argues, rest on a misunderstanding of the aim of the Ordinance, which 'was not about censorship but was an attempt at radical [feminist] law reform' (Kelly, 1988: 52).

Smart (1989) is also critical of MacKinnon and Dworkin's approach because it means working within a framework circumscribed by traditional judicial attitudes rather than one defined by feminism. Once the law is used, it may be invoked against feminism. She expresses doubts about the viability of legal solutions as a means of enforcement of feminist initiatives. Once feminism enters the legal arena, she argues, it is confronted by a set of standards and institutions predicated on traditional ideas. Using the law to regulate pornography means working within an established framework of harms and wrongs in which the complexity of feminist arguments is obscured. Working within legal discourse requires compromises, concessions and alliances with groups whose aims may be antithetical to feminist goals.

Smart characterises law as 'a discourse which disqualifies other forms of knowledge' as it translates them into law's own terms, for example, in the context of the rape trial. By working within law, feminism strengthens law's power when it should instead be seeking to decentre law by developing non-legal strategies. Law's ability to disqualify other forms of knowledge means that it is resistant to feminism. But the problem with this position is that few alternatives are offered, and in the absence of legal devices there is little prospect of change. While the remedies and solutions offered by the Ordinance may seem inadequate, they still constitute an advance on the *status quo*.

Smart is also sceptical regarding the use of censorship to achieve feminist goals: because the censorship lobby is hostile to feminism, and controlled by the 'moral right', censorship may be used against feminism. But the slippery slope argument is problematic for the reasons given earlier. She is critical of the definition of pornography in terms of sexual explicitness and coercion. It over-emphasises the sexual content of the degradation rather than degradation itself. It does have the merit of rejecting the liberal view of sexuality as natural, which obscures the coercive representation in pornography. Treating pornography as a form of sex discrimination is also useful, she says, in that it avoids debates on conservatism and permissiveness, and treats the issue as a matter of public policy. Smart construes MacKinnon's definition as implying any representation of explicit heterosexual activity involves coercion. This, she says, leaves little room for erotica other than lesbian erotica. Sexual explicitness and coercion are conflated. The focus on sexual domination, she says, diverts attention from other crucial forms of dominance, principally the economic one. Yet MacKinnon has written extensively on a range of areas of exploitation and domination, including sexual harassment in the work place and its implications for women's position in the labour market. There is nothing in the definition which denies the significance of these other dimensions of women's subordination. The definition also emphasises dehumanisation rather than sexual explicitness *per se*.

While many of the arguments raised against regulation in general, and the Ordinance in particular, are problematic for the reasons given, the usefulness of the Ordinance as a model for other jurisdictions may be limited. For example, if it were transplanted from an American constitutional context into the English legal system, there would be problems, as each system has a distinct structure. The Indianapolis Ordinance had to be charted through local, state and federal legal structures. It was ultimately constrained by a written constitution and Bill of Rights, and was defeated on the question of constitutionality. England has no Bill of Rights against which any Parliamentary legislation regulating pornography could be judged. Moreover, the principle of Parliamentary sovereignty raises the problem of entrenchment, so there would always be a risk that legislation passed to regulate pornography could be repealed by future Parliaments. In the United States there is also more scope for class actions than in England, where each individual complainant would have to bring an action. It would be harder for women to bring an action on behalf of women as a group. In England, women pursuing sex discrimination claims have received no legal aid for representation in industrial tribunals, and the level of compensatory awards on a finding of unlawful discrimination has been low. Women receiving support from unions and from the Equal Opportunities Commission have, however, achieved some notable successes.[6] Alternative methods of dispute resolution might be preferable or, at the opposite extreme, boosting the criminal law or introducing a new criminal offence of incitement to sexual hatred.

This raises the question of whether a civil or criminal law is preferable to deal with the issue of the regulation of pornography. The criminal law relating to obscenity has been criticised in both England and United States for its vagueness and problems of variability. The standard of proof is also higher, so it might be argued that civil law is a better option. If a civil measure were defeated in the United States, then a stronger criminal law would be unlikely to succeed. The advantage of a civil law is the use of the injunction to remove material and undermine profitability, compared to the fines and custodial sentences available under the Obscene Publications Act. On the other hand, it could be argued that a civil action does not give due weight to the seriousness of the problem. It treats the issue as a problem between individuals, to be resolved by compensatory payments, rather than as a problem for society as a whole, protecting itself against those who violate the rights of others.

While a civil Ordinance was favoured by reformers in the United States, in England other possibilities might include a criminal offence of incitement to sexual hatred modelled on the Race Relations and Public Order Acts. The case for and against an incitement to sexual hatred provision will be considered following a review of the current English law on obscenity.

Chapter 12

Freedom of speech and the regulation of pornography in English law

In England, unlike the United States, the protection of speech does not rest on fundamental constitutional grounds but has developed through the common law and statutory provisions. Consequently there has been less scope within English law for judicial consideration of the underlying philosophical principles which might be used to justify free speech, although discussions may be found in the Parliamentary debates on the passage of legislation rather than in the courts. Because England lacks a written constitution, it could be argued that the protection of free speech receives less support from the judiciary than in the United States. Less attention has been given to issues which have dominated First Amendment jurisprudence, such as the definition of speech, the relationship between speech and conduct and the problems of symbolic speech. There is also less hostility to prior restraint. The 'right' to free speech in English law exists in so far as it is not specifically precluded by relevant statutes and the common law.

However, although there is no comparable constitutional equivalent of the First Amendment, the right of free speech is to some extent protected by Article 10(1) of the European Convention of Human Rights, which guarantees freedom of expression. In the *Sunday Times* case, in 1979, the European Court of Human Rights held that an order prohibiting publication of an article on thalidomide by the newspaper did breach Article 10. While the Convention is not binding, it offers a framework which British courts may use when considering the scope of statutes which appear to limit free speech. The Convention also permits restraints on free speech, specifying the grounds on which this freedom may be curtailed or restricted. Article 10(2) states that this freedom:

> may be subject to such formalities, conditions, restrictions or penalties as ... are necessary in a democratic society, ... for the prevention of disorder or crime, for the protection of health or morals.

Otherwise there is a presumption in favour of free speech. Free speech is given less weight than the protection from torture in Article 3, which does not permit derogation. The infringement of the right to freedom of expression, when issues of public welfare and national security prevail, is thus built into the Convention. If legislation based on the Indianapolis Ordinance had been enacted in the United Kingdom, it could have been legitimately construed as falling within the scope of Article 10(2) so that the protection of public morals could provide a ground for intervention. However, one could anticipate opposition on the basis of the problems of establishing causal links with crime.

In the *Little Red School Book* case, *Handyside* v. *U.K.* (1976) 1 EHRR 737, the applicant was convicted under the Obscene Publications Act for publishing a book likely to deprave and corrupt children, and the book was confiscated. Although purporting to be a sex education text, it included advice on under-age sex. But the conviction did not violate the Convention. The European Court of Human Rights accepted a public interest defence, saying that it was open to states to apply their own standards. While Article 10 demanded free speech protection, states were entitled to impose restrictions based on their values.

In Britain the major means of regulation have been through the Customs Consolidation Act 1876, which controls imports, the Obscene Publications Act 1959, and the 1981 Indecent Displays (Control) Act 1981. Following a consideration of the law prior to 1959, the difficulties with the current English legislation will be considered.

Prior to the eighteenth century, there was little formal regulation of pornography. Obscenity laws developed in the eighteenth century. With the growth of technology, the development of new means of dissemination of materials and the rise of the novel, directed at a female as well as a male readership, the quest for stricter controls developed. This gathered pace in the nineteenth century, as Nielsen (1988) notes, with the rise of religious revivalist groups and moral entrepreneurs such as the Society for the Suppression of Vice, who began to take an interest in the suppression of obscene literature.[1]

The Obscene Publications Act was enacted in 1857 to crush a trade described as more deadly than prussic acid, arsenic or strychnine. No definition of obscenity was given in the 1857 Act, but in *R.* v. *Hicklin* (1868) LR 3 QB 360, Lord Cockburn defined the test for obscene libel as the tendency to deprave and corrupt those whose minds are open to immoral influences, and into whose hands these kinds of materials may fall. Whether the book had literary merit was irrelevant. Corruption suggested provoking impure thoughts.

Annie Besant and Charles Bradlaugh were convicted in 1877 under the Act for publishing a pamphlet on sex and contraception, although they were later acquitted on a technicality. Havelock Ellis' *Sexual Inversion,* a study of homosexuality, was also the basis of the prosecution of a bookseller. Homosexual and lesbian material was particularly vulnerable. Radclyffe Hall's *The Well of Loneliness* was subjected to a hostile press campaign and the book was publicly burnt in 1928. Trials were also conducted in the 1930s and 1940s of the publishers of sex education manuals. Subsequently a series of trials of commercial publishers of literary works generated a campaign which led to the reform of the obscenity law.

The history of the law of obscenity has generated concern about a slippery slope and partly explains why some critics of pornography are sceptical regarding the value of further legislation, which they fear will be used against lesbians and homosexuals.

THE OBSCENE PUBLICATIONS ACT 1959

The reform of the obscenity law may be seen as part of a general climate of permissiveness in the late 1950s and 1960s, reflected in the decriminalisation of homosexuality following the publication of the Wolfenden Report in 1957. However, this permissive ideology developed alongside campaigns by the police against prostitution, homosexuality and pornography, following public concern over the increasing visibility of prostitutes, and a moral panic over American horror comics. The prosecution of mainstream publishers had generated considerable criticism although, as Newburn (1992) argues, the Act which finally emerged in 1959 was a compromise reflecting the move towards both permissive ideology and increased regulation. The repressive changes in the 1970s, he says, can therefore be seen as a development of strategies already present in the 1960s and 1950s.

The Wolfenden Report (1957) was predicated on the harm principle, and on a sharp distinction between other-regarding and self-regarding action and the public and private spheres. In the public sphere it accepted that regulation and constraint were required. In the private sphere it maintained that individuals should be free to act:

> Unless a deliberate attempt is to be made by society, acting through the agency of the law, to equate the sphere of crime with that of sin, there must remain a realm of private morality which is, in brief and crude terms, not the law's business.
>
> (1957, paragraph 61)

The law should, instead, limit itself 'to those activities which offend against public order and decency or expose the ordinary citizen to what is offensive or injurious' (1957, paragraph 257).

The apparent liberalisation of the 1960s was followed by a reaction in the 1970s in favour of stronger regulation and the development of feminist critiques of pornography. They emerged in the context of increasing interest in the victims of sexual assault and the evolution of feminist theory, which has subjected the notions of choice and consent to critical scrutiny.

The issue of the law's intervention in the private sphere was revived in the 1990s by Operation Spanner, where a group of men who had consented to sado-masochistic activities in private were prosecuted, tried and imprisoned.[2] The defendants received support from civil libertarians and sexual libertarians. But the libertarian defence of sexual activity assumes a simple public–private distinction which is difficult to sustain and has been subjected to rigorous criticism by feminist theorists.

The Wolfenden Report was a major landmark in the deregulation of the private sphere, and the Williams Report continued that liberal tradition. The permissiveness of the 1960s has not been completely undermined by New Right individualism, because it sees the private sphere as the supreme realm of individual choice rather than a complex web of political relations.

Under the 1959 Act, amended in 1964, the crime of obscenity constitutes publishing an obscene article for gain. Mere possession for one's own use is not sufficient to commit an offence, in contrast to child pornography, where possession would be sufficient. The material may include written material, pictures and films and now includes video-cassettes.[3]

The test of whether the article in question is obscene is formally the same under the Act as at common law, namely the tendency to deprave and corrupt, whether:

> its effect . . . is, if taken as a whole, such as to tend to deprave and corrupt persons who are likely, having regard to all relevant circumstances, to read, see or hear the matter contained or embodied in it.
>
> (section 1(1))

This goes beyond the common-law test in *R. v. Hicklin* (1868) LR 3 QB 360 in looking at the work as a whole, and at all the relevant circumstances, when assessing the likely effects of reading the material.

The Act included a new statutory defence of public good, to prevent works of artistic and literary merit from being stifled. Whether the work contributes to the interest of science, literature, art or learning is taken into account in evaluating whether the material is likely to deprave or corrupt. Section 4(1) states that:

> A person shall not be convicted of an offence . . . if it is proved that publication of the article in question is justified as being for the public good on the grounds that it is in the interests of science, literature, art or learning, or of other objects of general concern.

Section 3 of the Obscene Publications Act 1959 allows for forfeiture of materials. Where the police have reasonable grounds to suspect that obscene materials are kept for publication for gain, they may apply to a Justice of the Peace for a search and seizure warrant. This allows for the seizure of large numbers of materials, but it is now rarely used. It has been subject to criticism because it excludes a jury trial and because the public good defence is not available to those who have been prosecuted under section 3. It was used to challenge the publication of *Fanny Hill* in 1963. The publishers argued that they should have been prosecuted under section 2 rather than subject to forfeiture, to allow them a jury trial, where they could have raised a public good defence.

A defence is given under section 2(5) of the 1959 Act. It provides that an offence is not committed if the person can prove that he has not examined the article and had no cause to suspect that his publication of it would make him liable to be convicted under section 2.[4]

When the Act was passed, Penguin Books announced their intention to publish an unexpurgated edition of Lawrence's *Lady Chatterley's Lover* to test the public good defence of the new Act. They won, and since then there have been relatively few 'obscenity' trials.

While the Obscene Publications Act was intended to deal primarily with pornography, it has been applied to other areas. The depravity to which the Act refers is not confined to sex. Articles encouraging violence,[5] or drug abuse can be construed as obscene. In *John Calder Publications Ltd v. Powell* (1965) 1 QB 509, 515, Lord Parker said that an account of a drug user's life which stressed the beneficial effects of drug use could raise issues of depravation and corruption. In *R. v. Skirving; R. v. Grossman* (1985) Crim LR 317, a conviction under the Obscene Publications Act was upheld in relation to the publication of a pamphlet entitled 'Attention coke lovers: free base, the greatest thing since sex'.

The drafting of section 1 has been criticised for its vagueness and for allowing too much scope for jury discretion. Problems have arisen in measuring depravity and corruption. Because juries' verdicts may be unreliable, from the pornographer's standpoint it may be worth taking the risk of prosecution and conviction if the profits at stake are high. The legislation has been criticised for being too weak to control pornography but also for being too strong, in running the risk of prohibiting works of merit. The drafting of the legislation reflects the desire to satisfy the anti-censorship lobby, critical of the prosecution of genuine literary works as well as the anti-pornography lobby.

Thomas (1978) questions the wide discretion granted the jury by the vague statutory definition of obscenity, which permits the jury to determine for itself what the relevant standard should be. This is the most unsatisfactory form of discretion, he says, because it is not easily structured, whether by formal administrative guidelines or informal discussion and consultation. A sharper definition of the prohibited conduct should be drafted in the legislation to confine the jury. The problems of relying on juries to draw the boundaries of free speech were also referred to by Dicey (1959: 246): 'Freedom of discussion is, then, in England, little else than the right to write or say anything which a jury, consisting of twelve shopkeepers, thinks it expedient should be said or written.'

Since the 1959 Act was passed, the courts have held that shock or disgust on the part of the jurors themselves is insufficient to establish obscenity. It is not clear from the wording of the Act whether the standpoint to be used is the ordinary person or the person most likely to read it, or the most vulnerable reader. In *Knuller Ltd* v. *D.P.P.* (1973) 2 All ER 435 the court referred to publications encouraging a departure from 'current standards of ordinary decent people', which suggested that the reference point even after the Obscene Publications Act was still the ordinary person rather than those most likely to read it, which is problematic in a pluralist society characterised by a range of values. In *Calder* v. *Boyars* (1969) 1 QB 151 reference was made to the effect on a significant proportion of likely readers.

In *D.P.P.* v. *Whyte* (1972) AC 849 it was stated that the 'Act has adopted a relative conception of obscenity. An article cannot be considered obscene in itself: it can only be so in relation to its likely readers' (at 860). The jury must decide who are the likely readers and whether the material is likely to deprave and corrupt them. In *Darbo* v. *D.P.P.*, The Times, 11 July 1991, the Divisional Court stressed that articles of a sexually explicit nature were not necessarily obscene. The category of sexually explicit articles was much wider than the category of obscene articles. Here a warrant issued under section 3 of the Obscene Publications Act had given authority to search for any other material of a sexually explicit nature, also any material relevant to the running of a business. As section 3 refers only to 'obscene articles', the search exceeded the powers authorised by section 3.

In determining the effects of the material, the jury will not normally hear expert evidence unless knowledge of the effects of the material is likely to fall outside the bounds of the ordinary juror's experience. Jurors are presumed to be aware of the effects in most cases. But in *Skirving*, expert evidence was admitted on the characteristics of cocaine and their likely effects on the user, and methods of taking the substance. This did not usurp the function of the jury in determining the effect of the text on the likely reader and whether it was likely to deprave or corrupt. Where the average jury member is as capable as the expert of reaching a decision on these issues, expert evidence should not normally be admitted. This poses problems when assessing likely harms, as it means that most of the social scientific research on the impact of pornography would be excluded, even though it is arguable whether this lies within the realm of common sense rather than specialist knowledge, particularly as the presumption of the harmlessness of pornography is a widely held common-sense view.

The focus in English law is on the state of mind of the consumer rather than the generation of specific acts. It is not necessary to believe that actual patterns of behaviour may be changed. In this way it avoids becoming involved in questions of physical harm, or the vexed question of the effects on sexual offences, although the issue has arisen at the sentencing stage where comments on this connection have been made.

In the *Oz* trial, the defence argued that articles in *Oz* may have actually deterred people from indulging in the sexual practices and drug-taking described in the magazine.[6] It was found on appeal that the judge had not properly put this to the jury in summing up, and this was one reason why the convictions under the Act were quashed. But this defence would lead to the absurd position that the more revolting the material, the more likely it would be protected, which cannot be what Parliament intended. The editors were given custodial sentences, although these were subsequently suspended. In the end the convictions under the Obscene Publications Act were quashed but upheld under the Post Office Act 1953. Expert evidence was given on the public good implications by a range of witnesses including Ronald Dworkin.

In *D.P.P. v. Whyte* (1972) AC 849 it was made clear that the key issue is the effect on the mind or emotions, rather than behaviour. Depravity and corruption are conditions of the mind, although 'evidence of behaviour may be necessary to establish their presence' (at 871). Lord Wilberforce argued that:

> At least since *Reg. v. Hicklin*, L.R. 3 Q.B. 360 and, as older indictments show, from earlier times, influence on the mind is not merely within the law but is its primary target.
>
> (at 863)

This was supported by Lord Pearson, who added that 'it is not essential that any physical sexual activity ... should result' (at 867). In *Whyte* the magistrates had acquitted the respondents because they were already depraved and corrupted, and could not be further corrupted. But the House of Lords allowed the appeal, saying that the magistrates had misunderstood the purpose of the 1959 Act, because if the goal was to prevent corruption, this would include the further corruption of those already depraved as well as corruption of the innocent. It was unnecessary that bad behaviour had to be brought about as well, although examples of behaviour might be used in certain cases to show corruption.

Stone (1986) argues that this presents problems for the admission of expert evidence in *Skirving*. The fact that a text encourages unlawful acts does not of itself render it obscene. For example, if a text advocated breaking the Road Traffic Act, this would not run the risk of prosecution under the Obscene Publications Act. But if it relates to sex, drugs or violence, it might be prosecuted, and if the effect on behaviour is not significant, then it must be because of the effect on shared moral values. If so, this issue lies within the capabilities of the ordinary juror, so that expert evidence is not necessary.

Either side may submit expert evidence on the artistic or other merits under the public good defence in section 4(1) but not, as we saw earlier, on the substantive issue of obscenity itself, which must normally be left to the jury. Expert evidence on the psychotherapeutic benefits of pornography would also be inadmissible, according to *D.P.P.* v. *Jordan* (1977) AC 699. This excludes evidence on the cathartic effects of pornography in releasing sexual tensions or providing a harmless release for potential sexual offenders, although pornography has been used in psychiatric programmes.

The jury embarks on a two-stage procedure. First it decides whether the work is obscene and whether it has a tendency to deprave or corrupt. Once a decision has been reached on this, it considers whether the publication furthers the public good or has any merits which justify its protection, even though it is obscene. As Barendt (1985) observes, this is a difficult task for the jury, as it is hard to balance obscenity against a work's merits. It might make sense to balance the harm to particular individuals against the general good to the community as a whole if publication were permitted, but it is difficult for the jury to weigh the depraving and corrupting effects against the literary merit. Although expert witnesses do give evidence on the literary merits, this, he says, is elitist in presupposing two different readerships, the persons susceptible to corruption and the superior persons who can recognise the work's merits. Section 4 is also problematic, he says, in its reference to 'other objects of general concern'. While this has been construed as comparable to scientific or literary merits, it would not seem to include sexual therapy, and this, as we saw earlier, has been widely used by defenders of pornography as a legitimate and useful purpose of such material.

Since the 1950s, then, the obscenity law has been subject to criticism. The debate continued in the 1970s with the publication of the Longford Report in 1972, which argued for reform of the Obscene Publications Act, including revoking the public good defence, harsher penalties, controls on indecent displays and extension of the Obscene Publications Act to television and cinema. The legislation was also reviewed by the Society of Conservative Lawyers and the Arts Council and criticised by the Williams Committee. The regulation of pornography was also subject to consideration by feminist writers, who focused primarily on the effects on women. A range of other statutes also regulate the dissemination of pornography, and there are anomalies in the current legislation in the different meanings of obscenity and indecency.

THE POST OFFICE ACT 1953

Section 11 of this Act prohibits sending a packet through the post which encloses any indecent or obscene print, painting, photograph, lithograph, engraving, cinematograph film, book, card or written communication, or any indecent or obscene article, or which has on the packet or its cover any words, marks or designs which are grossly offensive or of an indecent or obscene character. The offence is punishable on summary conviction by a fine or imprisonment.

The mail has been used to disseminate obscene material and to evade detection by the police, as Manchester (1983) notes, since the 1860s. Sending indecent or obscene material through the post was criminalised in 1884 by the Post Office (Protection) Act. The prohibition on sending obscene materials through the mail is now contained in section 11 of the 1953 Post Office Act but this provision is rarely used by the Post Office because of the difficulties of intercepting mail. Manchester gives a figure of fifty casesfor 1982, which probably accounts for only a small proportion of materials actually transmitted by post. Obscene items are likely to come to light only if they are damaged in transit or cannot be delivered. The mail is more likely be used for soft-core pornography, while hard-core pornography is likely to be carried in private vehicles.

'Indecent' and 'obscene', under the 1953 Act, are construed as 'offending against the recognised standards of propriety', rather than the tendency to deprave or corrupt, used in the 1959 Obscene Publications Act.[7] It would cover violence, cruelty, sexual and excretory functions, and favourable accounts of drug use. The Post Office may destroy the material or refer the case for prosecution. The Post Office deals with internal mail, while imports are covered by Customs and Excise.

THE CUSTOMS CONSOLIDATION ACT 1876

Section 42 of the Customs Consolidation Act 1876 prohibits importation into the United Kingdom of indecent or obscene prints, books, cards, lithographs, engravings, photographs or other indecent or obscene articles. The goods may be impounded, condemned and forfeited. The procedure for seizure and condemnation is governed by section 139 of the Customs and Excise Management Act 1979 and schedule 3 of that Act. Under the Act 'obscene' is given its ordinary meaning, of filthy, loathsome, repulsive, lewd, rather than the specific meaning given in the 1959 Obscene Publications Act.[8] There is no public good defence under the Customs Consolidation Act, in contrast to section 4 of the Obscene Publications Act. In R. v. Bow Street Magistrates Court ex parte Noncyp Ltd (1990) 1 QB 123, books imported from the Netherlands by Gay's the Word Bookshop, including Men in Erotic Art, were seized. This case intensified fears of a slippery slope arising from stronger regulation of pornography. The Divisional Court held that the magistrates were not entitled to call expert evidence on the public good, even though a successful public good defence would have meant that no offence would have been committed under the Obscene Publications Act. The applicant sought judicial review of the magistrates' decision on the ground that if publication of the book was not an offence under the 1959 Act, then prohibition of its importation would contravene Article 30 of the EEC Treaty. Article 30 prohibits restrictions on imports. While Article 36 of the Treaty allows restrictions on grounds of public morality, this cannot be used to evade Article 30.

This issue had been considered previously in *Conegate Ltd* v. *Customs and Excise Commissioners*, (1986) 2 All ER 688, where the relationship between European law and the Obscene Publications Act and the Customs Consolidation Act was reviewed, as the case was referred to the European Court of Justice for a preliminary ruling. The Court ruled that member-states could not rely simply on public morality to restrict the importation of goods if it would not have been prohibited under the Obscene Publications Act. The prohibition on imports of obscene articles imposed by section 42 of the 1876 Act survived only to the extent that the Obscene Publications Act prohibited publication of the specific article in the United Kingdom.[9] The question was whether there was a lawful trade in the relevant articles in the United Kingdom. If the articles were of such a kind as to fall under the prohibitions in the Obscene Publications Act, as well as under the Customs Consolidation Act, then restrictions on imports would not constitute arbitrary discrimination or a disguised restriction within the meaning of Article 36.

In *Noncyp*, however, Croom-Johnson L.J. distinguished *Conegate*, as it concerned the importation of life-size dolls with orifices, described variously as 'rubber lady' dolls and 'sexy vacuum flasks', rather than books. Their sale in England was legal, provided certain licensing conditions were met. If a prosecution had already failed under the Obscene Publications Act because it did not meet the test of obscenity in section 1 or the public-good defence in section 4, then this would constitute an abuse of the Commissioner's discretion to seize material, but this was not the case in *Noncyp*.

THE PROTECTION OF CHILDREN

Specific legislation addressing the use of children in pornography is provided by the Protection of Children Act 1978 and the 1988 Criminal Justice Act. Section 1 of the Protection of Children Act 1978 makes it an offence to publish, distribute or take an indecent photograph of a child. A defence is given in section 1(4) if the accused has a legitimate reason for distributing or possessing the photograph. Possession of an indecent photograph of a child is prohibited by section 160 of the 1988 Criminal Justice Act, and this has enabled the police to make advances in the regulation of child pornography. The earlier child-protection measures focused on the child as consumer and reflected anxiety regarding horror comics rather than pornography. The Children and Young Persons

(Harmful Publications) Act 1955 prohibited the dissemination of comics which are harmful to children and young persons.

THE INDECENT DISPLAYS [CONTROL] ACT 1981

This is predicated on the notion of offensiveness rather than the depraving and corrupting potential. It makes it an offence to display in public material which is indecent, that is, which may cause offence or embarrassment to the public (section 1(1)). Material may be confiscated if it is on display and likely to offend others. Material should be removed or transferred to high shelves. Indecency is not defined in the Act, but is broader than obscenity.[10] Specialist sex shops are required to display warning signs to potential customers and to keep their shop fronts blank rather than festooned with the material available for sale. Soft pornography is still available in corner shops and high-street retailers, albeit on the top shelf, and has been the target of the Campaign against Pornography's Off the Shelf campaign.

THE PAGE THREE BILL

Clare Short introduced her Page Three Bill in 1986. It progressed as far as a second reading in April 1987. The bill sought to make illegal displays of pictures of naked or partially naked females in sexually provocative poses in newspapers. If found guilty, the offender would be fined 1 pence per copy of the newspaper published, and 2 pence if the offence was repeated. The aim here was to deal specifically with newspapers rather than pornography *per se*, because of the visibility of newspapers and the fact that women are constantly confronted by newspapers.

Although the bill failed in the face of tremendous hostility from the press, particularly the *Sun*, Short received over 5,000 letters of support.[11] A survey conducted by *Woman* magazine showed that 90 per cent of the respondents supported the aims of the bill because of perceived links between the pictures and violence against women, and hypocrisy in attitudes towards breast-feeding women. The respondents included a rape survivor who was told by her attacker that he was raping her because she looked like a particular page three model. Short used the harm argument in support of her bill, in terms of the effect on violence against women; she also stressed that women found these pictures offensive. The campaign also raised the question of the law as a feminist strategy. Some feminists were apprehensive about using a legal device because of the fear of its repressive deployment; others questioned the importance of the issue compared to other forms of sexual discrimination and oppression. The significance and meaning of the sexual imagery and representation in page three pictures were also subject to debate. Smart (1989) contrasts the hilarity and derision and comments on the size of her breasts which greeted Short's proposal with the serious consideration given by the media and Parliament to Winston Churchill's unsuccessful Bill to reform the Obscene Publications Act in 1986.

THE LOCAL GOVERNMENT [MISCELLANEOUS PROVISIONS] ACT 1982

This Act covers the licensing of sex shops by local authorities and permits them to determine the number of shops. Under section 2, schedule 3, the local council has the power to license sex cinemas and shops. A sex shop is defined as a shop used to a significant degree to sell articles concerned with the portrayal of sexual activity. The local authority can, if it chooses, demand licences, and if the council decides that there are too many in the area, it may refuse a licence and may take account of the feelings of local people.

CONSPIRACY TO CORRUPT PUBLIC MORALS

A prosecution may be brought under the common law of conspiracy to corrupt public morals, as illustrated by two cases in the 1960s and 1970s, the *Ladies' Directory* case, *Shaw* v. *D.P.P.* (1962) AC 220, and the *International Times* case, *Knuller*, although it is now rarely used. There is no public-good defence comparable to that in the Obscene Publications Act.

Shaw published *The Ladies' Directory*, a directory of prostitutes. It included nude photographs and a code describing the sexual practices on offer. He was convicted for the common law offence of conspiracy to corrupt public morals as well as publishing an obscene book, under the Obscene Publications Act 1959, although the content was mild compared to many pornographic works. He was also convicted of being a male living on the earnings of prostitution, contrary to section 30(1) of the Sexual Offences Act 1956, an offence aimed at pimps, although the women had paid him to run the advertisements.

In the House of Lords his conviction for conspiracy to corrupt public morals was upheld. Lord Simonds thought that it might be desirable to use the conspiracy offence if it was difficult to establish obscenity within the meaning of the Obscene Publications Act. He referred to the court's residual power to 'enforce the supreme and fundamental purpose of the law, to conserve not only safety and order but also the moral welfare of the State' (at 268). Lord Reid dissented, arguing that the intervention of the law to punish immoral acts was seen as ultimately a question for Parliament rather than the courts. The courts should not rush in where Parliament fears to tread.

In *Knuller Ltd* v. *D.P.P.* (1973) 2 All ER 435, the appellants, publishers of the magazine the *International Times*, had included columns of advertisements under the heading 'Males' which were mostly inserted by homosexuals to make contact with others in order to engage in homosexual activities. The magazine had a large circulation of over 30,000 copies, with many readers under 21, but the likelihood of members of that group responding to the advertisements was not in issue. The appellants were charged with conspiracy to corrupt public morals and with conspiracy to outrage public decency by publishing the 'lewd, disgusting and offensive' advertisements. They were convicted on both counts and the Court of Appeal dismissed their appeal. The case then went to the House of Lords, which dismissed their appeal on the first count but allowed their appeal on the second count. The question of whether there was an offence of outraging public decency was considered. The majority held that there was such an offence.

The prosecution had argued that the appellants had conspired by means of the advertisements to induce readers to meet those placing the advertisements to engage in homosexual practices, to encourage readers to engage in those practices, with intent to corrupt the morals of youth. Lord Reid accepted that section 2(4) of the Obscene Publications Act does not explicitly preclude prosecution for the offence of corrupting morals, but, he said, the policy underpinning the Act needs to be considered. Had Shaw's case been foreseen at the time of drafting the Act, it might have been worded differently. The Solicitor-General had given an assurance to the House of Commons in 1964 that a conspiracy to corrupt public morals would not be charged as a means of getting round the section 4 defence, which suggested some anxiety about *Shaw*.

Lord Reid addressed two points arising out of *Shaw*. The conspiracy to corrupt public morals is rather a misnomer, he said, as it really means conspiracy to corrupt the morals of such members of the public as may be influenced by the matter published by the accused. The meaning of corruption needs clarification, he said, as the effect of *Shaw* leaves too much to the jury. In *Shaw*, a direction which construed corruption as 'leading morally astray' was upheld. Lord Reid was critical of this:

> We may regret that we live in a permissive society but I doubt whether even the most staunch defender of a better age would maintain that all or even most of those who have at one time or in one way or another been led astray morally have thereby become depraved or corrupt. The jury should be told that although in the end the question of whether a matter is corrupting is for them, they should keep in mind the current standards of ordinary decent people.

The appellants argued that as homosexual acts between adult males in private are now lawful, persons cannot be guilty of an offence if they merely put in touch with one another two males who wish to engage in those acts. But this was rejected by the court. Procuring was still an offence. The fact that homosexual acts had been decriminalised did not mean that they were not corrupting, or that a licence had been given to encourage others to engage in them.

The appeal was dismissed on the first count. The conviction on the second count of conspiracy to outrage public decency was quashed because the jury had been misdirected, but their Lordships affirmed that such an offence existed. Lord Reid was critical of this. To recognise this new crime, he said, would go against the whole trend of public policy followed by Parliament in recent times. It would have a chilling effect on publishers. Without a public good defence, respected literary works would be at risk if they offended particular jurors.

In *R. v. Gibson* (1991) 1 All ER 439 the Court of Appeal upheld Gibson's conviction on a charge of outraging public decency for exhibiting at an art gallery a 'human earring' made from a freeze-dried human foetus. The court followed *Shaw* and *Knuller*, where the House of Lords made clear that it is an offence to outrage public decency whether or not the work also tends to corrupt and deprave those who see or hear it. The common law offence of outraging public decency did not depend upon proof of a tendency to corrupt public morals. Nor was it necessary to prove intention or recklessness. In *Gibson* there was no suggestion that anyone would be corrupted by viewing the exhibition.

The conspiracy to corrupt public morals is unlikely to be used if a substantive offence is available. The use of the conspiracy law in *Knuller* was widely criticised and may account for the support for a slippery slope argument.

THEATRE AND FILM CENSORSHIP

Theatre censorship was also placed on a statutory basis in the eighteenth century. It has subsequently been subject to regulation by a number of statutes, but control was relaxed by the Theatres Act 1968. Although an offence is committed if one directs a play whose effect taken as a whole is to deprave and corrupt the audience, a public good defence is available under section 3(1) of the Theatres Act 1968 if it can be shown that the play is in the interests of art, drama, literature or learning. The aim of the earlier legislation was to control material deemed to be a challenge to the established religion and to control political dissent, rather than pornography. The Revels Office was set up in 1545, and the Master of the Revels had the power to censor work. It enacted the recommendations of a Joint Select Committee which argued that there was no legitimate ground for distinguishing between books and plays. It also argued that the prevailing system was vague, allowed no appeals against decisions and had a chilling effect on artistic creativity. Its only merits were speed and economy.

Although this Act reflected the Committee's view that there could be no rational distinction between the law's treatment of books and plays, a distinction between books and the cinema and videos may still be found in English law.

The English system of film censorship demonstrates the tolerance of prior restraint in English law. A system of licensing of cinemas, including private clubs, was established by the Cinematograph (Amendment) Act 1982. The cinema is subject to greater control than the theatre, and this might be defended on the ground that the cinema has a much larger audience, is much cheaper, and more likely be attended by children, although the last problem could be solved by admission restrictions based on age. It may also reflect the elitism found in the law of obscenity, if it is thought that middle-class theatre audiences but not working-class cinema-goers can cope with risqué material.

Under the Cinematograph Act, local authorities can decide whether films should be shown, but usually the decision is made by the British Board of Film Censors. It, and the local authorities, may ban films or demand that parts of the film are cut on grounds of offensiveness, the degradation of women or the glorification of violence. Film exhibitors and distributors may also be prosecuted under the Obscene Publications Act 1959.

The Video Recordings Act 1984 was passed following a moral panic over video nasties. It gave the Home Secretary the authority to designate a person to classify video films. The British Board of Film Censors is now empowered to outlaw the sale or hire of any video not approved by the censor. The system of classification used for public showings of films is now applied to home videos, although, of course, access to them is difficult to control given the problems of policing the private sphere. The opportunities to copy censored videos means that circulation of illegal videos is possible. A number of prosecutions under the Obscene Publications Act 1959 have concerned the sale and circulation of videos in corner shops, available to inquiring customers.

REGULATION OF THE MEDIA

Controls on the media consist of statutory controls complemented by various forms of self-regulation.[12] The Broadcasting Standards Council was established in 1988, initially on a non-statutory basis, but given a statutory foundation in the 1990 Broadcasting Act (part VI). Its duty is to draw up and from time to time review a code giving guidance as to:

a practices to be followed in connection with the portrayal of violence in programmes to which this Part applies,

b practices to be followed in connection with the portrayal of sexual conduct in such programmes, and c standards of taste and decency for such programmes generally.

The Council was set up following the Hungerford killings and public concern over film and television violence. It also deals with individual complaints and monitors programmes in the light of its code of practice. A Broadcasting Complaints Commission was set up in 1981. Its powers and functions are now contained in the 1990 Broadcasting Act (part V). The press is regulated by the Press Complaints Commission. In addition the National Union of Journalists has its own Code of Practice, Ethics Committee and disciplinary procedures. Newspaper editors have appointed their own Ombudsmen. Although the emphasis has been on self-regulation by the press, there has been increasing criticism of press standards, particularly in relation to privacy (Calcutt, 1990), and demands for stronger and more effective forms of regulation.

Notwithstanding the range of legislation available, the pornography market has continued to expand. The 1980s and 1990s have also witnessed the paradoxes of deregulation of broadcasting in some areas in order to promote competition, combined with attempts to bring broadcasting under greater state control in certain areas, such as national security. To some extent this soft approach to pornography reflects the deeper contradictions of New Right social policy, evidenced, for example, in its commitment to the family as an institution and giving greater rights to parents – for example, in the Children Act 1989 – while failing to protect vulnerable family members experiencing violence in the home.

SENTENCING POLICY

The appropriate sentences for offenders involved in the commercial exploitation of pornography were considered by the Court of Appeal in *R. v. Holloway* (1982) Cr App R (S) 128. Here it was stressed that custodial sentences were appropriate for first offenders involved in commercial exploitation, including salesmen, projectionists, owners and suppliers of pornography. Pornography needed to be seen as a hazardous occupation. The appellant had been convicted on six offences of having obscene articles for publication for gain. Lord Justice Lawton stressed that:

> the only way of stamping out this filthy trade is by imposing sentences of imprisonment on first offenders and all connected with the commercial exploitation of pornography: otherwise front men will be put up and the villains will hide behind them.

(at 131)

Fines were ineffective as they could simply be passed on to consumers in price increases and sales would continue, but they could be effectively combined with custodial sentences. The annual profit from the two clubs involved in *Holloway* was estimated at £25,000 in 1982. But the guidelines in *Holloway* were intended for commercial cases. A distinction was drawn between those cases and the newsagent who is carrying on a legitimate business selling newspapers but who sells the odd pornographic magazine and has been careless in failing to check the contents of his stock, or 'the young man who comes into possession of a pornographic video tape and who takes it along to his rugby or cricket club to amuse his friends by showing it'. In the latter cases a fine would be appropriate. Since *Holloway* there have been a number of appeals concerning corner shops.

However, in dealing with traders and producers, sentences are still relatively light. This may partly reflect the problems of remoteness, referred to earlier, so strong sentences are deemed appropriate for perpetrators of direct harms, but the commercial industry is seen as further removed from the ultimate criminal act. In *R. v. Knight* (1990) Cr App R (S) 319 a twelve-month sentence for possession of obscene videos and magazines for publication for gain was reduced to six months and a fine. Knight had no previous convictions and pleaded guilty on seventeen counts. In *R. v. Doorgashurn* (1988) Cr App R 195 pornographic videos and books were sold in a corner shop which also sold sweets, children's comics and newspapers. It was not a large-scale operation. The appellant's sentence of twelve months, for fourteen counts of having obscene articles for gain, was reduced on appeal to six months. The videos involved buggery, sado-masochism and bestiality but not children. Lord Justice May referred to the dispiriting similarity of this case with an increasing number of cases of this type coming before the Court. In *R. v. Calleja* (1985) Crim LR 397, a sentence of twelve months' imprisonment for having an obscene article for gain on a second conviction was seen as appropriate for a part-owner of a club exhibiting pornographic films. Reference was made to the fact that the film included buggery but not children or animals.

POLICING PORNOGRAPHY

A particular difficulty with the English legislation has been the problem of enforcement. Regional variations have been found in enforcement, depending on the concerns of local communities and the priorities of particular Chief Constables. A major problem for the police has been the sheer volume of material handled by them, seized under section 3 of the Obscene Publications Act, which may run into millions of items per year. This may lead to delays in processing cases, as Stone (1986) notes, and this problem is increasing with the expansion of the pornography industry.

The difficulties with the existing law are reflected in the problems of policing pornography both in London and the provinces. It may take several months to classify materials, and once the case comes to court, the tribunal is still confronted with a huge amount of material to assess, which includes magazines, books, films and videos. Sampling procedures may be used to divide the material into classes or categories, ranging from the least obscene to the most obscene, and to select items from each class for consideration by the court. The use of sampling by the police was accepted by the Court of Appeal in *R. v. Snaresbrook Crown Court, ex p. Commissioner of Police for the Metropolis* (1984) 79 Cr App R 184, where Watkins L.J. noted that:

> The courts in this country which are seized of cases of pornography are facing a very, very considerable problem. Obtaining the services of justices to spend weeks on end looking at material of this kind is becoming almost impossible, and, of course, judicial time is being wasted to an inordinate and unacceptable degree.

> (at 189)

But clearly this raises the problem of leaving to the police, rather than the jury, the consideration of what counts as obscenity. Although the appellant could select the samples from each class if there was a disagreement over their classification, a better approach, Stone argues, would be for a standard procedure agreed by Parliament.

The work of the Obscene Publications Branch of the Metropolitan Police has shifted in recent years.[13] It now focuses principally on child pornography, using the Protection of Children Act 1978 and the 1988 Criminal Justice Act. In the past its work has mostly centred on adult pornography, using the Obscene Publications Act 1959. The advantage of the law is its flexibility in allowing for shifts in attitudes through time, in assessing the likely impact on the person's mind, whether he or she is likely to be depraved or corrupted. But the price paid is a degree of uncertainty. The major problem for the police has been the vagueness of the definition of obscenity, which has led to problems of unpredictability of jury verdicts and magistrates' decisions. The same materials could meet with different results in different courts. These problems may be apparent in the gap between London and the provinces, if stipendiary magistrates in London see themselves as more sophisticated than their rural cousins. Rural communities may exert more pressure on the police to act against material carried in the local newsagents.

Consequently, it may not be cost-effective to seize and store large amounts of material which need to be processed and described prior to trial. Even if a prosecution succeeds, another court might deem that the material is not obscene. The size of the market in adult pornography is huge, which again confirms its importance as a popular taste rather than the province of 'abnormal individuals'. In recent years the Obscene Publications Branch in London has moved away from large-scale raids of shops and suppliers. Outside London, periodic raids have netted sizeable quantities of obscene materials from sex shops. In 1992, in Operation Rouge, a series of raids was undertaken by vice squad officers in Southampton, Dorset, the West Midlands, Leicestershire and Derbyshire, on adult shops as well as private homes. The videos and magazines seized had an estimated sales value of £100,000.

Because of the abundance of material available, it is usually possible to select items where there is no doubt of obtaining a conviction, for example, bestiality, buggery, sado-masochism and child pornography, so many items seized may be obscene within the meaning of the Act even if not selected for prosecution under section 2. The forfeiture provisions of the Act under section 3 may also be used. While materials may be forfeited and destroyed under the 1959 Act, material seized from shops may be replaced immediately after a raid from secret stashes because the trade is so lucrative.

Much of what is seized includes sado-masochism, bestiality and coprophilia. Those depicting 'normal heterosexuality' include scenes of multiple rape, in which women are depicted as ultimately welcoming the rape, despite initial resistance. Materials seized by the Branch in recent years include scenes of a woman with her labia nailed to a board. In this respect the police experience suggests that the content is far removed from the benign view of liberal philosophers. It does mean a high success rate for those prosecutions launched.

Considerable legal and academic argument has focused on the slippery slope, the fear that prosecutions may be launched against the publishers of literary or artistic works or against radical bookshops. But the experience of policing in the capital shows that these fears may be exaggerated. In practice the public good defence is rarely run in obscenity trials. Few of the prosecutions concern literary works. Although in 1992 a prosecution of work by the Marquis de Sade was considered, where the defence might well have been raised, it was decided not to proceed. Given the vast amount of material which can be seized, officers and staff may be working through a huge backlog of materials. Control of pornography is an area of policing which is under-resourced.

The work of the Branch is now centred on child pornography. The experience of the Metropolitan Police is that different methods of production, distribution and exchange operate for child and adult pornography. The child pornography market is smaller than that of adult pornography and is, in the main, produced by and for paedophiles. Because of its secrecy, it may be harder to detect, although possession *per se* is an offence. Child pornography is more likely to be home-made and may be intended for private consumers rather than a commercial market, although it could be distributed more widely, and Amsterdam is used as a clearing-house. It may also be used to blackmail or coerce a child into silence or into further participation. It also serves to reinforce the process of legitimation and may be used as masturbatory material in which the child is frozen in time at the preferred age. The decision to focus on child pornography reflects the crucial importance of child protection and the limited resources available for policing pornography. Currently sixteen officers are responsible for policing obscene publications in London.

The Branch also trains Child Protection Teams in what to look for when visiting the homes of people suspected of abusing children, so their specialist knowledge may be used in other areas of child protection. It works closely with social services and provincial police officers examining child sexual abuse. Officers may be called in to assist with cases of child abuse or may themselves initiate contact once material has been found. As child pornography contains the scene of the crime, the assaults on children, identifying the children and adults involved will be crucial to ending the exploitation of children. Interviews may be conducted with convicted sex offenders who may have been involved in child sexual abuse over a number of years. This demonstrates the inadequacy of viewing pornography as mere representation or images, open to a variety of meanings depending on the code used to interpret them.[14] Rather we are dealing here with the substantive offence. It also shows that policing in practice is concerned primarily to protect those abused in the production of pornography, rather than the minds and morals of consumers. Most of the adult material encountered by the Branch is imported from the United States, Germany, France and Holland. Very little is manufactured in Britain. The Metropolitan Police have close links with customs officers in Britain and in the United States and with the FBI and the United States Postal Investigation Service and Interpol, as well as with Post Office investigators in the United Kingdom. International cooperation is increasing.

The British pornography industry is not centralised, but might be described as a cottage industry. The technical facilities for duplication and the use of mobile phones have allowed smaller-scale operators to become involved. Overseas material can be copied in the United Kingdom to avoid going through customs. Materials may also be distributed through larger mail-order firms. While in the United States organised crime is heavily involved in the pornography industry, this does not seem to be the case in the United Kingdom. The use of computer software to disseminate pornographic materials is also likely to figure in future work. In this sense the penetration of the home by pornography may be complete as these disks may be on sale at low prices, bought and watched by children and adults.

THE WILLIAMS REPORT

The Williams Committee was set up in 1977 to review the laws concerning obscenity, indecency and violence in publications, displays and entertainments, other than broadcasting, and to review the question of film censorship. At the time the law was seen to be inconsistent and inefficient. The

Committee surveyed a range of material and relied on Mill's formulation of the harm principle in *On Liberty* in considering whether regulation was necessary. Its approach was generally permissive in leaving adults to decide for themselves but seeking to protect children. It was willing to countenance restraints only if it could be shown that harm resulted from pornography. It examined a range of possible harms to those involved in production, as well as viewers, including children, and the general effect on society. Where it did consider regulation necessary, it advocated restrictions and relied on prohibition only in certain extreme cases. So while the Report accepts a general presumption against censorship, it is rebuttable if, for example, the harm is grave and probable. At the same time it could find no conclusive evidence of causal links between sexual crime and pornography, or that relaxations on the circulation of pornography had led to more violence and sexual crime. The Committee could find little evidence of harm other than the possibility of harm to participants in the production. The harms caused must be tangible harms, so it recommended legislation to prohibit films and photographs involving real rather than simulated violence. The Committee was also willing to countenance restrictions if it could be proved that pornography did generate sexual assaults, but not in the absence of such evidence. It therefore concluded that adults should be free to decide for themselves whether or not to read or view pornographic material, while special protection was needed for children. As we cannot know in advance which social, moral and intellectual developments are necessary for human flourishing and development, the Committee was reluctant to inhibit publication of pornography, not least because human development is constituted in part by free expression. Like Mill, the Committee recognised that some paths are more desirable than others, but saw the best society as one where individuals make their own decisions about the kind of life to lead.

The Committee also used a slippery slope argument, referring to the difficulty of finding a reliable criterion separating work of no value from valuable work, and of relying on juries to reach decisions on such matters. Clearly the slippery slope is less significant if the emphasis is on restriction rather than prohibition, as pornography is still permitted to enter the market place of ideas. Restriction is less likely to bar the potential contribution pornography might make to the exchange of ideas.

Restrictions on public display were advocated where the material was such that it would be offensive to reasonable people, because of the way it dealt with violence, and limitations on access by young people and the display of warning notices were suggested. The advantage of restriction, in the Committee's view, is that it avoids the pitfalls of the public good defence, while maintaining accessibility for willing consumers. Written works were excluded from restrictions. Restrictions would be justified on grounds of offensiveness, while prohibition would apply only where the production of the material appeared to involve the exploitation of a person who at the time was under 16, or suggested that actual physical harm was inflicted on that person. The Committee proposed that it should be an offence to send restricted material, including advertisements for pornography, to a person who the sender knows, or ought reasonably to have known, is under 16, or who he knows, or ought reasonably to have known, did not request that material. Any prohibited material should also be prohibited from postal transmission. This should also apply to exports, where importation of such material would be prohibited in the country of reception. The Committee also advocated stronger penalties for postal transmission of prohibited works.

Prohibition, the Committee argued, should be be limited to extreme cases, as offensiveness can be reduced by segregation. What the Committee had in mind here was that prohibition would be based on the harms of production, where physical harm was inflicted on the participants, or where the participants were under the age of 16 at the time the film was made. The Committee also advocated prohibition of live performances involving sexual activity of a kind offensive to reasonable people, or involving people under 16. Simulated activity was excluded, again to allow for artistic works. It also advocated a more formal and open system of film censorship in which reasons would be given for decisions.

The Committee's approach is essentially a goal-based rather than a rights-based approach, although not a crude utilitarian one. It seeks to protect the long-term goal of obtaining the best conditions for human development.

The Williams Report was not in favour of increasing the powers of the local authority, because it thought it would try to drive shops selling pornography out of the area altogether, and already there were variations in local practice. But the effect of recent laws such as the 1982 Local Government (Miscellaneous Provisions) Act considered earlier gives some control to local authorities.

Barendt (1985) argues that the distinction between restriction and prohibition may be difficult to justify on free speech principles but at least has the merit of being practicable. A restriction is easier to enforce than a total ban and does not prohibit written material, because it is less visually offensive. Implicit in the Williams approach is the asumption that obscene material is not fully speech, therefore it has less claim to protection than political speech. But if we see pornography as a form of speech, he says, then it should receive as much protection as other forms of speech. Restriction is still an infringement of a speech right even if less draconian than prohibition. It mitigates but does not transcend the slippery slope problem. He is critical of the appeal to visual criteria and offensiveness in justifying restrictions, which may mask a moral condemnation of the activity. In practice the local authority is likely to rely on a community standard or local feeling criterion.

Smart (1989) is also critical of the Williams definition of pornography, based on the Wolfenden model, which construes sexuality as an expression of individuality considered as politically neutral. Pornography is defined in terms of the intention to arouse the audience or having that function, and explicit representations of sexual material. There are two aspects here, explicitness and the intention to arouse, although, she says, explicitness is the more important as it is easier to measure empirically how much of the body or sexual activity is revealed. The assumption here is that the more explicit it is, the more sexually arousing it becomes. It offers a means of identifying what is pornographic and also offers a way of distinguishing between medical books and pornographic material. She sees this as typical of the liberal definition, focusing on explicitness rather than the more important issues of the degradation and the objectification of women.

Following publication, the Williams Report was criticised by liberal, conservative and feminist writers on a number of grounds: failing to recommend the use of the criminal law to enforce morality, dismissing the causal link between crime and pornography too readily and failing to take account of feminist work on this issue. The Report of the Committee was shelved, although the Indecent Displays (Control) Act 1981 addressed the issue of environmental nuisance and reflected the Committee's recommendations to some extent, by making it an offence to present an indecent display, although the Committee had found it difficult to define indecency. The Williams Report also provided a focus for Ronald Dworkin's defence of pornography, which will now be considered.

Chapter 13

The 'right' to consume pornography

'Rights-talk' has dominated the discussion of free speech in the United States in First Amendment jurisprudence. Although various types of harm have figured in the debate, these have been seen as weak compared to the right of free speech. The right to consume pornography is articulated by Ronald Dworkin (1986a) in his essay 'Do we have a right to pornography?', where he defends the freedom to publish and read pornography in terms of fundamental rights which trump majoritarian considerations. This is consistent with his general approach, which places rights in a privileged position, protected from erosion by appeals to general welfare. For Dworkin the right to free speech is in a paramount position over public interests, and its value is explained in terms of an appeal to moral independence. His defence of the right to consume pornography will be considered. It will be argued that it is difficult to reconcile this defence with other dimensions of his work.

DWORKIN'S CRITIQUE OF THE WILLIAMS REPORT

Dworkin develops his analysis of the right to consume pornography in the context of a critique of the Williams Report, which he sees as resting on a 'goal-based strategy' in contrast to his rights-based approach. From the goal-based perspective, it might be argued that even if we accept that publishing pornography is bad for the community as a whole, the consequences of suppression would be worse in the long run. By calculating the consequences, one can make the appropriate decision regarding prohibition or restriction. On a rights-based view, however, even if pornography makes the community worse off, it would still be wrong to restrict it, because it violates the moral or political rights of those affected by prohibition.

The Williams Report, as we have seen, adopts the harm principle: 'no conduct should be suppressed by law unless it can be shown to harm someone'. Dworkin draws attention to the problems of using the harm condition as the basis of its recommendations. If by 'harm' we mean physical harm or 'direct damage to property and financial interests, then this condition is too strong', and would preclude numerous forms of accepted regulation (1986a: 336). If it means mental distress or annoyance, then it would bring an enormous range of conduct within the scope of the criminal law.

Dworkin argues that the goal-based strategy, which the Report relies on, cannot in fact justify the Committee's conclusions. He focuses on the Report's approach to live sex shows to see if its goal-based strategy supports its recommendation that they be prohibited rather than restricted, and whether they can be treated differently from those with simulated sex or films incorporating sex scenes. The Report fails to provide a plausible argument as to why live shows may be distinguished from films. It refers to the presence of a spectator in the same space as people engaged in real sex as a degrading form of voyeurism. But this cannot be because others find the thought of the situation upsetting, as the Committee rejects that as a basis for regulation. Even if the activity is degrading, this still fails to explain why it applies only to live sex shows. Because these shows are expensive and appeal to only a small audience, their 'culturally polluting' effects, Dworkin says, are minimal. It is therefore difficult to justify this exception to its permissive approach. Its approach focuses on the best outcomes for society rather than the recognition of rights, even where this means accepting less than the best outcomes for the community as a whole.

Dworkin acknowledges that the arguments in favour of freedom of publication for pornographers are not necessarily of the same order as those used to justify publishing unpopular political texts; the established justifications for free speech and freedom of the press are a weak basis for dealing with pornography. Much of what we might say about political convictions, such as the need for competing viewpoints for spirited political debates, cannot be applied to pornography. It is also difficult to see how restraints on pornography could encroach on the realm of political speech. Few defenders of the right to read pornography would say the individual or community benefits from access to pornography, says Dworkin, although perhaps he underestimates the pornographers' robust defence of their practice here. For Dworkin the question is whether it is wrong to prohibit people publishing and reading pornography, when the community would be better off as a result. If people have moral or political rights they should not be infringed even if we thereby promote conditions for development.

The restriction–prohibition distinction central to the Williams strategy, which confines prohibition to very limited cases, is also problematic. It favours restrictions on the open display of pornography on the grounds that the personal harm and cultural pollution caused by display is greater than that caused by private consumption alone, and that restriction is less likely than prohibition to run the risk of stepping on to a slippery slope. Even if valuable artistic works are netted by restriction, they still join the market place of ideas. But Dworkin finds this unpersuasive because restrictions, he says, may amount to a qualitative change as well as a quantitative one. He also questions the Committee's argument that although pornography, by its nature, violates the line between public and private, this is compounded when it is publicly displayed. If pornography brought the day closer when sex occurred routinely in public this would not mean that the public–private distinction would collapse. The boundaries of the public and private constantly change, but the distinction is more likely to be threatened by a 'legally enforced freeze' on the boundary, argues Dworkin, than by allowing the free market to determine those boundaries.

As the Report rejects the link between pornography and violence and sexual offences, it cannot prohibit public display on the grounds of harm. Rather, it justifies restrictions by referring to 'offensiveness'. But if offensiveness is not sufficient to limits one's liberty in private, then it is unclear why it should limit it in public. Furthermore, if offensiveness is used as the criterion for control, this does not explain why we should stop short at the disgust caused by display. If the right to liberty is invoked instead, however, this conflicts with the goal-based strategy of the Report. If this right means not having one's liberty infringed because others are offended by one's proposed actions, then there would seem to be no reason why that liberty should not extend to acting as one likes in public, without having to take account of possible offence to the majority which may be caused by their seeing one's actions. The Williams strategy, Dworkin argues, does not provide coherent arguments for the distinction between restriction and prohibition underpinning the Report's proposals.

Dworkin also argues that scepticism about the most desirable developments for human flourishing need not necessarily preclude the prohibition of pornography. There is nothing in the Williams strategy *per se* to rule out a prohibiting or 'enforcement hypothesis' rather than the permissive stance it adopts. What the Report lacks is a positive argument that freedom of choice to survey pornographic films and books is essential to human flourishing. Although this might seem a difficult task, Dworkin claims that an argument can be found in the appeal to a right to privacy and a right to moral independence. But this argument cannot be extracted from the goal-based strategy. It belongs to a quite distinct rights-based stategy of the kind he advocates.

THE RIGHT TO MORAL INDEPENDENCE

The right on which Dworkin bases his defence of pornography is the right to moral independence, drawn from classical liberalism and associated with Mill, that is: the right not to suffer disadvantages in the distribution of social goods and opportunities or in liberties, just because one's fellow citizens think that one's opinion about the correct way to lead one's own life is flawed. He argues that even if the conditions for human flourishing are undermined by access to pornography, the right should still be respected.

His view therefore diverges from Raz's perfectionist approach and that of the Williams Committee. The right to moral independence is seen by Dworkin as a 'powerful constraint' on regulation. This right would be violated if the only ground for regulation were that the attitudes to sex found in pornography were demeaning, bestial or otherwise unsuitable to human beings of the best sort even if this were true, or that others were disgusted and offended by them (1986a: 354). The only circumstances in which Dworkin would see intervention as potentially justifiable would be if a significant increase in crimes of sexual violence, or other serious social consequences, could be shown to result from the consumption of pornography. He also hypothesises the example of an increase in absentee-ism from work due to pornography, but in neither case is offensiveness the ground for intervention. Moreover, if it were established that all types of 'emotionally powerful' literature generated an increase in crime, and a prohibition were imposed but the state selectively allowed the publication of Shakespeare's plays because of their cultural and literary value, this would not violate moral independence, he says, because it would not rest on the argument that those who enjoy pornography are inferior to those who do not. Rather the judgment would be one of literary value, and few devotees of pornography would claim that it has any literary merit. In any case, says Dworkin, this is 'only academic speculation, because there is no reason to suppose a sufficiently direct connection between crime and either *Sex Kittens* or *Hamlet* to provide a ground for banning either one as private entertainment' (1986a: 355). As we saw earlier, there are difficulties in determining what would be persuasive evidence, but having excluded that link, Dworkin treats the consumption of pornography as a self-regard-ing action.

He considers whether the prohibition of public display violates the right to moral independence. If one relies on aesthetic arguments here, one is not condemning the consumer of pornography as a bad person. However, it may be that such moral judgments do partly enter into the unease felt at the idea of public displays, says Dworkin. Mixed preferences may shape reactions to pornography. If a society wants to defend the abstract right of moral independence, he says, it might deny regulation altogether, because the above arguments are tainted with moral conviction; or strike a compromise by saying that no one should suffer '*serious* damage through legal restraint' when mixed preferences are involved. He considers whether taking account of such mixed preferences can generate a scheme of regulation which still recognises the right to moral independence. The inconvenience to consumers resulting from zoning the sex industry into specific locations, for example, is not excessive and unlikely to impose greater financial costs. Indeed one might go further than Dworkin here and argue that it would reduce costs, because of the greater competition generated by the concentration of suppliers. Although it might mean greater embarrassment to the consumer entering the pornographic zone, the right of moral independence, he says, does not demand a governmental guarantee that one may consume pornography without others knowing. On his argument, following Mill, persuasion and disapproval would be the worst the consumer might expect. Running the gauntlet of a picket of a sex club, for example, would be more intrusive if it were sufficiently strong to deny access. Dworkin also finds aesthetic arguments against zoning dubious, because usually pornography is zoned into the least attractive parts of the city. But one might argue against Dworkin here that these areas are most in need of improvement rather than further deterioration. For this reason zoning policies in the United States have been strongly opposed by neighbourhood groups.

What the right to moral independence demands, argues Dworkin, is a 'permissive legal attitude towards the consumption of pornography in private' (1986a: 358). His argument would permit a restriction scheme similar to that advocated by the Williams Report. He therefore does not reject restriction *per se* but argues that the goal-based strategy cannot adequately support it, but it can be justified on a rights-based strategy. The individual's right to independence cannot be breached simply on the ground that the community as a whole will benefit. For Dworkin, the right trumps considerations of public benefit which promote human development.

He hypothesises the situation where the prohibition of pornography enables citizens to fulfil more preferences and desires, so that the preferences of publishers and consumers of pornography are outweighed by the preferences of the majority. How could one resist granting prohibition in such circumstances? One might argue that the appeal of utilitarianism lies in its egalitarianism, in treating people as equals, when their preferences are balanced 'with no distinctions for persons or merit' (1986a: 361). People's preferences should be weighed on an equal basis with no double-counting: each counts for one and one only.

Dworkin gives the example of a community where Nazis think that Aryans' preferences should be given more weight and Jews' preferences should count for less. Should the Nazi preference for differential weight prevail? This could not be justified, because people's preferences should be weighed on an equal basis. Officials in such a community should therefore strive to defeat the Nazis' claims. Even if members of a benevolent community want a particular individual to have more preferences, on the basis of affection, their preferences should still be defeated, otherwise some individuals will suffer disadvantages in the distribution of goods or opportunities and the egalitarianism essential to (neutral) utilitarianism will be undermined. Utilitarianism must be modified to restrict the preferences that count by excluding formal and informal political preferences. One way is through rights, for example, the right to political independence: 'No one should suffer disadvantage in the distribution of goods or opportunities on the grounds that others think he or she should have less because of who he or she is or is not, or because others care less for him or her than they do for other people' (1986a: 364). This right of political independence would have the effect of protecting Jews from the preferences of Nazis in the above example.

Similarly, if all preferences are to be weighed on an equal basis in the same scale, then the views of sexual minorities, including homosexuals and pornographers, cannot be prohibited just because others see them as degrading. Otherwise greater weight would be given to the preferences of those with conventional tastes and preferences in sexual matters. The right of moral independence can trump utilitarian demands for prohibition where the majority find the idea of reading pornography offensive. Although prohibition would then be excluded on this argument, restrictions of the kind advocated by the Williams Committee might be permitted as a compromise for the reasons discussed above, without violating the right of moral independence itself. Restrictions may be justified, even though we cannot be sure that those references are unmixed, if the adverse effects consequent on restrictions on pornographers and consumers are not serious.

DWORKINIAN ANALYSIS AND THE DEFENCE OF REGULATION

Dworkin's argument offers a plausible way of combating demands for prohibition: it has the merit of recognising the inferior quality of pornography, it avoids the slippery slope problem of finding a rational and coherent cut-off point, and it does not exclude *a priori* the potentially harmful effects of pornography, but sees this as an empirical question. Dworkin's account is of interest because while there are difficulties with his analysis of pornography, it will be argued that a defence of the regulation of pornography may be justified by reference to Dworkinian arguments. The problems and potential of his approach will therefore be considered.

Dworkin wrongly assumes that consumers of pornography constitute a sexual minority, and that the critique of pornography represents the majority view. From this starting point he defends the right to consume pornography of this sexual minority when, as has been demonstrated, pornography is a mass taste fed by a sizeable industry. He says that the majority would prefer substantial censorship of sexually explicit books and films, but this is questionable if we take account of the 'soft pornography' found in magazines with a high circulation. This perception of pornography as a minority taste, vulnerable to attack by the moral majority, is a recurring theme in liberal thinking. It is also found in the Williams Report and in First Amendment jurisprudence, yet the reverse is the case. The analogy is often drawn between consumers of pornography and other sexual minorities such as homosexuals, but this is difficult to sustain, for we are not dealing in the case of pornography with a deviation from the norm, or a repressed group, but something approaching the scale of a dominant cultural form. In this respect women, as a subordinate social group, are closer than consumers of pornography to the position of homosexuals.

To see the pornographer as the modern icon of personal freedom is to misconstrue Mill's aim in *On Liberty*. When Mill attacked the closure of customary thought and the way in which consensus inhibits rational discussion and breeds intolerance, he envisaged issues of political and religious toleration rather than sexual libertarianism. Mill's defence of freedom of thought and the need for diversity encompassed more than sexual behaviour. The figures he refers to as the objects of persecution including Christ and Socrates can hardly be placed in the same category as the twentieth-century purveyor of pornography.

If a Dworkinian argument were construed on this arguably more accurate premise of pornography as mass culture, then from this different starting point, one could accept a rights-based argument and yet reach the opposite conclusion to Dworkin. If the right to autonomy is given more weight and regulation introduced on this basis, this would not rely simply on the condemnation of the consumer as a bad person, and so would not violate the consumer's right to moral independence.

From this premise, one could accept the rights-based argument and reach the opposite conclusion to Dworkin to launch an argument in favour of regulation. In doing so, one could also draw from Dworkin's analysis of adjudication in *Law's Empire* (1986b). Using Dworkin's notion of integrity, one could further argue that integrity demands that the Supreme Court should have upheld rather than struck down the Indianapolis Ordinance. In *Law's Empire* he advances a normative and descriptive theory which sees judges engaged in an interpretative enterprise, interpreting the constitution in terms of moral and political principles. In so-called 'hard cases' where the law seems uncertain or indeterminate, a decision can and should be reached by interpreting new situations and problems, from the standpoint of existing moral and political principles held by the community. Dworkin uses the notion of 'integrity' to explain this approach to legal reasoning. Integrity demands that consistency is achieved so that these principles apply equally to all members of the community, in all areas of the legal system. The 'right answer', in hard cases, will be the one which best fits those principles. An analogy is drawn with the chain novel, where a succession of authors individually write the chapters of a novel, while seeking to give the effect of a single-authored text. Each author in turn must take account of the content and meaning of previous chapters, aiming at the highest literary standards as well as unity, to arrive at the best interpretation of the preceding chapters. Similarly, judges should ask themselves which interpretation would best reflect these fundamental moral principles central to the community. Because these principles are bound up with the identification of what the law is, judges, in explaining past decisions, are at the same time offering a justification of them. Dworkin challenges approaches, such as Bork's, which appeal to the original intent of the framers of the constitution.[1] In doing so, he can defend the attempts of the Supreme Court to extend the existing law into new areas, such as extending the right to privacy to homosexuals. Similarly when he considers the case of *Brown* v. *Board of Education* 347 US 483 (1954), he interprets the decision in terms of the basic principles of equal concern and respect which, although embodied within the Constitution, also extend beyond it. On the principle of integrity, the Supreme Court when considering the Ordinance could have followed through the existing exceptions to free speech principles, to uphold its constitutionality, rather than making new law. The regulation of pornography might be construed as compatible with existing principles in terms of the established limits on free speech considered earlier.

An analogy might also be drawn between the control of pornography and the prohibition of segregation, and the ideals of gender equality and racial equality. MacKinnon (1984) argues that both racial segregation and pornography express the idea of the inferiority of a particular group and the justification of that subordination. At the same time they constitute practices of discrimination. The harm of the segregation was finally recognised by the Supreme Court in *Brown* v. *Board of Education* 347 US 483 (1954). It acknowledged that separating black children on racial grounds 'generates a feeling of inferiority as to their status in the community that may affect their hearts and minds in a way unlikely ever to be undone'. Although welcomed by most liberals, the decision was criticised by Wechsler (1959) as a violation of First Amendment rights of association. The relationship between civil rights, discrimination and the pornography debate is also explored by Rae Langton (1990), who considers whether a Dworkinian case for regulation of pornography can be advanced based on his analysis of reverse discrimination, of the cases of *Sweatt* and *DeFunis*, and his theory of equality (Dworkin, 1977b). She argues that 'Dworkin's principle of equal concern and respect requires a policy about pornography that conflicts with commonly held liberal views about the subject, and that coincides instead with the restrictive or prohibitive policy favoured by his feminist foes' (Langton: 312). Dworkin's theory of equality demands that all citizens be treated with equal concern and respect. This means the right to be treated as an equal rather than equal treatment. Governments should not constrain the liberties of some citizens because they differ in their conception of the good life. If this principle of equal concern and respect conflicts with utility, it should prevail. Rights as trumps should be used to protect individuals from others' external preferences.

Dworkin uses this analysis to distinguish the cases of Sweatt and DeFunis. Sweatt was refused admission to the University of Texas Law School because it operated a whites-only segregationist policy. DeFunis could not gain admission to the University of Washington Law School because his grades were not acceptable even though ethnic-minority candidates were admitted with similar scores. Although segregation violated the Fourteenth Amendment, this could be distinguished from the Washington programme which was challenged in the *DeFunis* case.

The Texan policy rested on the external preferences of citizens that others should be excluded because they do not merit equal concern. Dworkin recognises that preferences may be mixed, including personal and external preferences. Sweatt could demand that he be protected from the effects of others' external preferences, including those based on racial prejudice. Even if Sweatt were unaware of the policy and did not feel personally insulted, the policy would still conflict with the principle of equal concern and respect.

In Washington, however, DeFunis did not have a right to a place, but only a right to be considered as carefully as other candidates, which had not been violated. The policy did not rest on external preferences of citizens, but on the view that a more equal society is a better society even if its members prefer inequality.

Yet Dworkin does not apply this argument to the problem of pornography. He assumes that pornographers' rights to publish and consume pornography freely should prevail because they should be protected from the external preferences of others. But if we place the pornography debate in a civil rights context, still using a Dworkinian argument, a case for prohibition can be advanced.

Pornography undermines sexual equality, by contributing to practices in society which perpetuate women's subordinate status. Many women feel distressed and insulted by pornography, just as Sweatt felt insulted by the desires of fellow citizens as embodied in the segregationist policy. Even if women did not feel insulted, a permissive policy on pornography could still be seen as strengthening patriarchal ideology, with an adverse impact on sexual equality. We may not be able to prove this conclusively, any more than we could conclusively prove that Sweatt was harmed by exclusion. But in both cases it may be appropriate to accept a lower standard of proof than beyond reasonable doubt, and it is clear that such a presumption was applied by Dworkin in Sweatt's case.

We need to consider why many people would prefer pornography to be permitted. If, as seems likely, it depends on a particular view about the low status of women, then it is based on external preferences which should not prevail over the right to equality. Of course these preferences may be mixed, but the important point is that women have rights which trump the permissive policy. This does not rely on a simple harm-based argument. It is not necessary to argue that serious harms will result from a permissive policy, for we are focusing on the external preferences concerning the value of women.

The aim of the prohibition of pornography is a more equal and just social order. Even if pornographers do have a right of moral independence, and their liberty is curtailed by regulation, this may be justified by the independent ideal of a more equal society. The ideal of equality here is comparable to the ideal of racial equality in the case of Washington Law School. So prohibition would be justified even if members of society would prefer women to be treated as inferior. Regulation is justified on the grounds of undermining equality rather than appealing to harm-based arguments. If liberty and equality conflict 'it is indeed liberty that loses, assuming that one regards the conflict through the lens of Dworkinian liberal theory' (Langton, 1990: 359).

Similarly, if incitement to racial hatred were permitted this would give too much weight to racist preferences, which a government committed to egalitarianism should ignore. The regulation of pornography may be justified on Dworkinian arguments, using the principle of integrity in *Law's Empire* and his analysis of reverse discrimination and racism. It is also compatible with the strong defence of rights in Dworkin's work. While Dworkin would not see public interests as occupying equal grounds to rights, he acknowledges that competing rights are more difficult to deal with, and rights may need to be conceded in favour of competing rights or where a consideration on which the original right is based is in issue.[2] This is clearly highly relevant to the pornography issue, as it raises issues of competing rights. If we consider it from the standpoint of the autonomy and self-fulfilment of women as moral agents and their right to dignity and to equal respect, then the free market in pornography would be a less compelling way of dealing with the issue. Dworkin does not refer to Raz in his discussion, but it is arguable whether the Razian appeal to autonomy considered earlier would be trumped by the right of moral independence if we were dealing here with a competing right, rather than a consideration of public benefits. This in turn depends on whether or not one construes autonomy as extending the harm principle.

As well as misconstruing the quantity of pornography, Dworkin also misinterprets its quality, in so far as he accepts that it may be unpleasant but seems to underestimate the extent of the violence and degradation. His reference to *Sex Kittens*, for example, fails to capture the sadistic nature of much pornography. Those unfamiliar with the content are usually surprised by this. Much of the material seized by the Obscene Publications Branch involves children, animals and extreme violence; not the milder forms of titillation which are frequently cited by defenders of the right to consume pornography. In de Sade's *Juliette*, published for the first time in Britain in 1991, over two thousand women and children are raped, murdered and mutilated and many more are tortured, disembowelled, burnt and degraded. These practices are praised and recommended to the reader. Schwartz[3] describes her shock as a juror in a pornography case when she realised that the books in question were far removed from her perception of pornography prior to trial. Previously she had seen pornography as consisting of the type of material found in *Playboy* and similar magazines, and had not even imagined the primarily violent type of material with which she was confronted at trial. This was marked by an association of sexual pleasure with brutality, or women screaming with pain on being raped and assaulted, and thereafter depicted as welcoming the assault. Sex was presented as indissociable from pain and degradation; the books were also prefaced by pseudo-scientific observations presenting the acts as normal human behaviour. Similarly, Polly Toynbee, a member of the Williams Committee, described the material she watched as part of the Committee's investigation, which included bestiality and the rape of children. It is hard to reconcile these reports with the tame picture of pornography running through Dworkin's analysis.

The centrality of rights to free speech jurisprudence has been questioned by Schauer (1982), who argues that the truth and democracy justifications of the First Amendment raise questions of social welfare and public benefit rather than fundamental rights issues. There are problems in conceiving of the debate in terms of rights versus utility, for it wrongly presupposes a fundamental distinction between the individual and society. On this liberal individualist model, the individual is abstracted from society. On an organic communitarian model of society, the individual and society are two sides of the same coin and cannot be so easily distinguished. Individual flourishing and autonomy are essential to a healthy democratic society and to public welfare, rather than in conflict with them.

Dworkin's assumption that the consumption of pornography is essentially a self-regarding activity is contentious. While it may be difficult to prove harm conclusively, for the reasons given earlier, clearly the interests of others are affected. In any case, speech may be protected despite the fact that it harms others, because the harmful effects are seen as less serious than the harms resulting from constraints on free speech. However, the feminist case for regulation does not rest solely on the harm condition but focuses on questions of autonomy. Neither does it rest on the moral condemnation of the consumer as a bad person, even if it is likely that the individual's sensibilities are blunted by constant exposure to degrading sexual images.

The difficulties with Dworkin's analysis also illustrate some of the problems in using a rights perspective in the context of the feminist critique of pornography. The problems of rights analysis have received critical attention in a number of areas of feminist theory and practice. Concepts of equal rights and equal concern and respect fail to take account of the fundamental differences between the experiences and position of men and women. The disadvantages experienced by women may be difficult to rectify by an egalitarian solution. While fundamental rights may provide some protection from discriminatory political and social structures, they fail to strike at the underlying practices of subordination. While the Supreme Court in *Brown* critically reviewed for the first time the practices of a racist society, its judgment by no means combated racism. Nor did the ruling in *Brown* challenge informal segregation in American educational institutions.

Smart (1989) considers the example of equal rights at work which may have negative implications for women who are pregnant. Similarly the rights to family life, enshrined in the European Convention, she says, can be used to extend the power of unmarried fathers over their children against single mothers. Feminists in the nineteenth century used the fight for rights to combat legally imposed constraints on women's freedom, including the bars to professions and to university education, but now these objectives have been achieved, says Smart, a rights-based approach is less useful. The 'rhetoric of rights', she argues, has been exhausted, and may be detrimental to feminist concerns because liberal rights analysis assumes the neutrality of law rather than seeing it as part of the oppression feminism is seeking to overcome. Rights claims can involve more surveillance, and once rights exist, anyone can use them, including the most powerful and oppressive groups. Rights, she says, gloss over the complexities of power relations. Non-molestation and ouster orders cannot deal with the deeper causes of violence against women or the problem of enforcement. Similarly, the major new areas of rights, relating to reproduction and abortion, are meaningless in the context of laissez-faire politics because they are not matched by access to facilities.

The construction of the free speech debate in terms of either rights or utility has also been criticised by Lee (1990). Our moral thinking may reflect a number of values, not all of which are strictly speaking rights: we can also criticise rights without necessarily resorting to utility. He gives the example of telling a child that Father Christmas does not exist; clearly one has a legal right to do so, but it would not be morally commendable to tell the child. No one would seriously suggest prohibiting such speech or deny an individual's right to free speech here, but most people would argue that others should voluntarily 'censor' themselves. The issue would not be whether they possessed a legal or moral right but whether it was right to act in that way. It is this latter issue which Lee sees as most relevant to contemporary free speech debates.

He argues that moral philosophy has advanced beyond the simple dichotomy of rights and utility. Rights approaches are too rigid, he says, to deal with a plurality of conflicting values. How these conflicts are to be resolved will depend on the specific context. This also means that 'inconsistency' may be a merit rather than a failing of a legal system which recognises the complexity of issues, and that the watertight resolution of problems is not possible.

The analogy of racial and gender inequality may be further pursued in the context of the English debate on pornography and censorship, by considering the possibility of an incitement to sexual hatred offence modelled on legislation prohibiting incitement to racial hatred.

Chapter 14

Incitement to sexual hatred

Given the differences between the English and American legal systems, and specifically the absence of a written constitution or Bill of Rights, which may render it difficult to transplant a civil rights Ordinance of the kind used in Indianapolis to England, and given the problems faced by the Ordinance, incitement to racial hatred may provide a viable alternative model on which to base the regulation of pornography. This chapter considers the utility of the offence of incitement to racial hatred as a possible model for regulation. The experience of enforcing that offence also provides a means of testing the effectiveness of this form of legislation. The development of the law in this area is outlined and the problems with the current law are considered. A critical review follows of the major objections to enacting a sexual hatred offence, including its ineffectiveness and undesirability and problems with the comparison of racial and sexual hatred.

INCITEMENT TO RACIAL HATRED

The development of the law in this area is complex, and reflects the uncertainty over whether race hate speech is best dealt with through public order or anti-discrimination law. Prior to the Public Order Act 1936, there were various common law offences including criminal libel, public mischief and seditious libel, but prosecutions were rare and the law was generally seen as inadequate and ineffective.

The 1936 Public Order Act provided some limited protection and was aimed principally at the activities of the British Union of Fascists. Although some members of the British Union of Fascists were fined and bound over, by the end of 1936 local communities had largely lost confidence in the police; it was widely felt, as Jacobs (1978) recounts, that the police were indifferent to the problem or sympathetic to the fascists. In the post-war period demands for legislation to deal directly with racism and for a specific offence of incitement to racial hatred increased. This was finally achieved in 1965, when the offence of incitement to racial hatred was created in section 6 of the 1965 Race Relations Act, as part of a number of measures designed to combat discrimination. It was subsequently inserted into the 1936 Act by the 1976 Race Relations Act. The current law is contained in Part III of the 1986 Public Order Act, which consolidates all the former offences relating to racial hatred in one place and tries to deal with some of the problems of the earlier legislation. In Northern Ireland, but not England and Wales, there are prohibitions on incitement to religious hatred. Under the 1970 Incitement to Hatred (Northern Ireland) Act, it is necessary to prove intent, and that the words in question were likely to stir up hatred towards a particular section of the public rather than a particular individual or church. But very few cases have been brought, and in this respect it has been less successful than the Race Relations Act. Although the Public Order provisions may be used today, the older offences of seditious libel and powers to deal with breaches of the peace remain, even where they overlap with the Public Order Act. In addition, incitement to racial hatred is recognised in international law, by Article 20 of the International Covenant on Civil and Political Rights.[1] Incitement to racial hatred legislation is also valid under Article 10(2) of the European Convention on Human Rights, to prevent disorder or crime. In the European context, these provisions have particular significance because of the historical experience of persecution. Furthermore, in other European jurisdictions, such as France and Germany, there are specific criminal offences of revisionism to deal with the denial of the Holocaust.

THE 1936 PUBLIC ORDER ACT

Prior to the race relations legislation, the major provision dealing with incitement to racial hatred was found in section 5 of the Public Order Act 1936. Section 5 of the 1936 Act made it an offence to use 'threatening, abusive or insulting words or behaviour, with intent to provoke a breach of the peace or whereby a breach of the peace is likely to be occasioned' in a public place, or public meeting. It was punishable by three months' imprisonment or a £50 fine, this offence being triable only summarily. In *Jordan* v. *Burgoyne* (1963) 2 QB 744, Lord Parker emphasised that the speaker must take the audience as he finds it, even if ordinary people would be unlikely to respond in a violent way. The test is not that of whether a reasonable person is likely to be incited. Jordan had said that Hitler was right, Jews were the enemy, and this provoked a riot in the crowd.

In *Brutus* v. *Cozens* (1973) AC 854, it was held that 'insulting' had no special meaning beyond its ordinary meaning. It was also necessary to establish causation, that the words caused the breach of the peace, so a close link in time would be necessary. In *R.* v. *Ambrose* (1973) 57 Cr App R 338 the Court of Appeal said that we should look at the short-term effect rather than the long-term effect. Similar considerations would need to apply to an incitement to sexual hatred offence.

The development of the law in this area has raised important free speech issues, including the problem of the heckler's veto. It has been claimed that sometimes English courts have been too willing to control marches where a hostile audience will be present, effectively giving the opponents the power to censor.

When the 1936 Act was passed it was thought that the reference to threatening, abusive, or insulting words gave wide discretion to the courts in applying the law, but in practice it was used very conservatively.[2] The next major development was the 1965 Race Relations Act.

THE RACE RELATIONS ACT 1965

This Act made racial discrimination illegal, and set up bodies to enforce and monitor the law and to work towards racial equality, initially the Race Relations Board and subsequently the Commission for Racial Equality. Although the Act is primarily concerned with civil wrongs and remedies, section 6 makes incitement to racial hatred a criminal offence.[3] The Act represented a compromise between free speech interests, public order interests and respect for the groups subjected to racial hatred.

Section 6 provided that:

A person shall be guilty of an offence under this section if, with intent to stir up hatred against any section of the public in Great Britain distinguished by colour, race or ethnic or national origins –
a) he publishes or distributes written matter which is threatening, abusive or insulting;
b) he uses in any public place or at any public meeting words which are threatening, abusive or insulting being matter or words likely to stir up hatred against that section on grounds of colour, race or ethnic or national origins.

To obtain a conviction it was necessary to prove the following elements of the offence:

1 The material published or words used had to occur in a public place or public meeting.
2 The words spoken or published had to be threatening, abusive or insulting.
3 Intention to stir up racial hatred was required, whereas section 5 of the 1936 Public Order Act did not require intention if a breach of peace was likely.
4 The material or speech had to be likely to stir up racial hatred.

The offence was triable either way and was punishable by six months' imprisonment and/or a fine of £200 on a summary conviction. In the Crown Court it was subject to a maximum term of two years' imprisonment, and a fine of £2,000. Prosecution required the consent of the Attorney-General, and this was justified as a brake on prosecutions and in view of the higher penalty.

While the concern in the 1930s had been with anti-Semitic attacks, the 1965 Act was passed in the context of racism directed at black and Asian communities, as well as in the context of immigration controls. The two areas of legislation reflected what the governments of the time saw as a difficult political problem, namely how to pacify racist sections of society while gaining the support of black and Asian voters. This dilemma was resolved by appearing to tackle racism through the enactment of the Race Relations Act while at the same time toughening controls on immigration. In practice very few prosecutions for incitement to racial hatred were initiated. In the period 1966–80 only fifteen people were prosecuted for the offence of incitement to racial hatred.[4] Between 1965 and 1976 there were 15 convictions and 24 prosecutions, so its impact was limited.[5]

THE 1976 RACE RELATIONS ACT

Section 70 of the Race Relations Act 1976 added a new section 5A into the 1936 Public Order Act. Since 1976 incitement to racial hatred has been dealt with under public order legislation and not race relations provisions. Amendments to the Race Relations Act were made in 1976 following criticism in Lord Scarman's report on Red Lion Square. The Public Order Acts were seen at the time as a better vehicle than the ordinary criminal law for dealing with this issue, although the reasoning behind this is unclear.

Under the new provision it became an offence to publish or distribute matter which is threatening, abusive or insulting, or to use in any public place or at any public meeting words which are threatening, abusive or insulting where having regard to all the circumstances, hatred is likely to be stirred up against any racial group in the United Kingdom. Consent of the Attorney-General was retained and the sentence increased.

The courts' response was mixed. There were still few convictions or prosecutions, and sentences tended towards leniency. It was argued in one case that racist speech was more likely to arouse sympathy for black people than hatred. Some members of the National Front were convicted, but the legislation was also used against black people. As Gordon (1982) notes there were 21 prosecutions under section 5A of the Public Order Act between 1977 and January 1982, of which 13 resulted in convictions. Although this amounted to a success rate of 70 per cent the actual number of prosecutions was low, and racist groups evaded the legislation by circulating material published outside the United Kingdom or publishing material anonymously. In some cases consent to prosecute was refused because the material had been distributed to *anti-racist* groups and organisations and therefore was seen as unlikely to stir up racial hatred. Geographical variations were found in the willingness of the police to enforce the law.

The lukewarm response to the legislation by the courts in the 1970s reflected both a fear of censorship and a fear of escalating conflicts by giving racist groups a high media profile through prosecution, and a general failure to take racial harassment seriously. In 1980 the Commission for Racial Equality recommended broadening the legislation to include broadcasting but also to include ridicule or contempt as well as hatred. Legislation which extends to ridicule has been enacted in other jurisdictions.

THE 1986 PUBLIC ORDER ACT

The law on racial incitement was reconsidered in the 1980s as part of a general review of public order law. The offence of racial incitement was retained in the new Public Order Act in 1986, which is broader than the earlier legislation. It includes behaviour and the display of written material, in private and public places, but not if it is in a private house and words cannot be seen or heard by those outside. It may be used where there is intent to stir up racial hatred, or the words or behaviour are likely to stir it up.

The new Public Order Act therefore covers a wider range of behaviour than the 1936 Act. It is necessary to prove either intent or, alternatively, likelihood. Intentional conduct is punishable whether or not it has the desired effect. The requirement of consent of the Attorney-General has been retained.

Racial hatred is defined in section 17 of the Public Order Act 1986 as hatred against a group of persons in the United Kingdom who are defined by reference to colour, race or nationality, including citizenship, ethnic or national origins. This follows the definition of a racial group in section 3 of the 1976 Race Relations Act. Hatred is not specifically defined in section 17 but would suggest intense dislike and animosity but not contempt or ill-will.

Under section 18

[1] A person who uses threatening, abusive or insulting words or behaviour or displays any written material which is threatening, abusive or insulting, is guilty of an offence if –
  [a] he intends thereby to stir up racial hatred, or
  [b] having regard to all the circumstances racial hatred is likely to be stirred up thereby.
[2] An offence under this section may be committed in a public or private place, except that no offence is committed where the words

or behaviour are used, or the written material is displayed, by a person inside a dwelling and are not heard or seen except by other persons in that or another dwelling.

The acts which are intended or likely to stir up racial hatred at which the Public Order Act is aimed include the use of words or behaviour or the display of written material (section 18), publishing or distributing written material (section 19), the public performance of a play (section 20), distributing, showing or playing a recording (section 21), broadcasting or including a programme in a cable programme service (section 22) and possession of racially inflammatory material (section 23).

The Act also incorporates section 5 of the Theatres Act 1968, under which the presenter or director of a play which contains threatening, abusive or insulting words is guilty of an offence if he or she intends to stir up racial hatred and that was a likely consequence. Section 21 introduces a new offence of distributing, playing or showing a recording. The Act tries to update the law, to deal with the effects of video-recordings and film. Although scientific research is not prohibited, the researcher has to bear the risk that the dissemination of his or her research findings will stimulate racial hatred.

Section 24 governs powers of entry and search. Section 25 gives the power to order forfeiture of the material. Section 27 refers to procedure and punishment. The penalty on indictment is imprisonment for a term not exceeding two years or a fine or both; on summary conviction, a maximum of six months' imprisonment, a fine not exceeding the statutory maximum or both.

The other provisions of the 1986 Act deal with general issues of public order and the likelihood of immediate violence. In *R. v. Horseferry Road Metropolitan Stipendiary Magistrate, ex parte Siadatan* (1991) 1 All ER 24, the Divisional Court again emphasised the importance of the violence being immediate and unlawful, but said that immediate did not mean instantaneous. But it does connote 'proximity in time and causation, that it is likely that the violence will result within a very short period of time and without any intervening occurrence'.

The legislation regulating incitement to racial hatred was framed in the light of free speech concerns similar to those found in the pornography and censorship debate. Its scope was limited to satisfy the protection of free speech interests. In retrospect the free speech arguments were voiced with far less intensity than those employed by libertarians in the United States or England when resisting proposals for the regulation of pornography. A number of jurisdictions have accepted constraints on free speech in relation to incitement to racial and religious hatred, but have been much more reluctant to accept corresponding incitement to sexual hatred provisions.

If incitement to racial hatred is to be considered as a possible model for the regulation of pornography, then two isues need to be addressed: first the effectiveness of the legislation as a remedy for racial hatred, and second, the problems which may arise in applying it to sexual hatred, even if improvements were made to the existing law.

PROBLEMS WITH THE OFFENCE OF INCITEMENT TO RACIAL HATRED

A number of problems have been found in both the drafting and the implementation of the legislation in the Race Relations and Public Order Acts. One consequence of the law had been a shift towards less blatant racist propaganda, which may take on an appearance of rationality if couched in less emotive language. As Horkheimer and Adorno (1973) have pointed out, in the context of Nazi hate speech, such propaganda is usually so crude that not even its supporters could treat it seriously, but a more subtle approach may be harder to combat.

The legislation has rarely been used, even in the late 1970s when assaults on black people were increasing. It might be argued that using the provision will give greater publicity to a racist group by drawing the media's attention to it, particularly given that media coverage of the National Front and its goals, for example, has been disproportionate to its share of vote, compared to other small parties. If members of racist groups are prosecuted, this may generate further support for their ideas because they are seen as martyrs.

It may be hard to establish that the conduct was intended to arouse or foment racial hatred. An alternative offence of intimidation was considered at the time the 1986 Act was enacted, but this was rejected. There are also difficulties if the hatred is already present, for example, if a leader of a racist group is addressing his or her supporters. There is a range of emotions, including hostility, contempt, prejudice and ill-will, which fall short of hatred, but which could be included or substituted. Although some convictions of members of the National Socialist Movement were obtained in the 1960s, the actual number of convictions and prosecutions was still relatively low. But black people were also prosecuted under section 6 of the 1965 Race Relations Act. For example, Malik (Michael X), a member of the Racial Action Adjustment Society, was convicted in 1967 of incitement to racial hatred, and sentenced to twelve months' imprisonment and refused leave to appeal.[6] Members of the Universal Coloured Peoples' Association were also convicted and fined for using words at Speakers' Corner which, it was claimed, stirred up racial hatred against white people.[7]

The treatment of such cases may be contrasted with the generally lenient response to white racist groups in the *Southern News* case.[8] Here members of the Racial Preservation Society in 1968 were charged with incitement to racial hatred by distributing their Society's newspaper. They successfully argued that the paper, which drew attention to the perils of racial mixing, was intended to educate politicians regarding the dangers of immigration practices and were acquitted.

Since 1986 the number of prosecutions has fallen, as Bindman (1992) notes, even in the context of an increase in the activities of right-wing and neo-Nazi groups, and there were only two prosecutions in 1988. One offender received a suspended sentence for making a racist speech and distributing racist literature, while the other was fined £100 for pasting Nazi stickers on lamp posts. Prosecutions are more likely to be brought today, he observes, under planning statutes such as the Town and Country Planning (Control of Advertisements) Regulations 1989. When the black Conservative Party candidate for Cheltenham was subjected to racist abuse in public by a fellow party member during an election campaign, a prosecution was brought against the maker of the statement but he died before the case came to trial.

The failure to take incitement to racial hatred seriously is reflected in the earlier case law in the *Read* case in 1976.[9] Kingsley Read addressed a meeting using racially offensive epithets. He also referred to a recent Asian murder in Southall, saying 'one down a million to go'. When the jury failed to agree the case was retried. At the retrial Judge McKinnon described the use of such epithets as merely jocular, and said that section 6 of the Race Relations Act did not preclude reasoned argument advocating restraints on immigration or repatriation. Read was acquitted. After the case was over, he praised Read for having the courage to stand up in public to say what he believed.

The experience of litigating the 1986 Public Order Act raises questions about the efficacy of such legislation in dealing with racial hatred and has implications for a similar sexual hatred offence. The conduct must be threatening, abusive or insulting and does not include more subtle messages which, in some circumstances, may be more damaging than a clear-cut race-hate message, for example, if couched in neutral 'factual' language. It focuses specifically on the far end of the continuum of race-hate speech, although such speech may not be radically different in content to everyday racist speech.[10] The effectiveness of the Act also needs to be considered in the light of procedural changes such as the loss of peremptory challenge of jurors.

To mount a prosecution under the Act the consent of the Attorney-General is still required, and he may be reluctant to authorise prosecution. The current legislation, as Bindman (1992) points out, also means a convoluted procedure, of first reporting to the local police, who then report to the Crown Prosecution Service. If the CPS consider prosecution using racial incitement provisions is appropriate, the matter will be referred to the Attorney-General. This requirement was intended to discourage mischievous prosecutions to discredit the legislation by racist individuals and groups and to prevent the harassment of particular individuals, but the effect seems to have been a lukewarm approach to prosecution. These constraints partly reflect the anxiety to protect free expression and to prevent a 'floodgates' problem, although this is hardly a realistic fear given the under-reporting of such offences. Moreover, in other areas of law, such as defamation, the interest of the citizenry in free speech has not constrained the development of law explicitly holding individuals accountable for the exercise of free speech.

Notwithstanding these problems, there have been some convictions in the 1990s, including convictions of members of the Ku Klux Klan, but the numbers remain very low. The sentences are still mild. But these could be amended and more prosecutions could be initiated. More use is being made of section 5 of the Public Order Act to control racist speeches, as Bindman (1992) observes, which does not require the Attorney-General's consent. If a person uses threatening, abusive or insulting words or behaviour within the hearing or sight of another person likely to be caused harassment, alarm or distress, and if the person does not refrain from doing so after being warned by the police, he or she may then be arrested without warrant. There is also the possibility of using the Malicious Communications Act 1988 to deal with racist letters and telephone calls. The disadvantage is that these are summary offences with minor penalties, compared to the incitement to racial hatred offence, which can be tried on indictment.

In any event because race-hate speech is for many an everyday rather than an unusual experience, the likelihood is that cases may not be reported or pursued. Racism may promote a sense of powerlessness, so that complainants feel it is not worth pursuing an action, or do not wish to report incidents because of expectations that the police will not take them seriously, or be sympathetic.

The individuals and groups seeking to enforce the racial incitement legislation in Britain have confronted similar problems to feminist activists campaigning against pornography: namely problems of proof of effects and causation, and difficulties in adducing evidence which will be sufficient to persuade the jury or magistrates to convict. The difficulties with the law on racial incitement reflect the general failure of anti-discrimination law to solve the problems of discrimination.

INCITEMENT TO SEXUAL HATRED

The case for an incitement to sexual hatred offence has been advanced by a number of commentators including Itzin and the Campaign against Pornography and Censorship. The CPC (1988) argued that the freedom to manufacture and distribute pornography may be justifiably limited on the grounds that it acts as an incitement to sexual hatred and violence against women in the same way that racist and fascist literature acts as an incitement to racial hatred and which is now prohibited under the Public Order Act 1986. Itzin (1987) proposed the use of incitement to racial hatred legislation as a model for the regulation of pornography, by rendering it unlawful to publish or distribute material which is likely to stir up sexual hatred. Pornography which is 'threatening, abusive and insulting' or degrading or damaging to women would be subject to a degree of regulation. This would be defined in terms of the depiction of violence or the use of criminal force in the course of its production. She defined pornography in terms of the combination of sex and violence and degradation of women, and proposed its prohibition on the grounds of its harmful effects as indicated by the evidence available at the time, which had been accepted by the Federal Courts in the United States.[11] Following her proposal the National Council of Civil Liberties reviewed its policy on pornography.

The major objections to an incitement to sexual hatred offence are as follows: first, that the above problems which have been encountered in the case of incitement to racial hatred suggest that a similar offence covering sexual hatred is unlikely to succeed. Second, some see the use of the law in relation to sexual hatred as inherently undesirable. Third, the value of the analogy of sexual hatred with racial hatred *per se* has been questioned, irrespective of the issue of its effectiveness.

THE LIMITS OF THE LAW

Given the experience of the incitement to racial hatred offence, would an incitement to sexual hatred offence be more successful? The incitement to racial hatred provision is rarely used, but would a law aimed at incitement to sexual hatred be more frequently used by women? If physical assaults on women are under-reported, are women more likely to proceed on the basis of 'rape speech'?

There are also fears that the problems encountered with the incitement to racial hatred legislation would recur if it were used as the basis for a sexual hatred offence. Similar concerns regarding vexatious litigants have been voiced in relation to the regulation of pornography, and one way of dealing with these fears would be to require the Attorney-General's consent to prosecute, although clearly this might constrain its effectiveness. As few prosecutions have succeeded under the Public Order Acts and Race Relations Acts, one might argue that the success rate is unlikely to be greater for a sexual hatred offence and that other methods should be used to control pornographic materials, such as education. But equally one could argue the other way, that once such legislation is in place, it might be used more frequently than the Public Order provisions. Already the Sex Discrimination legislation is used more frequently, and with more success than the Race Relations Act. There are also more prosecutions relating to pornography under the Obscene Publications Act than prosecutions for incitement to racial hatred. It is possible that the offence of incitement to sexual hatred would yield a higher number of prosecutions and convictions.

Parmar (1988) is sceptical regarding the use of the Race Relations Act as a model because, she claims, it has been relatively ineffective in protecting the interests of black people. She is also concerned that ultimately any form of censorship could be used against black activists. It is partly because of the experience of Malik and the UCPA that some have opposed an incitement to sexual hatred offence, which, it is feared, could be used against feminist and lesbian writers and film-makers, for stirring up hatred against men. State regulation of pornography may be particularly problematic for black feminism because of the largely negative experiences black women have of the state and state officials. This particularly applies in the context of social security, where the welfare state has been used as a form of internal immigration control adversely affecting black and Asian women already settled or born in the United Kingdom. As Williams (1989) has argued, black and white women stand in quite different relationships to the welfare state. But for all women, the state and legal apparatus may be problematic, and for this reason it is frequently argued that feminists should resist seeing law or the state as the best vehicle for the protection of women's interests. Even where a benign law is vigorously enforced, it is questionable whether it changes the underlying social attitudes and practices. It rather operates at a cosmetic level, giving the impression that 'something is being done'.

If we set the Race Relations legislation in the context of immigration law and the regulation of asylum seekers and refugees, the law's potential to legislate for equality is problematic. But even where a particular law is benign, if it operates within a racist and patriarchal society, this will limit its effectiveness. The protections afforded ethnic minorities by benign laws may be fragile.

An incitement to sexual hatred offence conceivably may be used by a man against a feminist journal. Furthermore, in the current political climate the prospect of enactment is unlikely, partly because of pressures on Parliamentary time and in view of the composition of the House together with the low importance given to women's issues.

If incitement to racial and sexual hatred raise similar problems, how useful is the racial incitement model for the development of an 'incitement to sexual violence' or 'sexual hatred' offence? Osman (1988) questions whether such a law would work in women's interests any more than the existing anti-discrimination laws work in the interests of ethnic minorities or women. A campaign on benefits issues, she says, may offer a better way of protecting women's interests than the regulation of pornography.

But even if there are difficulties, this avenue should not be ruled out. Existing legislation, as Gregory (1987) and Leonard (1987) argue, could be made more effective. Even if the number of prosecutions is low, the existence of the incitement to racial hatred legislation is important in demonstrating a public rejection of racism and marking the boundaries of acceptable speech. Similarly, a stronger regulation of pornography would acknowledge the importance of women's interests.

There may be problems in defining the scope of a new sexual hatred offence, given the range of behaviours which might be perceived as violent, ranging from verbal abuse to harassment and assault. There is also the question of whether the civil or the criminal law is the more effective vehicle for regulation. Clearly the existence of a criminal offence would demonstrate the seriousness of the issue compared to a civil action. But a criminal prosecution has the disadvantage of requiring a higher standard of proof, beyond reasonable doubt, compared to the lower civil standard of balance of probabilities. The courts might be more cautious in interpreting a criminal than a civil statute, construing it more narrowly.

If we view the incitement offence in the context of the wider problems of enforcement of the race relations provisions, one might conclude that the law is of limited value in combating racism and by analogy equally unlikely to succeed in changing patriarchal attitudes. But this view is flawed. Of course the mere prohibition of racist or sexist speech will not swiftly change the entrenched attitudes and practices of patriarchal and racist societies, but at the very least it marks the law's recognition of the unacceptability of those ideas and beliefs. The purpose of the criminal law is to express society's moral position on appropriate behaviour, and to define the limits of accceptable behaviour, and to include racism and sexism within its compass is a significant step forward. Notwithstanding the short-comings of the Race Relations Acts, there have been some changes in the development of affirmative action programmes, the ethnic composition of the labour force and the implementation of equal opportunities policies.

THE DESIRABILITY OF THE LAW

While many liberals and some feminists have been reluctant to countenance the regulation of pornography, they have nonetheless acknowledged the legitimacy of the legal regulation of racist material. Many of the discussions of censorship and pornography have dwelt at great length on the impli-cations of regulation for free speech rights, on whether the law will be abused by over-zealous prosecutors and complainants. Similar fears were expressed in the earlier debates on incitement to racial hatred but were not found to be justified. When the incitement to racial hatred legislation was enacted, although the free speech issue was raised, the question of censor-ship did not figure so prominently as it has in the pornography debate.

While the weakness of the racial incitement legislation in part reflects attempts to reconcile speech controls with freedom of speech, there has been far less concern over the free speech question in the courts, in academic writings and the media on the issue of racism than in relation to the regulation of pornography. Fears of a heckler's veto have been expressed in relation to a sexual hatred offence. But if one hypothesises that feminist objectors might challenge the showing of a pornographic film, raising public-order considerations, the quixotic nature of these fears become apparent. Official statistics and self-report studies show that women as a social group are more likely to be victims than perpetrators of violent acts and are far less likely to engage in violent confrontations. They can hardly be compared to National Front or neo-Nazi thugs.

Prominent leading liberal writers, such as Ronald Dworkin (1986a, 1986b), readily accept legislation aimed at combating racial discrimination and have enthusiastically endorsed Supreme Court decisions such as *Brown* v. *Board of Education* 347 US 483 (1954) which constitute crucial advances in this direction. Yet they have displayed much greater hestitation and caution when addressing issues of sexual discrimination. While both the courts and academic commentators have accepted limited evidence of harm when dealing with racism, a much higher standard of proof has been required when assessing the harms caused by pornography. Relatively few objections to the offence of incitement to racial hatred have been voiced in academic circles compared to the tremendous resistance to the regulation of pornography, whether in the form of incitement to sexual hatred, a stronger obscenity law, the Page Three Bill or a Civil Rights Ordinance. It is now widely and rightly accepted that ethnic minorities should not be subject to racist insults and expressions of hatred, yet attempts to give legal protection to women from expressions of sexual hatred have been strongly resisted.

The fact that limitations on racist speech may be countenanced shows that in certain cases the commitment to free speech is not paramount. The underlying justifications of prohibitions on speech likely to cause racial violence include the desire to maintain social order, which has been given more weight than the desire to protect the feelings of a minority group. Yet in many cases the issue may not be one of immediate risk of disorder, as defined by the clear and present danger test in *Schenck* v. *United States* 249 US 47 (1919), although this could apply in some instances. If racist speech is permitted to flourish, then the long-term effects are likely to be a hardening of racist attitudes and the creation of a climate in which disorder becomes more likely, as exemplified by the link between racism and disorder in the Los Angeles riots of 1992.

The popular counter-argument, of course, is that repression of racist or patriarchal attitudes drives them underground, and if anxieties are not freely discussed, disorder may occur and possibly lead to attacks on ethnic minorities or women. This is a form of the 'bad speech should be challenged by more speech' cathartic argument. Defenders of free speech have argued, both in relation to racism and pornography, that the best way to deal with hate speech, whether in the form of racist remarks or rape speech, is for the offended groups to respond with more speech to put forward their own viewpoints.[12] Any move towards constraints on speech, however well-intentioned, opens up the danger of censorship which may adversely affect the disadvantaged group.[13] But it may be difficult for a weak group to gain access to the means of communication. In any case, there are a number of areas where the law already accepts limits on speech in order to respect competing rights, for example, in the law of defamation.

Although feminist arguments for the regulation of pornography do not need to rely solely on 'mere offensiveness', it could justifiably be argued that if injury to feelings is sufficient to protect victims of racist speech, then women's feelings demand equal consideration and respect.

But if restraints on racist speech have been accepted in terms of a general tendency or likelihood, then surely the case for constraints on pornography is equally compelling: even if there are difficulties with a criminal law of incitement to sexual hatred, the possibility remains of a civil measure such as the Indianapolis Ordinance. But it may be that the low level of interest in the effects of pornography on women's feelings reflects the low status of women or the size of the group of consumers and producers of pornography who would resent the denial of access to pornography.

While free speech objections to racial hatred provisions have been voiced by some writers, they have not been so vociferously expressed or as widespread as in the pornography debate, but have been largely confined to academic commentators. In contrast, the free speech defence of pornography has dominated popular thinking and ultimately legislation has been enacted in the former case, but resisted in the latter case.

THE PROBLEMS WITH THE RACIAL AND SEXUAL HATRED ANALOGY

While some have ignored the racial–sexual hatred analogy, others have explicitly rejected it. Criticism has emanated from two quite distinct sources; first, the pornographer with an interest in a continued free market in pornography, and second, some feminists and political activists.

A pornographer might argue that while racist speech is motivated by hatred and has no merits or public benefits, the prime purpose of pornography is the exploration of sexuality, albeit within a commercial context. Racist speech and pornography should therefore be distinguished. The benefits of pornography, including its sexually liberating effects, have been extolled by defenders of pornography and focus on sexual liberation. Lynn (1988), for example, argues that the range of motifs in pornography, namely the portrayal of a variety of groups including disabled, pregnant and older women as sexually active, liberate us from the stereotype of the young white woman as the paradigm of sexual activity and offer one of the few vehicles for positive images of these other groups. This denial of hatred as a defining feature of pornography is hard to reconcile with the pervasiveness of denigratory and hostile views of women in pornography, for example, of bound and gagged women enjoying rape and domination.

Some feminist writers also find the comparison between racial and sexual hatred unsatisfactory, albeit on quite different grounds. The fundamental differences between the position of ethnic minorities and women, it is argued, render the use of the analogy inappropriate and over-simplistic. The position of ethnic minorities within Europe and the United States has to be understood in the context of distinct historical experiences, including black slavery, genocide and persecution, which do not compare to white European women's experiences. Feminism is divided on the validity of this analogy, depending on the primacy given to gender and ethnicity as the source of oppression.

Parmar (1988) is critical of the use of the race analogy to understand pornography, and of the proposal to use the Race Relations Act 1976 as a possible model for regulation. She is particularly critical of the comparison of the experience of black slavery with the objectification of women in pornography. As well as reflecting a failure to understand the complexity of slavery, she argues, it 'diminishes both African history and women's struggle for control over our sexuality' (1988: 128). These two distinct processes of exploitation, she argues, cannot be treated as equivalent to each other.

But Parmar's sharp distinction between racial hatred, epitomised by slavery, and sexual hatred expressed in pornography is problematic, as the two may not always be easy to distinguish, either at the level of ideology and representation or as social reality. First, we find an overlap of the two in the genre of racist pornography, which uses motifs drawn from both slavery and Nazism to convey ideas of control and domination, couched in racist language and imagery. The genres of pornography may be mediated by the cultural context of racism, expressing, for example, white male perceptions of black female sexuality. Although critics of the analogy might contrast the mere *perceptions* of women in pornography with the *actuality* of slavery, for example, it is difficult to separate ideologies from the practice of subordination. If we consider the depiction of slavery in celluloid, for example, it may well fail to capture the subjective experience of those enmeshed in those relations of production, whether seeking to legitimise or expose them; yet it may still have an effect on practice. Similarly pornography may be construed as both ideology and practice, as a legitimisation of sexual violence, and as a practice of sexual discrimination.

Second, when we confront the reality of racist persecution we find that the manipulation of women has a special significance and centrality. Control of women's sexuality and reproductive power is an enduring feature of racist practice, particularly associated with biological reductionist forms of racism. It was an essential feature of the Nazi project and the SS state and must be an essential element of its critique. This is illustrated by the Nazis' control of the reproductive faculties of both Jewish and non-Jewish women: the sterilisation and experiments on Jewish women and, in contrast, baby farms for selected groups who conformed to the Nazi ideal of womanhood, and the theft of Polish children who met the desired characteristics. Also essential to the control of reproduction was the extermination of children and adults who did not fit that ideal because of genetic abnormalities, such as Down's Syndrome and the sterilisation and killing of the mentally ill.[14]

It is difficult to drive a wedge between racial and sexual hatred at the level of either ideology or practice, even though we must acknowledge the distinct historical experiences of each group on the receiving end of such hatred. Both modes of oppression have a long-standing history. The earliest historical records of ancient societies show the sale of women as chattels, and demonstrate that the oppression of women is as old as the history of slavery.[15] Both women and ethnic groups have been systematically excluded from privileges, power and education and subjected to persecution and genocide. Thousands of women regarded as witches were exterminated in the seventeenth century; historians have only recently begun to document this seriously.

The analogy of slavery with sexual oppression is not fanciful. A substantial literature within feminist theory argues strongly for the view that the relations of production in the modern domestic mode of production are essentially slave relations, as Delphy (1984) argues, in being excluded from the realm of exchange. Control over women's labour-power has been an enduring feature of a variety of modes of production.[16] Furthermore, relations between prostitutes and pimps within the sex industry itself can be seen as a form of slavery involving total control of the sex worker's labour power.[17] Feminist Hegelians have used Hegel's master–slave dialectic to understand gender relations.[18] Moreover, both systems of institutionalised subordination have been legitimised by the appeal to biological or natural inequalities.

We can and should acknowledge the existence of the two systems of oppression, of patriarchal and slavery-based modes of production. These may sometimes support each other and at other times contradict each other, depending on the particular historical circumstances and cultural contexts. But one can still profitably study each form to gain insights into the other.

It is not difficult to infer hatred from the depictions of rape, abuse, mutilation and denigration found in 'hard' pornography. The focus on hatred would also provide a potential way of distinguishing pornography and erotica, if the latter is seen as based on desire and on a positive rather than a negative view of sexuality, celebrating and enhancing rather than brutalising sexual relationships.

The drafting of a suitable provision would need to be carefully considered. A public good defence, to cover academic or literary works, could be inserted. If this legislation were interpreted too broadly, it would not satisfy offended groups, but it would be difficult to argue for the literary or scientific merit of pornography or race-hate tracts.

A group libel provision might also be considered where a remedy is provided to a group whose reputation is harmed by a statement or publication which suggests hatred or contempt. It would then be open to any member of that group to initiate an action.[19] This might raise similar problems to the existing law, such as the appropriate level of damages and the waywardness of juries, but as these are now being revised to deal with inappropriate awards, the inadequacies of the existing law would not necessarily be transplanted into a group libel provision. Libel law has been used in the United States as a way of controlling racist speech.[20]

The enactment of a law marks the beginning rather than the end of change. Racist and patriarchal attitudes may not be changed immediately by legal intervention, but in the long term it can have an impact. Furthermore, it puts the racist on the defensive, rather than legitimising racist speech.

A law to regulate pornography would by itself be insufficient to combat the oppression of women, just as the legislation has failed to combat racism. But no one involved in the critique of pornography would see this as the only strategy or solution but as part of a wider campaign against patriarchy. Constructing the debate in terms of the free speech versus censorship divide, as pornographers and civil libertarians have attempted to do, fails to take account of the fact that already inroads have been made and that these are, in many cases, accepted as legitimate. The feminist argument against pornography is not an isolated assault on free speech rights, but could be seen as a recognition of the difficulty and undesirability of an absolutist position on free speech in a pluralist society.

Chapter 15

Conclusion

The problem of pornography has been used as a testing ground for the use of law as a feminist strategy. A number of approaches may be identified, including the approaches of those who reject law outright and those who welcome legal advances in principle, but are sceptical of their value in practice. Critics have pointed to the inherent problems of relying on law as well as specific problems of implementing particular laws which seem *prima facie* advantageous to women. Others argue that law may be effective, for example, in the provision of welfare rights, but that it is inappropriate in dealing with the complex issue of pornography.

Smart (1989) is sceptical of the use of law in regulating pornography. We have no guarantee, she says, that the legal regulation of pornography would be any more effective than equal pay legislation or the law of rape. It is also difficult to contemplate a legal solution when there is no consensus within feminism regarding the nature of the problem of pornography. Underpinning her critique is a concern with the way in which feminism is constrained to work within boundaries set by law. Although influenced by Foucauldian analysis, she challenges Foucault's claim that law's power is diminishing as other discourses become powerful, eclipsing legal discourse. While non-legal forms of knowledge and regulation have become more important, nonetheless law is retaining and enhancing its power, as new opportunities for legal regulation arise, for example, in charting foetal rights and defining death. In this way law is extending its territory. By developing a feminist jurisprudence, she says, we may concede too much to law by placing it at the centre of feminist thought when we need to develop alternative strategies, and to deconstruct law. Otherwise feminism may fall into the trap of presenting itself as the truth, claiming epistemic supremacy and thereby assuming an essentially positivist notion of objectivity, when it should be challenging dogmatism.

The use of state institutions to implement legal reforms has also been subject to criticism by Parmar (1988), who argues that expecting the patriarchal state to behave benevolently to protect women's interests through intervention, such as the implementation of the Ordinances, is naive. If these institutions are seen as part of the political apparatus of a patriarchal, racist society, then this will limit their viability. If a civil rights ordinance or similar legislation were enacted, it would still need to be interpreted so that its impact could be neutralised, given the composition of the judiciary and the constraints operating in the culture. Legislation may not be the best means of dealing with sex discrimination, whether expressed in pornography or in the labour market.

For those apprehensive about the repressive power of the state, strengthening its power through censorship controls is undesirable as legislation might be used against women. Women would still be relying on state functionaries to deal with complaints. If the law is already used to protect the sex industry, for example, in some European countries, to license prostitution, then can we expect it to intervene effectively in the regulation of pornography?

How persuasive are these objections? The first point that should be made is that advocates of law reform have themselves reflected on the difficulties of using law as a feminist strategy. Catherine MacKinnon and Andrea Dworkin, the architects of the Indianapolis and Minneapolis Ordinances, have written extensively on the difficulties, and have deployed legal measures despite the difficulties, rather than being oblivious to them. The slippery slope argument, reviewed earlier, is also a weak ground for resisting regulation.

The remaining arguments against the use of law are also problematic. The rejection of regulation on the ground that existing forms of anti-discrimination law are ineffective is unpersuasive. We can highlight problems within the law which may be remedied, for example, specific problems relating to the defences invoked in equal pay and sex discrimination claims, and the failure to deal with occupational segregation. Feminist lawyers have been active in drawing attention to these flaws. We could envisage reshaping the current law to rectify weaknesses and loopholes and strengthening legal aid, if the political climate changed. Existing provisions have improved women's rates of pay and narrowed the gap between male and female earnings. Over time women have become more confident about using industrial tribunals to pursue their claims. Weaknesses within the Act could be addressed if Parliament was so minded. In the long term the law may affect attitudes. Initially, racist and sexist attitudes may be expressed covertly if open expression arouses disapproval, but in the longer term we may see a genuine shift if racist or sexist views are not legitimised.

Similarly in other areas of law, such as criminal law, feminist lawyers have tried to reconstruct and reshape the law to make it more amenable to feminist goals.[1] In campaigns on issues such as abortion, marital rape, and the development of the law of provocation and self-defence to reflect women's experience of domestic violence, one can find areas where the law may be improved to empower and protect women rather than oppress them. Similarly, in the context of recent attacks on the welfare state, women have fought to retain state benefits. A total rejection of law is therefore too defeatist, especially as no viable alternatives have been offered by those who reject the use of law as an appropriate strategy.

Moreover, it is possible to see a role for theorising without a commitment to objectivity. Theories can be recognised as fulfilling various pragmatic requirements without dogmatic appeals to truth. The perception of the masculinist nature of law seems to posit a static view of law. It fails to capture the dynamism of law, and the way in which it may be moulded and captured to reflect feminist ideals. The indeterminacy of legal outcomes provides an arena in which feminist demands may be voiced and fought for, so the recuperation of victories by patriarchal institutions is not inevitable.

Using the law in territory occupied by groups who may be hostile to feminist objectives can be seen as an opportunity for permeating and disseminating feminist ideas, rather than a 'dead end'. The challenge to feminism is to infuse its own ideas into competing modes of thought. Even if does not always succeed, at least specific practical advantages may be secured. As it becomes stronger it will need to make fewer concessions and compromises.

Crude instrumentalist theories of the state are hard to sustain but still find support. They rest on a naive and untenable model of the legal system, which sees judges interpreting laws in ways which reflect their interests. But judicial discretion is constrained by more than crude self-interest or the social composition of the judiciary. Precedent, the rules of statutory interpretation, public policy considerations and the content of the statutes would constrain both feminist and misogynous judges. The strongest critics of the state would acknowledge that reformist measures have a limited value in the short term, and would also accept that the state may have a considerable degree of autonomy from capital. The experience of struggling for them may have a mobilising effect on consciousness. Analogously, the struggle for the regulation of pornography arguably has had the effect of mobilising and chanelling women's anger as well as highlighting divisions within feminism. But this division should not be construed negatively. Divisions, whether between women from different classes, ethnic groups or sexual orientations, may reflect real differences of interest particularly in relation to law and the state, but it is important to understand and take account of them as this can strengthen campaigns on women's issues.

The establishment of women's presence in the media, press and publishing through equal opportunities policies, better employment practices and non-legislative strategies should be pursued in addition to legal measures. This means working within the media unions and developing more effective bodies to control standards of broadcasting and advertising in place of existing ones. Media regulation could be supplemented by democratisation of the media. Efforts to promote equal opportunities do not negate the need for regulation as well. These initiatives could be pursued alongside the campaign to regulate pornography to create a climate in which the demand and supply of pornography will decline.

While many of the strategies proposed to regulate pornography have been subject to accusations of censorship and the infringement of free speech rights, it has been argued that these accusations rest on a very narrow view of censorship.

Recent developments in Canada may be of interest. In *R. v. Butler* 89 Dominion Law Reports 449 (1992) the Canadian Supreme Court recognised the harms to women, children and society arising from pornography as justifying constraint on the free speech rights of pornographers. The expression found in obscene material, the Court concluded, lies far from the core of the guarantee of free expression. Pornography appeals only to the basest aspect of individual fulfilment, physical arousal, and it is primarily economically motivated. The aim of obscenity legislation is of fundamental importance in a free and democratic society; it is directed at the avoidance of harm which Parliament has reasonably concluded will be directly or indirectly caused to individuals and groups, such as women and children, and to society as a whole, by the distribution of these materials. Parliament is entitled to have a reasoned apprehension of harm resulting from the desensitisation of individuals exposed to materials which depict violence, cruelty and dehumanisation in sexual relations: 'While a direct link between obscenity and harm to society may be difficult, if not impossible to establish, it is reasonable to presume that exposure to pornography bears a causal relationship to changes in attitudes and beliefs' (Sopinka J. at 483). Although the relevant provision of the Criminal Code may be construed as violating the Charter of Rights and Freedoms, this is a reasonable limit prescribed by law. It meets the requirement of proportionality, in so far as there is a rational connection between the measures and the objective, it minimally impairs the right to freedom, and there is a proper balance between the effects of the limiting measures and the objective of the legislature. Education may be a helpful way to deal with negative attitudes to women, but it is not sufficient, and legal measures may also be required.

In England, there are a number of areas where the courts are already sympathetic to constraints on free speech, including national security and official secrets. In recent years the trend has been towards a steady increase in constraints on speech in areas relating to official secrets.[2] At the same time we find resistance to constraints on pornography, so the law's toleration of speech is highly selective. In the context of the specific characteristics of the English legal system, an incitement to sexual hatred offence may be the best means of regulating pornography.

Notes

INTRODUCTION

1 See, for example, Cocks (1989), Coward (1984), Valverde (1985) and Kappeler (1986).
2 Research is being undertaken at the University of Bradford by the Research Unit on Violence, Abuse and Gender Relations.

1 THE LIBERAL DEFENCE OF PORNOGRAPHY

1 Madeleine Smith, for example, as part of her defence to a charge of murder, argued that she purchased arsenic for cosmetic purposes.
2 See, for example, Bataille (1969) and the discussion of his work in Dworkin (1981).
3 The United States Supreme Court has been criticised for being too willing to impose restrictions on free speech on speculative grounds, although it has been more protective than the English courts. Ronald Dworkin (1977a), for example, has criticised the Supreme Court's handling of the draft cases for giving too much weight to speculation on possible harmful effects.

2 THE TYPES OF HARM

1 See *McLoughlin* v. *O'Brian* (1983) 1 AC 410, *Alcock* v. *Chief Constable of S. Yorks Police* (1991) 3 WLR 1057.
2 See Donnerstein (1980), Donnerstein and Berkowitz (1981), Malamuth and Check (1980), Malamuth and Donnerstein (1984).
3 See Hart (1968) and Devlin (1968).
4 For example, *Reservoir Dogs*, *Man eats Dog* and *Cape Fear*.
5 See Duggan (1985), Feinberg (1987a) and MacKinnon (1984, 1987).
6 *People* v. *Douglas and Hernandez*, Felony complaint no. NF 8300382, Municipal Court, Judicial District Orange County, California 5 August 1983.
7 See Clark and Lewis (1977).
8 See Renvoise (1982) and Dobash and Dobash (1992).
9 See, for example, Zillman and Bryant (1982, 1989), Malamuth and Donnerstein (1984), Malamuth and Check (1980, 1983), Malamuth, Check and Briere (1986), Linz, Donnerstein and Penrod (1988), Donnerstein (1980), Donnerstein and Berkowitz (1981).

10 See Temkin's (1993) critical discussion of the use of section 2 of the Sexual Offences (Amendment) Act 1976.
11 For example, *Re S and B* (1990) 2 FLR 489.
12 See Wilson's (1992) discussion of Operation Spanner and *R. v. Brown, Lucas, Jaggard, Laskey and Carter*, The Times, 21 February 1992, 12 March 1993.
13 A Minneapolis Ordinance was rejected by the Eighth Circuit Court of Appeals in 1977 because it was too limited.

3 PROVING HARM

1 Both Frederick Schauer, who contributed to the Meese Commission, and Bernard Williams, who conducted an inquiry into pornography and film censorship in Britain, are philosophers.
2 See Popper (1959, 1963 and 1972).
3 See, for example, Kuhn (1962), Feyerabend (1975), Stockman (1983) and Lamb (1991).
4 *American Booksellers* v. *Hudnut* 771 F 2d 323 7th Circuit (1985).
5 *R. v. Butler* 89 Dominion Law Reports 449 (1992).

4 DIVERSITY AND AUTONOMY

1 See Scanlon (1972) and chapter 10 *infra.*
2 Some have focused on the development of feminist rather than masculinist conceptions of rationality, placing rationality at the heart of the feminist project, while others have revealed the difficulties inherent in the notion of rationality itself. See Easton (1987), Cocks (1989), Pateman (1988), Rhode (1991), Moller Okin (1991).
3 Although Raz does consider freedom of speech in a subsequent paper, he addresses the issue from the standpoint of his analysis of toleration and moral pluralism rather than focusing specifically on the implications for autonomy. (Raz, 1991).
4 The actions of sado-masochists were defended on this basis in the Countdown on Spanner campaign, which campaigned against the conviction of five men for offences under the Offences against the Person Act 1861 where the parties had consented to the assaults and they occurred in private. See *R. v. Brown, Lucas, Jaggard, Laskey and Carter*, The Times, 12 March 1993.
5 See *American Booksellers* v. *Hudnut* 475 US 1001 (1986).

5 FEMINISM, TRUTH AND INFALLIBILITY

1 Mill's model of the development of knowledge might be seen as a Popperian one, although Feyerabend (1975) uses Mill as a springboard for his critique of Popper.
2 This view is also associated with Justices Frankfurter and Brandeis in *Whitney* v. *California* 274 US 357 (1927) and *Kovcas* v. *Cooper* 336 US 77 (1949). The problems of assuming infallibility also arise in *New York Times Co.* v. *Sullivan* 376 US 254 (1964).
3 See, for example, Kuhn (1962), Feyerabend (1975) and Lamb (1991).

6 FREE SPEECH AND MAJORITARIANISM

1 This may be partly due to the ambivalent status of those involved, on the margins of illegal activity, and the attempt to keep a low profile if they are also engaged in commercial enterprises outside the sex industry.

2 Some indication of popularity is given in the following figures for the period January–June 1993: *Fiesta*: 250,332; *Knave*: 92,685 (average sales per issue in the six-month period; Audit Bureau of Circulation), which showed a substantial increase for the same period in 1991. *Penthouse* estimates its circulation to be 100,000 in the United Kingdom.

3 See *American Booksellers* v. *Hudnut* 771 F 2d 323 7th Circuit (1985), *American Booksellers* v. *Hudnut* 475 US 1001 (1986) and chapter 11 *infra*.

7 THE SLIPPERY SLOPE

1 See *Brind* v. *Secretary of State for the Home Department* (1991) 1 All ER 720.
2 See introduction *supra*.
3 See chapter 11 *infra*.

8 FEMINISM AND PURITANISM

1 This term is used by Barry (1984).
2 For example, Carol Gilligan's *In a Different Voice: Psychological Theory and Women's Development* (1982).

9 THE PROTECTION OF FREE SPEECH

1 See *Spence* v. *Washington* 418 US 405 (1974), *Smith* v. *Goguen* 415 US 566 (1974), *Cahn* v. *Long Island Moratorium Committee* 418 US 906 (1974).
2 See *New York Times Co.* v. *Sullivan* 376 US 254 (1964).
3 *Cohen* v. *California* 403 US 15 (1971).
4 See Articles 3 and 19 of the International Covenant on Civil and Political Rights, Articles 19 and 29 of the Universal Declaration of Human Rights and Article 10 of the European Convention on Human Rights.
5 Although in England the press has been subjected to increasing criticism over its invasions of privacy, leading to demands for new legislation, for example, Clive Soley's Freedom and Responsibility of the Press Bill, 1993.
6 *New York* v. *Ferber* 458 US 747 (1982).

10 INTERPRETING THE FIRST AMENDMENT

1 *Gitlow* v. *New York* 268 US 652 (1925).
2 For example, Playboy's First Amendment Awards.
3 See Black (1960), Kalven (1967), *Roth* v. *United States* 354 US 476, (1957), *Smith* v. *California* 361 US 147, 155 (1959) and *Miller* v. *California* 413 US 15 (1973).
4 See Mendelson (1962) and Frantz (1963).
5 See, for example, *Mishkin* v. *U.S.* 383 US 502 (1966), *Paris Adult Theatre* v. *Slaton* 413 US 49 (1973) and *Schad* v. *Borough of Mount Ephraim* 452 US 61 (1981). In *Schad*, nude dancing was deemed to fall within the First Amendment.

6 See *Keller* v. *State* 606 SW 2d 931 (1980).
7 *U.S.* v. *12200 DT Reels* 413 US 123 (1973).
8 See *U.S.* v. *Reode* 402 US 35 (1971).
9 See *Doe* v. *Commonwealth Attorney* 403 Fed. Supp. 1199 (1975).
10 Brief on behalf of American Booksellers Association and ACLU, filed 4 March 1982.

11 THE CIVIL RIGHTS ORDINANCES

1 *Minneapolis Star and Tribune*, 19 October 1983.
2 Testimony to the Zoning Commission, City of Minneapolis, 18 October 1983.
3 Public Hearings on Ordinances to add Pornography as Discrimination against Women, Committee on Government Operations, City Council, Minneapolis, Minn. 12–13 December 1983; *Everywoman* magazine (1988).
4 Attorney-General's Commission on Pornography (1986).
5 *Linda R.S.* v. *Richard D.* 410 US 614 (1972).
6 *Hayward* v. *Cammell Laird Shipbuilders* (1988) AC 894, *Pickstone* v. *Freemans plc* (1989) AC 66.

12 FREEDOM OF SPEECH AND THE REGULATION OF PORNOGRAPHY IN ENGLISH LAW

1 See Robertson (1979), S. Nielsen, 'Books for bad women: a feminist looks at censorship' in Chester and Dickey (1988): 17–25.
2 *R.* v. *Brown, Lucas, Jaggard, Laskey and Carter*, The Times, 12 March 1993.
3 Attorney-General's Reference No. 5 of 1980.
4 *R.* v. *Love* (1959) 39 Cr App R 30.
5 *Calder* v. *Boyars* (1969) 1 QB 151.
6 *R.* v. *Anderson* (1972) 1 QB 304.
7 *R.* v. *Stanley* (1965) 2 QB 327.
8 *R.* v. *Bow Street Magistrates Court ex parte Noncyp Ltd.* (1990) 1 QB 123.
9 *R.* v. *Henn; R.* v. *Darby* (1980) 2 All ER 166.
10 *R.* v. *Stanley* (1965) 2 QB 327.
11 Tunks and Hutchinson (1991).
12 See Gibbons (1991).
13 This account is based on an interview with Michael Hames, Obscene Publications Branch, Metropolitan Police, 9 October 1992.
14 See Coward (1984).

13 THE 'RIGHT' TO CONSUME PORNOGRAPHY

1 See also Dworkin (1984).
2 See Dworkin (1977a).
3 See Schwartz in Chester and Dickey (1988): 11–16.

14 INCITEMENT TO SEXUAL HATRED

1 Any advocacy of national, racial or religious hatred that constitutes incitement to discrimination, hostility or violence shall be prohibited by law.
2 See *Duncan* v. *Jones* (1936) 1 KB 218.

3 *Thorne* v. *B.B.C.* (1967) 1 WLR 1104.
4 Review of the Public Order Act 1936 and related legislation, Home Office 1980, Cmnd 7891, paragraph 106.
5 *Ibid.*
6 *Malik*, The Times, 9, 10 November, 22 December 1967.
7 The Times, 29, 30 November 1967.
8 *Hancock, Hardy, Dominy and Budden*, The Times, 28, 29 March 1968; see also Heineman (1972) and Osman (1988).
9 *Read*, Daily Mail, 18 January 1972.
10 Hall *et al.* (1978) compared private race-hate mail and found that it did not differ greatly from the content of communications in the popular press in its references, for example, to miscegenation. Similar comments have been made by prominent politicans. Duncan Sandys was reported in the *Daily Telegraph* on 25 July 1967 as warning of the dangers of mixed marriages and proposing that the British government should finance the voluntary repatriation of immigrants: 'The breeding of millions of half-caste children would merely produce a generation of misfits and create increased tension.'
11 This issue had been considered in *American Booksellers* v. *Hudnut* 771 F 2d 323 7th Circuit (1985).
12 See Lee (1990) and Barendt (1985).
13 See Coliver (1992).
14 See Burleigh (1991).
15 See Hirschon (1984).
16 *Ibid.* and Mies (1986).
17 See Barry (1984).
18 See Hegel (1971), de Beauvoir (1972) and Easton (1987).
19 Lee (1990) argues that a group libel provision might also be preferable in race-hate cases and would be a better way of dealing with cases like that of Salman Rushdie. It would embrace all ethnic groups and religions and meet the objections to the partiality of the blasphemy law. A public-interest defence would have meant that he was unlikely to be prosecuted and even more unlikely to be convicted. Lee refers to the New South Wales Anti-Discrimination (Racial Vilification) Amendment Act 1989 as a 'half-way house' between group libel and incitement to racial hatred which might be considered as a possible model for dealing with hate speech.
20 In *Beauharnais* v. *Illinois* 343 US 250 (1952) Beauharnais had been circulating leaflets attacking the black community and specifically referring to their involvement in rapes and robberies. Illinois had enacted a statute prohibiting the depiction of depravity, criminality, unchastity or lack of virtue of a class of citizens of any group, colour, creed or religion which exposes that group to contempt, derision or obloquy or which leads to a breach of the peace. His conviction under the statute was upheld. The court treated group libel as comparable to individual libel and excluded it from the protection of free speech, although subsequently the court has preferred to control racist speech by reference to the public order and fighting words exceptions.

CONCLUSION

1 See Lacey, Wells and Meure (1990).
2 The Official Secrets Act 1989.

Bibliography

Abel, G. (August 1977) 'The components of rapists' sexual arousal', *Archives of General Psychiatry*, 34.

Attorney-General's Commission on Pornography, Final Report, (1986), Washington, D.C.: US Department of Justice (Meese Commission).

Barendt, E. (1985) *Freedom of Speech*, Oxford: Clarendon Press.

Baron and Straus (1984) 'Sexual stratification, pornography and rape', in N. M. Malamuth and E. Donnerstein, (eds), *Pornography and Sexual Aggression*, New York: Academic Press, 185–209.

Barry, K. (1984) *Female Sexual Slavery*, New York: University Press.

Bataille, G. (1969) *Death and Sensuality*, New York: Ballantine Books.

Beauvoir, Simone de (1972) *The Second Sex*, trans. H. M. Parshley, Harmondsworth: Penguin.

Ben-Veniste, R. (1970) 'Pornography and sex crime: the Danish experience', *U.S. Commission on Obscenity and Pornography*, Technical Report VII.

Berlin, I. (1967) 'Two concepts of liberty', in A. Quinton (ed.) *Political Philosophy*, Oxford: University Press.

Bindman, G. (1992) 'Outlawing hate speech', *The Law Society Gazette*, 14: 17–23 (8 April).

Black, J. (1960) 'The Bill of Rights', *New York University Law Review*, 857.

Burgess, A. (1970) 'What is pornography?', in D. A. Hughes (ed.) *Perspectives on Pornography*, New York: St Martin's Press.

Burleigh, M. (1991) 'Racism as social policy: the Nazi "euthanasia" programme 1939–1945', *Ethnic and Racial Studies*, 14: 4: 453–73.

Calcutt Report, Report of the Committee on Privacy and Related Matters (1990) London: HMSO, Cmnd 1102.

Campaign against Pornography and Censorship (1988) Policy Statement.

Chester, G. and Dickey, J. (eds) (1988) *Feminism and Censorship*, London: Prism Press.

Clark, L. and Lewis, D. (1977) *The Price of Coercive Sexuality*, Toronto: Women's Press.

Cocks, J. (1989) *The Oppositional Imagination*, London: Routledge.

Coliver, S. (1992) (ed.) *Striking a Balance: Hate Speech, Freedom of Expression and Non-Discrimination*, London: Article 19.

Coward, R. (1984) *Female Desire*, London: Paladin.

Delphy, C. (1984) *Close to Home: A Materialist Analysis of Women's Oppression*, London: Hutchinson.

Devlin, P. (1968) *The Enforcement of Morals*, Oxford: University Press.

Dicey, A. V. (1959) *Introduction to the Study of the Law of the Constitution*, London: Macmillan.

Dobash, R. and Dobash, R. (1992) *Women, Violence and Social Change*, London: Routledge.

Donnerstein, E. (1980) 'Aggressive erotica and violence against women', *Journal of Personality and Social Psychology*, 39(2): 269–77.

Donnerstein, E. and Berkowitz, L. (1981) 'Victim reactions in aggressive erotic films as a factor in violence against women', *Journal of Personality and Social Psychology* 41(2): 710–24.

Duggan, L. (1985) 'False promises: feminist anti-pornography legislation in the U.S.', in V. Burstyn (ed.) *Feminists against Censorship*, Toronto: Douglas and McIntyre; reprinted in G. Chester and J. Dickey (eds), *Feminism and Censorship*, London: Prism Press, 62–75.

Dworkin, A. (1981) *Pornography: Men Possessing Women*, London: The Women's Press.

Dworkin, R. (1977a) 'Civil disobedience', in *Taking Rights Seriously*, London: Duckworth, 206–22.

—— (1977b) 'Reverse discrimination', in *Taking Rights Seriously*, London: Duckworth, 223–39.

—— (1977c) 'Taking rights seriously', in *Taking Rights Seriously*, London: Duckworth, 184–205.

—— (1984) 'Reagan's justice', *New York Review of Books* (9 November).

—— (1986a) 'Do We Have a Right to Pornography?', in *A Matter of Principle*, Oxford: University Press, 335–72.

—— (1986b) *Law's Empire*, London: Fontana.

Easton, S. (1987) 'Hegel and feminism', in D. Lamb (ed.) *Hegel and Modern Philosophy*, London: Croom Helm, 30–55.

Everywoman magazine (1988) *Pornography and Sexual Violence, Evidence of the Links*, London.

Feinberg, J. (1987a) *Offense to Others*, Oxford: University Press.

—— (1987b) *Harm to Others*, Oxford: University Press.

Feyerabend, P. (1975) *Against Method*, London: New Left Books.

Foucault, M. (1979) *Discipline and Punish: The Birth of the Prison*, Harmondsworth: Penguin.

Fox Keller, E. (1985) *Reflections on Gender and Science*, New Haven, Conn.: Yale University Press.

Frantz, L. (1963) 'Is the First Amendment law? A reply to Professor Mendelson', 51 *California Law Review* 729.

Gibbons, T. (1991) *Regulating the Media*, London: Sweet & Maxwell.

Gilligan, C. (1982) *In a Different Voice: Psychological Theory and Women's Development*, Cambridge, Mass.: Harvard University Press.

Gordon, P. (1982) *Incitement to Racial Hatred*, London: The Runnymede Trust.

Gregory, J. (1987) *Sex, Race and the Law*, London: Sage.

Hall, S. *et al.* (1978) *Policing the Crisis*, London: Macmillan.

Harding, S. and Hintikka, B. (1983) (eds) *Discovering Reality: Feminist Perspectives on Epistemology, Metaphysics, Methodology, and Philosophy of Science*, Dordrecht: Reidel.

Hart, H. L. A. (1968) *Law, Liberty and Morality*, Oxford: University Press.

Hegel, G. W. F. (1971) *The Phenomenology of Mind*, trans. W. Wallace and A. Miller, Oxford: Clarendon Press.

Heineman, W. (1972) *The Politics of the Powerless*, Oxford: University Press.

Hirschon, R. (ed.) (1984) *Women and Property – Women as Property*, London: Croom Helm.

Hohfeld, W. N. (1919) *Fundamental Legal Conceptions as applied in Judicial Reasoning*, New Haven, Conn.: Yale University Press.

Horkheimer, M. and Adorno, T. (1973) *Aspects of Sociology*, London: Heinemann.

Howitt, D. and Cumberbatch, G. (1990) *Pornography: Impacts and Influences*, London: HMSO.

Itzin, C. (1987) *London Daily News* (20 April).

Jacobs, J. (1978) *Out of the Ghetto*, London: Janet Simon.

Jeffreys, S. (1988) 'The censoring of revolutionary feminism', in G. Chester and J. Dickey (eds), *Feminism and Censorship*, London: Prism Press, 133–9.

Kalven, H. (1967) 'Upon rereading Mr. Justice Black on the First Amendment', 14 *UCLA Law Review* 428.

Kappeler, S. (1986) *The Pornography of Representation*, Cambridge: Polity Press.

Kelly, L. (1988) 'False promises: the US Ordinances; censorship or radical law reform', in G. Chester and J. Dickey (eds), *Feminism and Censorship*, London: Prism Press, 52–61.

Kuhn, A. (1985) *The Power of the Image*, London: Routledge.

Kuhn, T. S. (1962) *The Structure of Scientific Revolutions*, Chicago, University of Chicago Press.

Kutchinsky, B. (1973) 'The effect of easy availability of pornography on the incidence of sex crime: the Danish experience', *Journal of Social Issues*.

Lacey, N., Wells, C. and Meure, D. (1990) *Reconstructing the Criminal Law*, London: Weidenfeld & Nicolson.

Lamb, D. (1991) *Discovery, Creativity and Problem-Solving*, Aldershot: Avebury.

Langton, R. (1990) 'Whose right? Ronald Dworkin, women and pornographers', *Philosophy and Public Affairs*, 19(4): 311.

Lee, S. (1990) *The Cost of Free Speech*, London: Faber.

Leonard, A. (1987) *Judging Inequality*, London: The Cobden Trust.

Linton, D. (1988) 'Why is pornography offensive?', in D. Braine and H. Lesser (eds) *Ethics, Technology and Medicine*, Aldershot: Avebury: 123–8.

Linz, D. G., Donnerstein, E. and Penrod, S. (1988) 'Effects of exposure to violent and sexually degrading depictions of women', *Journal of Personality and Social Psychology*, 55(5): 758–68.

Lynn, B. (1988) 'Pornography and free speech: the civil rights approach', in L. Gostin (ed.) *Civil Liberties in Conflict*, London: Routledge, 170–84.

MacKinnon, C. (1984) Brief, Amicus Curiae, *American Booksellers Association Inc. et al. v. William H. Hudnut III*, US District Court, Southern District of Indiana, Indianapolis Division.

—— (1987) *Feminism Unmodified*, Cambridge, Mass.: Harvard University Press.

—— (1989) *Toward a Feminist Theory of the State*, Cambridge, Mass.: Harvard University Press.

Malamuth, N. M. (1986) 'Predictors of naturalistic sexual aggression', *Journal of Personality and Social Psychology* 50(5) 953–62.

Malamuth, N. M. and Check, J. V. P. (1980) 'Penile tumescence and perceptual responses to rape as a function of victim's perceived reactions', *Journal of Applied Social Pyschology*, 10(6): 528–47.

—— (1983) 'Sexual arousal to rape depictions: individual differences', *Journal of Abnormal Psychology* 92(1): 55–67.

Malamuth, N. M., Check, J. V. P. and Briere, J. (1986) 'Sexual arousal in response to aggression: ideological, aggressive and sexual correlations', *Journal of Personality and Social Psychology*, 50(2): 330–40.

Malamuth, N. M. and Donnerstein, E. (1984) (eds) *Pornography and Sexual Aggression*, New York: Academic Press.

Malamuth, N. M. and Spinner, B. (1980) 'A longitudinal content analysis of sexual violence in the best-selling erotic magazines', *Journal of Sex Research*, 16: 226.

Manchester, C. (1983) 'Obscenity in the mail', *Crim LR* 64.

Marx, K. (1961) *Capital*, Moscow: Foreign Languages Publishing House.

Meiklejohn, A. (1960) *Political Freedom*, New York: Harper & Row.

Mendelson, W. (1962) 'On the meaning of the First Amendment: absolutes in the balance', 50 *California Law Review* 821.

Mies, M. (1986) *Patriarchy and Accumulation on a World Scale: Women in the International Division of Labour*, London: Zed Books.

Mill, J. S. (1970) *On Liberty*, in *Utilitarianism*, ed. M. Warnock, London: Fontana.

—— (1984) *The Subjection of Women*, Cambridge, Mass.: MIT Press.

Moller Okin, S. (1991) *Justice, Gender and the Family*, London: HarperCollins.

Newburn, T. (1992) *Permission and Regulation: Law and Morals in Post-war Britain*, London: Routledge.

Osman, S. (1988) 'Should it be unlawful to incite sexual violence?', in G. Chester and J. Dickey (eds). *Feminism and Censorship*, London: Prism Press, 151–60.

Parmar, P. (1988) 'Rage and desire: confronting pornography', in G. Chester and J. Dickey (eds), *Feminism and Censorship*, London: Prism Press, 119–32.

Pateman, C. (1988) *The Sexual Contract*, Cambridge: Polity Press.

Popper, K. (1959) *The Logic of Scientific Discovery*, London: Hutchinson.

—— (1963) *Conjectures and Refutations*, London: Routledge.

—— (1972) *Objective Knowledge*, Oxford, Clarendon Press.

President's Commission on Obscenity and Pornography (1970), Washington: US Government Printing Office.

Public Hearings on Ordinances to add Pornography as Discrimination against Women, Committee on Government Operations, The City Council, Minneapolis, Minn., 12–13 December 1983.

Racial Discrimination (1975), White Paper, London: HMSO, Cmnd 6234.

Radcliffe Richards, J. (1982) *The Sceptical Feminist*, Harmondsworth: Penguin.

Raz, J. (1986) *The Morality of Freedom*, Oxford: University Press.

—— (1991) 'Free expression and personal identification', *Oxford Journal of Legal Studies*, 11(3).

Renvoise, J. (1982) *Incest*, London: Routledge.

Review of the Public Order Act 1936 and related legislation, Home Office (1980), Cmnd 7891.

Rhode, D. (1991) *Justice and Gender*, Cambridge, Mass.: Harvard University Press.

Richards, D. A. J. (1977) *The Moral Criticism of Law*, Enrico, Calif.: Dickenson.

Robertson, G. (1979) *Obscenity*, London: Weidenfeld & Nicolson.

Sartre, J.-P. (1943) *Being and Nothingness*, trans. H. E. Barnes, London: Methuen.

Scanlon, T. (1972) 'A theory of freedom of expression', *Philosophy and Public Affairs*, 1(2): 204–26.

Scarman, L. (1975) *The Red Lion Square Disorders of 15 June 1974*, London: HMSO, Cmnd 5919.

Schauer, F. (1982) *Free Speech: A Philosophical Inquiry*, Cambridge: University Press.

Simpson, A. W. B. (1983) *Pornography and Politics*, London: Waterlow.

Smart, C. (1989) *Feminism and the Power of Law*, London: Routledge.

Smith, B. (1988) 'Sappho was a right-*off* woman', in G. Chester and J. Dickey (eds), *Feminism and Censorship*, London: Prism Press, 178–84.

Steiner, G. (1970) 'Night words: high pornography and human privacy', in D. A. Hughes (ed.) *Perspectives on Pornography*, New York: St Martin's Press, 47.

Stockman, G. (1983) *Antipositivist Theories of the Sciences*, Dordrecht: Reidel.

Stone, R. T. H. (1986) 'Obscene publications: the problems persist', Crim LR 139.

Temkin, J. (1993) 'Sexual history evidence: the ravishment of section 2', Crim LR, 3–20 (January).

Thomas, D. A. (1978) in P. Glazebrook (ed.) *Reshaping the Criminal Law*, London.

Tunks, K. and Hutchinson, D. (eds) (1991) *Dear Clare ... This is What Women Feel about Page 3*, London: Radius.

Tynan, K. (1970) 'Dirty books can stay', in D. A. Hughes (ed.) *Perspectives on Pornography*, New York: St Martin's Press, 111.

Valverde, M. (1985) *Sex, Power and Pleasure*, Toronto: The Women's Press.

Vance, C. S. (1986) 'The Meese Commission on the road', *Nation*, 80–1 (2 and 9 August).

Weber, M. (1965) *The Protestant Ethic and the Spirit of Capitalism*, London: Unwin.

Wechsler, H. (1959) 'Toward neutral principles of constitutional law', 73 *Harvard Law Review*, 1.

Williams, B. (1979) *Report of the Committee on Obscenity and Film Censorship*, London: HMSO, Cmnd 7772.

Williams, F. (1989) *Social Policy, A Critical Introduction: Issues of Race, Gender and Class*, Cambridge: Polity Press.

Wilson, W. (1992) 'Is hurting people wrong?', *The Journal of Social Welfare and Family Law*, (5): 388–97.

Wolfenden, J. *Report of the Committee on Homosexual Offences and Prostitution* (1957), London: HMSO, Cmnd 247.

Zillman, D. and Bryant, J. (1982) 'Pornography, sexual callousness and the trivialization of rape', *Journal of Communication*, 32(4): 10–21.

—— (1989) *Pornography: Research Advances and Policy Considerations*, Hilsdale, N.J.: Erlbaum.

Statutes

Broadcasting Act 1990 136–7
Children and Young Persons (Harmful Publications) Act 1955 131–2
Cinematograph (Amendment) Act 1982 138
Criminal Justice Act 1988 131, 139
Customs Consolidation Act 1876 66, 123, 130–1
Customs and Excise Management Act 1979 130
Incitement to Hatred (Northern Ireland) Act 1970 159
Indecent Displays (Control) Act 1981 5, 123, 132, 144
Indianapolis Ordinance 1985 xii–xiv, 2, 8, 16, 19, 21, 40, 61–3, 70–1, 73–4, 82, 93–4, 100, 107, 109–10, 112–21, 123, 152, 158, 171, 176
Local Government (Miscellaneous Provisions) Act 1982 133, 143
Malicious Communications Act 1988 166
Minneapolis Ordinance 1983 xii–xiii, xvi, 16, 21, 82, 109–13, 176
Obscene Publications Act 1959 xii, 66, 68, 73, 123–31, 133–4, 136–41, 168
Offences against the Person Act 1861 180n
Official Secrets Act 1989 74
Post Office Act 1953 128–30
Protection of Children Act 1978 131, 139
Public Order Act 1936 87, 121, 158–62, 164
Public Order Act 1986 87, 121, 159, 162–7
Race Relations Act 1965 121, 159–61, 164, 167
Race Relations Act 1976 121, 159, 161–2, 164, 167–8, 172
Theatres Act 1968 135–6, 163
Town and Country Planning (Control of Advertisements) Regulations 1989 165
Video Recordings Act 1984 136

Cases

Abrams v. *United States* 250 US 616 (1919) 55, 98

Alcock v. *Chief Constable of S. Yorks Police* (1991) 3 WLR 1057 10

American Booksellers v. *Hudnut* 77 F 2d 323 7th Circuit (1985), 475 US 1001 (1986) xi, 19, 62, 94, 107, 114–15

Beauharnais v. *Illinois* 343 US 250 (1952) 183n

Brind v. *Secretary of State for the Home Department* (1991) 1 All ER 720 67

Brown v. *Board of Education* 347 US 483 (1954); 349 US 294 (1955) 34, 152–3, 156, 170

Brutus v. *Cozens* (1973) AC 854 159

Calder v. *Boyars* (1969) 1 QB 151 127

Chaplinsky v. *New Hampshire* 315 US 568 (1942) 89

Cohen v. *California* 403 US 15 (1971) xiv, 55

Conegate Ltd v. *Customs and Excise Commissioners* (1986) 2 All ER 688 131

Darbo v. *D.P.P.*, The Times, 11 July 1991 127

DeFunis v. *Odegard* 94 S.Ct 1704 (1974) 153–4

Doe v. *Commonwealth Attorney* 403 Fed. Supp. 1199 (1975) 106

D.P.P. v. *Boardman* (1972) AC 241 18

D.P.P. v. *Jordan* (1977) AC 699 129

D.P.P. v. *Whyte* (1972) AC 849 127–8

Duncan v. *Jones* (1936) 1 KB 218 160

Feiner v. *New York* 340 US 315 (1951) 96

Gitlow v. *New York* 268 US 652 (1925) 94

Griswold v. *Connecticut* 381 US 479 (1965) 106

Handyside v. *U.K.* (1976) 1 EHRR 737 66, 101, 123

Hedley Byrne & Co. Ltd v. *Heller* (1964) AC 465 90

Hoggard v. *State* 27 Ark 117 640 SW 2d 102 (1982) 15

Jacobellis v. *Ohio* 378 US (1964) 184 xi

John Calder Publications Ltd v. *Powell* (1965) 1 QB 509 126

Jordan v. *Burgoyne* (1963) 2 QB 744 159

Keller v. *State* 606 SW 2d 931 (1980) 105–6

Knuller Ltd. v. *D.P.P.* (1973) 2 All ER 435 127, 133–5

Kovcas v. *Cooper* 336 US 77 (1949) 180n

Linda R. S. v. *Richard D.* 410 US 614 (1972)

Los Angeles v. *Taxpayers for Vincent* 466 US 789 (1984) 89

McLoughlin v. *O'Brian* (1983) AC 410 10

Makin v. *A-G for New South Wales* (1894) AC 57 17

Manual Enterprises v. *Day* 370 US 478 (1962) 104

Memoirs v. *Massachusetts* 383 US 413 (1966) 34

Miller v. *California* 413 US 15 (1973) 11, 61, 68, 93, 104–5, 107, 116
Mishkin v. *U.S.* 383 US 502 (1966) 104, 113
New York v. *Ferber* 458 US 747 (1982) 106–7, 112–13, 115
New York Times Co. v. *Sullivan* 376 US 254 (1964) 100, 180n
Olivia N., a minor v. *National Broadcasting Co. Inc.* (1977) App 141, Cal Rptr
     511 16
O'Moran v. *D.P.P.* (1975) QB 864 87
Paris Adult Theatre v. *Slaton* 413 US 49 (1973) 28, 32, 40, 96, 104–5
People v. *Mature Enterprises* 343 NS 2d 911 (1973) 73 Misc 2d 749 (1974) xiii
Pittsburgh Press v. *Pittsburgh Human Rights Commission* 413 US 376 (1973) 114
R. v. *Ambrose* (1973) 57 Cr App R 338 159–160
R. v. *Anderson* (1972) 1 QB 304 66, 128
R. v. *Bow Street Magistrates Court ex parte Noncyp Ltd.* (1990) 1 QB 123 130–1
R. v. *Brown, Lucas, Jaggard, Laskey and Carter*, The Times, 21 February 1992, 12
     March 1993 180n
R. v. *Butler* 89 Dominion Law Reports 449 (1992) xi, xvi, 178
R. v. *Calleja* (1985) Crim LR 397 138
R. v. *Doorgashurn* (1988) Cr App R 195 138
R. v. *Gibson* (1991) 1 All ER 439 135
R. v. *Hancock, Hardy, Dominy and Budden*, The Times, 28, 29 March 1968 164–5
R. v. *Henn; R.* v. *Darby* (1980) 2 All ER 166 131
R. v. *Hicklin* (1868) LR 3 QB 360 103, 123, 125, 128
R. v. *Holloway* (1982) Cr App R (S) 128 15, 137–8
R. v. *Horseferry Road Metropolitan Stipendiary Magistrates, ex parte Siadatan*
     (1991) 1 All ER 24 163
R. v. *Knight* (1990) Cr App R (S) 319 138
R. v. *Liddle* (1985) 7 Cr App R (S) 59 15
R. v. *Love* (1959) 39 Cr App R 30 126
R. v. *Malik*, The Times, 9 November, 10 November, 22 December 1967 164
R. v. *Penguin Books* (1961) Crim LR 176 126
R. v. *Skirving; R.* v. *Grossman* (1985) Crim LR 317 126–7
R. v. *Smith* (1914–5) All ER 262 17
R. v. *Snaresbrook Crown Court, ex parte Commissioner of Police for the Metropolis*
     (1984) 79 Cr App R 184 139
R. v. *Stanley* (1965) 2 QB 327 132
R. v. *Straffen* (1952) 2 All ER 657 17
R. v. *Taylor* (1987) 9 Cr App R (S) 198 14–15
Re S and B (1990) FLR 489 24
Renton v. *Playtime Theatres* 10 S Ct 925 (1986) 29
Roberts v. *United States Jaycees* 468 US 609 (1984) 89
Roth v. *United States* 354 US 476 (1957) 103, 115–16
Schad v. *Borough of Mount Ephraim* 452 US 61 (1981) 181n
Schenck v. *United States* 249 US 47 (1919) 98–9, 170
Shaw v. *D.P.P.* (1962) AC 220 133–5
Skokie v. *National Socialist Party* 373 NE 2d 21 (1978) 86
Spence v. *Washington* 418 US 405 (1974) 87
Stanley v. *Georgia* 394 US 557 (1969) 30, 106
Sunday Times v. *U.K.* ECHR Series A No. 30 (1979) 101, 122
Sweatt v. *Painter* 339 US 629, 70 S Ct 848 153–4
Texas v. *Johnson* 109 S Ct 2533 (1989) 87
Thorne v. *B.B.C.* (1967) 1 WLR 1104 160
Tinker v. *Des Moines School District* 394 US 503 (1969) 86

U.S. v. *Reode* 402 US 351 (1971) 106
U.S. v. *12200 DT Reels* 413 US 123 (1973) 106
Whitney v. *California* 274 US 357 (1927) 63, 99, 101, 180n
Young v. *American Mini-Theatres* 427 US 50 (1976) 28, 100–1

Index

Abel, G. 38–9
abortion 12
absolutism 95–8, 100, 174
Adorno, T. 164
American Civil Liberties Union 65, 70, 117
American Booksellers Association 117
animated pornography 20
Article 19 74, 76
Association of American Publishers 117
Austin, J. L. 93
autonomy x–xi, xviii, 42–51, 78, 81, 83, 95, 101–3, 151, 154
autopsies xiv, 20

balancing 95–8
Barendt, E. 54–5, 67, 77, 101, 129, 143
Baron, L. 22
Barry, K. xvi–xvii, 8, 22, 24–6, 36, 38
Bart, P. 110
Beauvoir, S. de 46
Ben-Veniste, R. 37
Berlin, I. 77
Besant, A. 123
bestiality xii, xvi, 113, 138, 140, 155
Bindman, G. 165–6
blackmail xiii, 14, 24, 89, 140
Bradlaugh, C. 123
bribery 89
British Broadcasting Corporation 77
Bryant, J. 22
buggery 138, 140
burden of proof 35–7, 59, 96
Burgess, A. xiv
'but for' test 16, 19

Calcutt Report 137
Campaign against Pornography 81, 132

Campaign against Pornography and Censorship xvii, 72–3, 81, 166–7
Campaign for Press and Broadcasting Freedom 74, 76
causal links 11–12, 14–19, 22, 31, 32–41
censorship ix–xi, 1, 65–78, 80, 118–19, 142, 162, 169, 171, 174
child pornography xvi, 20, 23–5, 83, 106–7, 115, 125, 131, 139–41, 155
children xvii, 2, 8, 15, 17, 20, 106–7, 131, 173
child sexual abuse 15, 20, 23–4, 36, 58, 108, 110–11, 141
child witness 21, 108
choice 7–9, 30, 43–4, 51, 82–3, 124–5
Churchill, W. 133
Citizens for Democracy through Law 117
citizenship ix
clear and present danger test 98–9, 170
coercion 40, 111–13, 118–19, 140
commercial interests 5, 24–5, 60
commercial speech 88, 90, 97, 100
community morality 10, 27–8
community standards 103–6
computer pornography 20, 141
consent xvii, 7–8, 19, 21, 25–8, 108, 111–12, 115, 118, 124
Conservative Party 74
conspiracy 89; to corrupt public morals 133–5; to outrage public decency 134–5
contract 7–9, 21, 82–3, 118
corroboration 21, 108
credibility 20–4, 108, 115, 118
crime rates 11
Cumberbatch, G. 11–12, 32
cultural sadism 8, 25–7

custom 44, 59, 60–1

Deep Throat xiv, 15, 61
defamation 73–90, 94, 171
Delphy, C. 173
democracy justification of free speech
xi, 62–4, 99–101, 103, 155
Denmark 22, 37
Devlin, P. 27–8
Dicey, A. V. 126–7
diversity 42–6, 67, 103, 151
domestic violence 21, 108, 176
Donnerstein, E. 13, 22, 110
Down's Syndrome 173
Duggan, L. 71, 118
Dworkin, A. xii–xiii, 16, 45, 82, 109–10,
117, 119, 176
Dworkin, R. x, 2–3, 49, 59, 61, 63, 81–2,
128, 144–6, 170, 179n

Easton, S. 180n
Eastwood, C. 16
Ellis, Havelock 123
Emmanuelle xv
environmental harms 10, 28–31
erotica xv–xvi, 29, 174
European Convention on Human
Rights 122–3, 156, 159
expert evidence 110, 127–9

Fanny Hill 126
falsifiability 53, 56
Falwell, J. 79
fascism 158, 167
Feinberg, J. xii–xv, 3, 13, 16–19, 26–7,
29–30, 34, 37–8, 67, 92, 104
feminism ix, 9, 34, 45, 48, 57–8, 68,
70–1, 73, 79–82, 156, 168, 172, 175–8
Feminist Anti-Censorship Task Force
71, 76, 117–18
fighting words 89, 114
film censorship 135–6, 141
First Amendment xi, xiv, 34, 45, 51–2,
53, 55, 59, 61–2, 68, 85–9, 91–2,
94–109, 114–16, 122, 145, 151–3, 155
flag-burning 86–7
Foucault, M. 2, 175
Fourteenth Amendment 106
Fox Keller, E. 33
freedom 49–50, 77–8, 151
free speech xi, xvii, 20, 34, 41–2, 49, 51,
55–6, 59, 62–4, 65, 67, 70, 86–93,

155–7, 160, 163, 166, 169–71, 174;
waiver of free speech right 62–4

Gay's the Word 66, 130
genocide 24
Gordon, P. 161–2
Gregory, J. 169

Hall, Radclyffe 123
Hall, S. 183
Harding, S. 33
harm principle x, 1–7, 15, 31, 47, 88–90,
95, 109, 124, 141–2, 146–7; types of
harm xvii, 7, 10–31, 145
Hart, H. L. A. 27
hate speech 6, 49, 54, 62, 74, 117,
158–74, 183n
heckler's veto 160, 170
Hegel, G. W. F. 173
Holocaust, 159
homosexuality xii, 18, 27, 66–7, 82, 104,
116, 123–4, 134–5, 150–2
Horkheimer, M. 164
horror comics 124, 131–2
Howitt, D. 11–12, 32

imitative harms 14–19, 38–9
incitement 6, 88–9, 93, 96, 120–1; to
racial hatred 154, 157–74, 183n; to
religious hatred 159; to sexual hatred
158, 163–4, 166–74, 178
indecency xii, 130–2, 141, 144
Independent Broadcasting Association
77
Index on Censorship 76
individualism 82, 125, 155
individuality 9, 42–3
infallibility xviii, 55, 57–8, 60, 95
integrity 151–2
International Covenant on Civil and
Political Rights 159
International Times 134–5
Itzin, C. 166–7

Jacobs, J. 158
Jaeckin, J. xv
Jeffreys, S. 76, 79, 83
Joyce, J. 66
judiciary xvii, 14, 66, 122, 152, 177
juries xiv, xvii, 32, 66, 69, 105, 126–9,
139, 142, 165

Kant, I. 21, 102
Kelly, L. 119
Kuhn, A. 71
Ku Klux Klan 166
Kutchinsky, B. 37

Labour Party 74
Ladies' Directory 133
Lady Chatterly's Lover 126
Lamb, D. 54
Langton, R. 153–4
law, use of as a feminist strategy 2, 68–9, 119, 132, 167–9, 175–8
Lawrence, D. H. 126
Lee, S. 35, 49, 69–71, 75–6, 87–8, 116, 156–7, 183n
Leonard, A. 169
lesbianism 66, 83, 104, 123
libel xiii, 6, 75, 88–90, 114, 174
liberalism ix–x, xvii, 1–7, 11, 31, 42, 50, 57–8, 65, 79, 82, 95, 106
libertarianism 7–9, 19, 31, 33, 49, 74
Liberty 76, 167
Linton, D. xv–xvi
Little Red School Book 66, 123
Lynn, B. 171–2

McCarthyism 65
machismo 26–7
MacKinnon, xii–xiii, 15–16, 19, 21, 34, 60, 80, 82, 89–90, 92, 105, 109–10, 112–15, 117, 119–20, 152, 176
majoritarianism xviii, 42, 59–63
Malamuth, N. M. 13, 22
Manchester, C. 130
Manet, E. xvi
Marchiano, L. 19
Meese Commission 11–13, 32, 39–40
Meiklejohn, A. 62–3, 97–100
Men in Erotic Art 130
methodological individualism 53
methodology xvii, 11, 32–40, 54
Michael X [Abdul Malik] 164, 168
Mill, J. S. ix–xi, 1–7, 9–10, 15, 23, 30–1, 42–7, 52–8, 60–2, 67, 69, 77–8, 88, 95, 101–2, 141–2, 148–9, 151
Minneapolis Hearings 11, 19, 22, 34
misrepresentation 114
moral entrepreneurs 2
moral independence x, 2–4, 95, 148–51
'moral police' 52–3
moral right 12, 68, 80, 82

National Council of Civil Liberties 167; *see also* Liberty
National Front 164, 170
national security 90, 95–6, 98, 123, 137
National Socialist Movement 164
National Union of Journalists 137
National Viewers' and Listeners' Association 57, 79
Nazis 13, 24, 54–5, 149–50, 164, 172–3
Neo-Nazis 165, 170
Newburn, T. 124
Nielsen, S. 123
Northern Ireland 159

Obscene Publications Branch 139–41, 155
obscenity xi, xii–xiv, 30, 60–1, 66–8, 73, 103–6, 125–31, 136; obscenity laws 12, 40, 71, 120–1, 123–33, 137–41, 170
offensiveness xiii–xvi, 6, 13, 28–30, 48, 104–5, 110, 132, 136, 147, 150
official secrecy 74, 90
Operation Spanner 125, 180n
organized crime 5, 25, 60, 141
Orwell, G. 61
Osman, S. 168
Oz trial 66, 128

paedophilia 24, 49, 140
Paedophilia Information Exchange 49
Page Three Bill 132–3, 170
Parmar, P. 168, 172, 175
Pateman, C. 9
paternalism 47, 51, 104
perfectionism 31, 46–51, 78, 148
Peirce, C. S. 54
Penthouse 9
philosophy of science 33, 54–5
Playboy 80, 155
political speech 68, 95, 97, 99–101, 146
Popper, K. 35, 56–7
pornography: art and xv–xvi, 68, 91, 125; autonomy and x, 43–5, 78, 81, 83, 103, 151, 154; censorship and ix; content of xii–xvi, 14, 20, 22, 24–5, 30–1, 43, 45–6, 61, 71–2, 173–4; definitions of xi–xvi, 110–13, 119; as fantasy 4, 22, 25–6, 38, 51; feminist critiques of 45, 50, 72–4, 76, 80, 124; harms to women and xi, xvii–xviii, 1–2, 4, 10–41, 43, 48, 72–3, 91–3, 104, 107, 109–121, 127–8, 142–8, 153–5,

166–7, 177; importation of 130–1, 141; literature and xiv–xv, 66–8, 91–2, 125–6, 135, 140, 148; policing of 138–41; as popular culture ix, 50–9, 60–2, 72, 151, 181n; private sphere and 30–1, 64; research into xvi; sexual liberation and 57, 71; soft-core and hard-core xvi, 35; as therapy 4, 129; women's consumption of 82–4
President's Commission 4, 11–12, 32, 37, 39, 112
prior restraint 69, 122, 136
privacy 27, 95, 106
prohibition 69, 143, 146–7, 153
prostitution xvii, 7–9, 29, 133
prurient interest 104–5
public good defence 70, 125–6, 129, 130–1, 135
public order 159–60, 163, 170
Puritanism 52, 79–82, 116

Racial Action Adjustment Society 164
Racial Preservation Society 165
racism 8, 29, 55, 62, 74, 76, 117, 152–6, 158–74, 176
Radcliffe Richards, J. 5, 57, 79–81
rape xii, xvi–xvii, 4, 14–15, 20–3, 25, 33, 37–9, 43, 45, 97, 108, 110–11, 113, 118, 132, 175
Raz, J. xviii, 42, 46–51, 180n
Read, K. 165
Red Lion Square 161
registration 5
regulation x, 2, 10–11, 13–14, 16–18, 28–30, 32, 37, 48, 64–9, 72–3, 77, 82, 92, 109–44, 158, 166–71, 174; of the media 137–8, 177–8
remedies 112–13, 116, 119
restrictions 5, 29, 48, 142–3, 146–7
reverse discrimination 153–4
Richards, D. xiv
right to pornography 145–57
ritual sacrifice 20
Rushdie, S. 71, 75

Sade, Marquis de xiii, 70, 140, 155
sadism xiii, 25–6
sado-masochism 49, 54, 82–3, 104, 125, 138, 140, 180n
Sartre, J.-P. 45
Saudi Arabia 37
Scanlon, T. 101–3

Scarman, L. 161
Schauer, F. xii, 6, 34, 39, 45, 63–6, 69, 85–6, 91, 97, 99, 155
Schwartz, R. 155
Searle, J. 93
segregation 34, 152–4, 156
sentencing xv, 137–8
sex clubs 5
sex discrimination 110, 114–15, 119, 152–4, 170
sex education x, 81, 123
sex industry xvii, 5, 7–9, 176
sex offenders 4, 11, 110, 141
sex shops 2, 28–9, 79, 132–3, 139–40
sex shows 146
sexual abuse 20–2
sexual harassment 21, 120
sexual liberation 28, 57, 171–2
sexual libertarianism 33, 37, 42, 79, 83, 125, 151
sexual offences 11–12, 14–18, 20–5, 33, 36–7; see also rape, sexual abuse, child sexual abuse
sexual slavery 8, 82
Short, C. 74, 132–3
similar fact evidence 17–18
Simpson, A. W. B. 45
Skokie 86–7
slavery 172–3
slippery slope argument x, 65–70, 116–17, 119, 135, 140, 142–3, 150, 176
Smart, C. ix, 68, 80, 119–20, 132–3, 144, 156, 175
Smith, B. 83
snuff movies 19–20
Society for the Suppression of Vice 123
speech 6–7, 85–94, 96, 104, 113, 118
speech acts 93
Spinner, B. 22
standard of proof 33–5, 169
state power 2, 14, 47–9, 55, 72, 75, 102, 175–7
statistics 33
Steiner, G. xiv
Straus, M. 22
Stone, R. T. H. 128, 138–9

taxation 6, 48
Temperance Movement 2
theatre censorship 135
The Story of O xv, 25, 82

Thomas, D. A. 126
Toynbee, P. 155
trafficking 111–13, 115
truth justification of free speech xi,
    52–7, 63, 67, 95, 103, 155
Tynan, K. xv

Ulysses 66
Universal Coloured Peoples'
    Association 164, 168
utilitarianism 149–50, 155,
    157

Vance, C. S. 12, 39–40

Vietnam 86

Weber, M. 36
Wechsler, H. 152–3
Wendell Holmes, O. 55
Williams, B. 3
Williams Committee 5, 45, 129, 141–4,
    150, 155; Williams Report 29, 32, 68,
    125, 141–51, 168
Wolfenden Report 27, 124
Woman 132

Zillman, D. 22
zoning 28–9, 109–10, 114, 149